Global politics in the information age

Manchester University Press

Global politics in the information age

edited by Mark J. Lacy
and Peter Wilkin

Manchester University Press
Manchester and New York

distributed exclusively in the USA by Palgrave

Copyright © Manchester University Press 2005

While copyright in the volume as a whole is vested in Manchester University Press, copyright in individual chapters belongs to their respective authors, and no chapter may be reproduced wholly or in part without the express permission in writing of both author and publisher.

Published by Manchester University Press
Oxford Road, Manchester M13 9NR, UK
and Room 400, 175 Fifth Avenue, New York, NY 10010, USA
www.manchesteruniversitypress.co.uk

Distributed exclusively in the USA by
Palgrave, 175 Fifth Avenue, New York,
NY 10010, USA

Distributed exclusively in Canada by
UBC Press, University of British Columbia, 2029 West Mall,
Vancouver, BC, Canada V6T 1Z2

British Library Cataloguing-in-Publication Data
A catalogue record for this book is available from the British Library

Library of Congress Cataloging-in-Publication Data applied for

ISBN   0 7190 6794 4 *hardback*
EAN   978 0 7190 6794 5

First published 2005

15 14 13 12 11 10 09 08 07 06 05   10 9 8 7 6 5 4 3 2 1

Typeset in Sabon with Gill Sans display
by Servis Filmsetting Ltd, Longsight, Manchester
Printed in Great Britain
by Biddles Ltd, King's Lynn

Contents

Figures, boxes and tables

Acknowledgements

We would like to thank the following for their help in the production of this book: Dr Lloyd Pettiford, Dr Olga Guedes Bailey, Dr Graham Chesters, Cathal Smyth, and most importantly Clare Coxhill.

Notes on contributors

Stuart Allan is Reader in the School of Cultural Studies, University of the West of England, Bristol. He is the author of *News Culture* (Open University Press, 1999; second edition, 2004) and *Media, Risk and Science* (Open University Press, 2002). His edited collections include, with Barbie Zelizer, *Journalism After September 11* (Routledge, 2002) and *Reporting War: Journalism in Wartime* (Routledge, 2004).

Sharon Beder is Professor in the School of Social Sciences, Media and Communication at the University of Wollongong in Australia. She is author of several books including *Global Spin: The Corporate Assault on Environmentalism*; *Power Play: The Struggle to Control the World's Electricity*; *Selling the Work Ethic*; *The New Engineer*; and *The Nature of Sustainable Development*.

Danielle Beswick is studying for an ESRC sponsored PhD at the Department of Politics and International Relations, Lancaster University. Her research focuses on interpretations and consequences of the Rwandan interventionist policy towards the Democratic Republic of Congo since 1996.

John Boyle is Lecturer in the Department of Social and Psychological Sciences at Edge Hill University College, Ormskirk. He is also completing doctoral research in the Department of Politics and International Relations at Lancaster University, UK. His research focuses on politics and mass communications within a neoliberal context.

James Compton is Assistant Professor in the Faculty of Information and Media Studies at the University of Western Ontario. He received his PhD in communication from Simon Fraser University in British Columbia, and is a former reporter and editor with Canadian Press/Broadcast News in Vancouver, B.C. He is the author of *The Integrated News Spectacle: A Political Economy of Cultural Performance*, New York: Peter Lang, 2004.

His work also can be found in the academic journals: *Journalism Studies*, *Journalism: Theory, Practice & Criticism*, and *UDC Communique*. He is currently co-editing a book on corporate convergence and its implications for journalism and democracy entitled *Converging Media, Diverging Politics* for Lexington Books.

Matthew David is Senior Lecturer in Sociology within the Department of Sociology, University of Liverpool. He is author (with Carole Sutton) of *Social Research: The Basics* (Sage, 2004), and of *Science in Society* (Palgrave, 2005). He has published articles on New Genetics, Science and Computing in a range of academic journals, books and encyclopaedias.

Jamieson Kirphope is currently undertaking doctoral research at the University of Plymouth, investigating conflicts over intellectual property and freedom of communication in virtual environments. He is undertaking empirical research in this field and has published work in the area of computers, freedom and surveillance more generally.

Mark J. Lacy is Lecturer in International Relations in the Department of Politics and International Relations in Lancaster University. He is author of *Security and Climate Change: International Relations and the Limits of Realism* (Routledge, 2005). He has published articles on ecopolitics, popular culture and International Relations theory in *Alternatives: Local, Global, Political, Millennium: Journal of International Studies*, and *Environmental Politics*.

Timothy W. Luke is University Distinguished Professor of Political Science at Virginia Polytechnic Institute and State University in Blacksburg, Virginia. He also is the Program Chair for Government and International Affairs in the School of Public and International Affairs, and Coordinator of the Alliance for Social, Political, Ethical, and Social Theory (Aspect) in the College of Liberal Arts and Human Sciences at Virginia Tech. His recent books are *Capitalism, Democracy, and Ecology: Departing from Marx* (University of Illinois Press, 1999), *The Politics of Cyberspace*, ed. with Chris Toulouse (Routledge, 1998), and *Ecocritique: Contesting the Politics of Nature, Economy, and Culture* (University of Minnesota Press, 1997). A cultural theorist as well as a political theorist, he is very interested in evaluating museums, memorials and monuments as examples of cultural discourse and political rhetoric at work in the development of the economy and society. The author of over 150 journal articles and edited book chapters, he writes extensively on the politics of museums as well media politics, international affairs and social theory. His latest book, *Museum Politics: Power Plays at the Exhibition* was published in Spring 2002 with the University of Minnesota Press.

Brian McNair is Professor of Journalism and Communication at the University of Strathclyde. He is the author of many books and articles on journalism, including *The Sociology of Journalism* (Arnold, 1998), *Journalism and Democracy* (Routledge, 2002), and *Mediated Access* (with Matthew Hibberd and Philip Schlesinger, University of Luton Press, 2003).

Ngai-Ling Sum is Lecturer in the Department of Politics and International Relations at Lancaster University. Her most recent publications are a co-authored book (with Bob Jessop) on *Beyond the Regulation Approach* (Edward Elgar 2006) and an edited book (with Marcus Perkmann) on *Globalization, Regionalization and Cross-Border Regions* (Pelgrave, 2002). She has also contributed to *Critical Asian Studies, Capital and Class, New Political Economy* and *Urban Studies*.

Peter Wilkin is currently Head of Department of Politics and International Relations at Lancaster University. He has published articles in *Third World Quarterly*; *The British Journal of Politics and International Relations*; *Social Theory and Practice*; *Media, Culture and Society*. He has written a number of books including *Noam Chomsky: On Power, Knowledge and Human Nature*, and *The Political Economy of Global Communication*.

Mark J. Lacy

Introduction: the excess of information

In *Immortality* the novelist Milan Kundera argues that we have moved from the age of ideology to the society of imagology, where political/economic ideas become translated and circulated through slogans and images. In the age of imagology everyday existence becomes permeated by images and stories of a distant reality, whether it be the images of traumatised children escaping or being stretchered out from a school-as-warzone in a small Russian town, the holiday fashions of Tony Blair and family as they enjoy the hospitality of Silvio Berlusconi, the internet blog of a young Iraqi writing on his countries 'liberation' and the latest *Massive Attack* download.

In the age of imagology politics becomes spectacle. Kundera writes:

> Of course, imagologues existed long before they created the powerful institutions we know today. Even Hitler had his personal imagologue, who used to stand in front of him and patiently demonstrate the gestures to be made during speeches so as to fascinate the crowds. But if that imagologue, in an interview with the press had amused the Germans by describing Hitler as incapable of moving his hands, he would not have survived this indiscretion by more than a few hours. Nowadays, however, the imagologue not only does not try to hide his activity, but often even speaks for his politician clients, explains to the public what he taught them to do or not to do, how he told them to behave, what formula they are likely to use and what tie they are likely to wear. We needn't be surprised by this self-confidence: in the last few decades, imagology has gained a historic victory over ideology. (Kundera 1991: 127)

Commanding media networks, imagologues work to create 'systems of ideals and anti-ideals, systems of short duration which are quickly replaced by other systems but which influence our behaviour, our political opinions and aesthetic tastes, the colour of carpets and the selection of books just as in the past we have been ruled by the systems of ideologues' (Kundera 1991: 130). The concept of social and political change that has been fundamental to European political thought takes on a new meaning, moving away from the idea of new stages of 'coherent' development to a *shift from one side to another*. Politics becomes the search for the most effective strategies to manage consumer society; and politics and consumerism become intimately connected to the point where you can buy a 12-inch Elite Aviator George W. Bush doll or Turkey Dinner George W. Bush: 'the Turkey Dinner George W. Bush Figure celebrates George W. Bush's surprise Thanksgiving 2003 visit to our troops in Iraq. This figure does not talk, but comes dressed in an Army jacket nearly identical to the one he wore on that historic day.' Or you can consume an album of fourteen ballads called 'Meglio Una Canzone' (Better a Song) featuring Silvio Berlusconi's lyrics sung by Mariano Apicella, a guitar-playing musician he met in a hotel bar in Naples in 2001.

Kundera is correct to remind us that the age of imagologues existed before spectacular election campaigns and media-friendly 'wars-at-a-distance'. Indeed, it is possible to argue that we see signs of imagology in the time of the Roman empire. In *Flesh and Stone: The Body and the City in Western Civilization* Richard Sennett discusses Hadrian's project in AD 118 to build a new Pantheon in order to emphasise to the Roman citizenry that the 'past would flow smoothly forward' (Sennett 1996: 92). Through the construction of buildings, emperors constructed their legitimacy in the eyes of the people, constructing the 'fiction of an essential character' through times of uncertainty and change, providing a belief in something fixed and secure: buildings asserted that 'stable values underlay the insecurity, misery, and humiliation' experienced by the populations of the city (Sennett 1996: 96). In order to create the fiction of an 'eternal city' it was necessary to dramatise the emperor's power and authority in the most powerful and spectacular way:

> The people also gained from believing that their buildings bore the stamp of absolute authority. To the Romans we owe the phrase *teatrum mundi*, later rendered by Shakespeare as 'all the world's a stage.' A Roman could give him- or herself over to that willing suspension of disbelief which is the essence of theatre, assured that power guaranteed as consequent and correct those places in which the spectacle of life unfolded. The Realm of certified stone in the city literally set the stage for Romans believing the evidence of their eyes. (Sennett 1996: 97)

Yet there has undoubtedly been an *intensification* in the uses of information technology and imagology for 'political' ends in an age of 24/7 news reporting, media-conscious terror networks, just-in-time delivery, wireless internet, mediagenic election campaigning and real time spectacles of violence and suffering.

The chapters that we have collected together in this book aim to explore this networked information society from a number of perspectives and locations, from the strategies used by the state apparatus through to the strategies of resistance that are opening up to those who feel that the 'global society' is not the route to a secure cosmopolitan space of freedom and security. In this chapter we are going to situate the essays collected together in this volume, essays that emerge from a number of perspectives and disciplines, in a broader intellectual context, speaking to their location as contributions to a broader project of critical thought across the social sciences.

All the world's a stage

What we want to do before outlining the chapters is provide some background to the perspectives that circulated in the twentieth century on media, politics and the Age of 'Enlightenment'.

For Theodor Adorno and Max Horkheimer, central figures in the Frankfurt School of Critical Theory, an intellectual movement that sought to revive Marxian-inspired critique of the modern world, the age of Enlightenment and Progress created news of dangers and domination. These dangers were often ignored in the sense of optimism on the ability of the 'enlightened' state and citizen to control nature and create new levels of security through transformations in science and techniques of social organisation: the world was moving from primitive barbarity, irrationality and insecurity to an existence where advances in culture and science would enable humans to take control of society and fashion it into something better, a society that enabled the citizenry to develop their potentialities in art, consumerism, science and politics. The age of Enlightenment promised a better tomorrow.

In *Dialectic of Enlightenment*, first published in 1947, Adorno and Horkheimer wrote that 'Enlightenment has always aimed at liberating men from fear and establishing their sovereignty. Yet the fully enlightened earth radiates disaster triumphant' (Adorno and Horkeheimer 1997: 1). We see the condition of 'disaster triumphant' in the bureaucratically organised factory of death in the concentration camp; in the potential for climatic disaster emerging from our addiction to car culture and fossil fuels; in the chaos that increasingly networked and efficient financial markets can create for human existence around the planet; in the ambitious economic and political projects designed to deliver human beings from fear and suffering.

Far from liberating human beings from fear, the emerging 'culture industries' used fear to keep humans disciplined and efficient for capitalist economies and war machines. For Adorno and Horkheimer, 'irrational' ideas circulate in 'enlightened' societies increasingly influenced by the culture industries, such as astrology columns in daily newspapers, the theme of Adorno's book *The Stars Down to Earth*, and through cartoons. In addition, the search for technological advancement often proceeded without reflection on the dangers for human and non-human existence. On this view, it is not that advances in science lead to irrationality. Far from it: science does lead to more sophisticated understandings of the world we live in. But from this pessimistic perspective, modern societies often suppress uncertainty about the dangers and accidents that technological innovation, innovations that emerge from advancements in scientific knowledge, can create. The same can be said for advances in economic knowledge, where intellectual uncertainty mutates into an ethos of economic fundamentalism and experimentation. For the Frankfurt School, suppressing dangers about technological 'advancement' and economic progress in the drive for a better tomorrow constitutes one form of irrationality.

Faced with the condition of 'disaster triumphant', disturbing the illusions of progress and technological advancement, we retreat into the spectacles provided by the culture industry. Writing about cartoons, Adorno and Horkheimer observe:

> In so far as cartoons do any more than accustom the senses to the new tempo, they hammer into every brain the old lesson that continuous friction, the breaking down of all resistance, is the condition of life in this society. Donald Duck in the cartoons and the unfortunate in real life get their thrashing so that the audience can learn to take their own punishment. (Adorno and Horkheimer, 1997: 138)

In the age of *Matrix Reloaded*, *The Day After Tomorrow*, *Spiderman* and *Revenge of The Sith*, with their computer-generated images that take spectacles of destruction, violence and speed to new intensities, Adorno and Horkeheimer's observations may seem rather quaint. The point they are making is that faced with the insecurity of existence brought about by rapid technological transformation and increasing discipline in the workplace (for those lucky enough not to be left as human waste), popular culture becomes a space to escape, watching Neo in *Matrix Reloaded* or Jack Bauer in *24* taking their 'punishment' (and give it back) to make us feel better about our own condition of powerlessness.

Writing at a similar time as Adorno and Horkheimer, Walter Benjamin wrote that in the culture of modernity, 'Mankind, which in Homer's time was an object of contemplation for the Olympian gods, now is one for itself. Its self alienation has reached such a degree that it can experience its own destruction as an aesthetic pleasure of the first order.' Sharing the pessimism of Adorno and Horkheimer on the fully enlightened earth that radiates disaster triumphant, Benjamin is arguing that our fantasies of destruction are a consequence of living through a state of emergency: the '"state of emergency" in which we live is not the exception but the rule' (Benjamin 2004: 248).

For Benjamin, like Adorno and Horkheimer, the culture of modernity was intensifying an aestheticisation of politics (from the symbolism of fascism through to the selling of Turkey Dinner Bush). This aestheticisation of politics permeates all aspects of everyday life. Writing in 1937, the Argentinean novelist Jorge Luis Borges comments in 'A Pedagogy of Hatred' on the illustrations and story in a German children's book, a book that sold 51,000 copies: 'Its goal is to instill in the children of the Third Reich a distrust and animosity toward Jews. Verse (we know the mnemonic virtues of rhyme) and color engravings (we know how effective images are) collaborate in this veritable textbook of hatred' (Borges 1999: 199). In the travelogue of Italo

Calvino's visit to the United States in 1960, the Italian novelist recounts a trip to Wall Street. Calvino explains that financial institutions in Wall Street 'do a huge amount of propaganda for investments, with brochures based on the principle that money breeds money, with maxims about money by the great philosophers, and this propaganda for the cult of money is constant in America: if by chance a generation grows up that does not put money above all else, America will go up in smoke' (Calvino 2003: 42). In this sense, the culture industries do much more than simply enable humans to take their punishment: they seduce the consumer into desiring the collective identities provided by the state, the goods on offer in the market place and the projects for delivering us from the state of emergency offered by the military-scientific-complex.

The culture industries offer fantasies of escape from the state of emergency, or the excess of biopower, that the modern state and corporations promise to deliver us from, their foundation for legitimation. They circulate desire for regimes of power and control that may actually contribute to the state of emergency we confront, limiting the search for alternatives to the condition of disaster triumphant. We learn to desire that which limits our freedom, limits our possibilities for living a less insecure existence.

The state of emergency and informational politics

Let's take the observations offered by Adorno, Benjamin and Horkheimer into the twenty-first century. In a move that appears on the surface to take us from the realm of fashion, fiction and gossip to 'reality', we see the aestheticisation of politics at play in an issue of *Vanity Fair* titled 'War and Destiny', an article that contains a collection of photographs by Annie Leibovitz that set out to capture 'the spirit of Washington's mission control'. The narrative that accompanies the photographs, the article 'War and Destiny: The White House in Wartime', is concerned with restoring a sense of security against the terror of uncertainty that has been experienced since 9/11. Indeed, the editorial of the issue makes this strategy explicit: Graydon Carter, after telling us of the memorable images that *Vanity Fair* has produced since World War I, informs us that it is not just 'strength but images of strength that matter in this 21st-century war'. *Vanity Fair*, Carter likes to believe, has taken on a 'status equivalent to the High Sierra of the Public Images' (Carter 2002: 18). As Kundera observes, the imagologues of contemporary politics have reached a level of self-confidence when they can openly acknowledge their activity and how they will achieve their objectives.

The pictures that dominate the article could have been produced by someone who had studied Roland Barthes essay on 'Photography and Electoral Appeal', where Barthes sets out the signs that are used to produce 'a veritable blackmail by means of moral values: country, army, family, honor, reckless heroism' (Barthes 1993: 92). Although, in this case, the narrative that develops is concerned with displaying considered and thoughtful heroism. In the text that accompanies the portraits the narrative is of someone viewed as inexperienced, and perhaps unsuited to the role of President, transforming into a great leader. This transformation is to be expected, although the article admits that Bush got off to a 'rough start' by flying *away* from Washington. And he 'evinced a Bushian aptitude for the jarring phrase: we would find 'those folks' who attacked us' (Buckley and Leibovitz 2002: 48). So the article is trying to silence anxieties about Bush's performance – they are exactly what makes this such a compelling story. But his transformation and overcoming into a war president has an easy explanation because 'Bushes are cool in crisis. It's the breeding, stupid – blue Wasp *sang* at its most froid' (Buckley and Leibovitz 2002: 48).

The War on Terror is the destiny of George W. Bush and a destiny for which breeding has prepared him. But the article does not reduce the War on Terror to the destiny of Bush, although the first main image is a close-up of the face of Bush. As Barthes observes, a full-face photograph underlines the 'realistic outlook' of the candidate: 'Everything there expresses penetration, gravity, frankness: the future deputy is looking squarely at the enemy, the obstacle, the 'problem' (Barthes 1993: 92). To be sure, Bush is not seeking re-election yet but he is still seeking the support of the electorate in a frightening and unprecedented situation. The article shows portraits of the whole team Bush has around him, aiding him to fight terror. On this view, the article is supporting the view that Bush is surrounded by an experienced and diverse team, a talented team that will deliver us from terror: the photograph of the First Lady observes that the person who is probably closest to Bush is not afraid to rein in her husband when 'he starts sounding like Jack Palance'.

The article is followed by another on 'The Big Guns' that tells us about the military experts that are securing us: here we learn that Tommy Franks, Commander in Chief of US Central Command, was raised in 'Bush country' whose family refers to him as 'Pooh', a move that humanises him, a family man who will look after us. The text that accompanies the 'War and Destiny' article tells us more about the family that is looking after us, an embodiment of the state through clearly defined characters, with the pictures titled with cinematic captions like 'The Rock' (for Dick Cheney), 'The Confidante' (for Condoleezza Rice) 'The Conscience' (for Colin Powell), 'The Protector' (for Tom Ridge), 'The Lieutenants' (for Richard Armitage, Paul Wolfowitz, and Stephen Hadley) and 'The Consiglieri' (for Karl Rove and Karen Hughes'), 'The Heat' (John Ashcroft). Put simply, the text for each player reduces their character to a simple archetype, producing an image of an administration that reads like a real-life performance of the television series of *The West Wing* (it even includes pictures and descriptions of the real life 'Spin Team'). The image produced is one where the sheer diversity of personalities of the administration will create a balanced and authoritative form of governance, overcoming individual frailty with a body that represents and embodies the values that make up the state (conscience, power, wisdom, optimism): there are a team of experts that represent the diversity of the nation working to protect us – and the descriptions and pictures are full of representations that have deep roots in the historical imagination of the United States. Dick Cheney is sat in front of what appears to be an antique map. The map is titled 'A Map Showing the Route taken by Samuel Fletcher Cheney Captain 21st Regiment'. These people have experience of war in their blood and breeding: we can feel safe that they are in control. The description of Tom Ridge, Director of Homeland Security, concludes with an observation from a White House Official that this imposing six-foot-three man is designed to become a 'brand': 'When people see him, we want them to think, My babies are safe' (Buckley and Leibovitz 2002: 53) The body and face of Ridge, circulated through informational networks, are part of an attempt to symbolise power, certainty and security in the same way that Hadrian's pantheon was.

The culture industries are working to create images of authority and security as we confront the state of emergency. Working to construct the image that although mistakes have been made, our leaders are rational agents of protection. In the state of emergency: threats selected on the basis that they can be located outside the territory that seeks to be defended, securing an existence that may be contributing to a condition of global danger. It is easier to consume the illusion of security, the spectacle of security, than recognise that our modes of existence may be dangerous or produce suffering. Thinking about (in)security politics can be developed further by taking the work of Michel Foucault as a point of departure. In many ways, Foucault's work can be located in the tradition of intellectuals such as Adorno and Horkheimer: writing about the Frankfurt School, Foucault comments in *Remarks on Marx* that 'I do so with the bad conscience of one who should have known them and studied them much earlier than was the case. Perhaps if I had read them earlier on, I would have saved useful time' (Foucault 1991: 119).

In his writings on biopower and the rise of the modern state, Foucault argued the society of surveillance works by making individuals internalise the fear that they may be watched by the network of technologies designed to make public spaces safer. And the mobilisation of 'official fear' is a cost-effective means of regulating public spaces and flows of bodies; at the same time, these strategies legitimate technological innovation in the sciences of protection. This internalisation of fear now utilises the media-entertainment networks of popular culture, from prime-time fiction cop shows to 'reality' shows depicting 'real-time' car chases. The television series *Crime Scene Investigation (CSI)*, for example, is a popular look at the sophisticated techniques used by the police to investigate brutal crimes. The agents don't always 'win' but we get to see the latest advances in police work in a fair amount of detail for a prime time cop show. *CSI* is produced by Jerry

Bruckheimer who has secured access to specialist advice (as he did on *Black Hawk Down*). It is not surprising that so much expert knowledge is deployed in the series: *CSI* is a warning, an attempt to internalise fear of policing/surveillance networks. Similarly, the illusionary proximity to the networked war machine, with its embedded journalism, in Iraq seems to have been designed to create a spectacle of fear, not only for the regime but for other states harbouring terrorists or terrorist ambitions. Indeed, as Andrew Marshall, who insiders at the Pentagon describe as the Yoda of network-centric war, discussing revolutionary developments in war that do not involve combat, told *Wired*:

> There are ways of psychologically influencing the leadership of another state. I don't mean information warfare, but some demonstration of awesome effects, like being able to set off impressive explosions in the sky. Like, *let us show you what we could do to you*. Just visually impressing the person. (Marshall 2002)

It could be argued that the Gulf War that began on 2003, which even 'realists' of International Relations argued was an 'unnecessary war', was an example of such a spectacle of deterrence. However, it can also be argued that this spectacle and performance of war, with its 'new tempo', also works to reassure citizens that the society of (in)security can deliver them from disaster triumphant: and the global audience gets to see what punishment they will be subject to if they threaten the United States and the 'free world'. The war in Iraq is the promise of control in the condition of disaster triumphant.

Adorno and Horkheimer would undoubtedly see the Enlightened earth continuing to radiate disaster triumphant, sharing the pessimism of more recent writers such as Virilio and Foucault on the 'global accident' or the 'excess of biopower'. In the text that accompanies *Unknown Quantity*, a collection of images from a Foundation Cartier exhibition on the 'accident' Virilio comments that whereas in the past 'the *local accident* was precisely situated (*in situ*) – the North Atlantic for the Titanic, for example – the *global accident* no longer is, and its fall out extends to entire continents' (Virilio 2003: 25) This integral accident becomes a deleterious effect of progress; Virilio cites Hannah Arendt's observation that 'Progress and catastrophe are the opposite faces of the same coin.' Or as Michel Foucault put it, writing during the 1970s on the biopolitical strategies designed to regulate, secure and order existence inside the modern state, an 'excess of biopower appears when it becomes technologically and politically possible for man not only to manage life but to make it proliferate, to create living matter, to build the monster, and ultimately, to build viruses that cannot be controlled and that are universally destructive' (Foucault 2004: 254) This excess of biopower is the darkside of the Enlightenment that the dream of progress seeks to suppress.

Not only would they see the project of liberating humans from fear leading to new formations of insecurity, they would see the global networks of the culture industry continuing to limit attempts to think differently about the fully enlightened earth. Indeed, they would probably see the mutation of culture industries with the information economy and military-scientific complex as an intensification of the totalitarian potential they saw in all modern formations of Enlightenment society.

Maybe what would surprise Adorno and Horkheimer is the expansion of the culture industry through the lifeworld: transformation in information technology allows the proliferation of image/information producers. The culture industry once produced cartoons of aesthetic barbarity for consumers; now aesthetic barbarity can be produced and circulated by anyone with a digital camera. From home-made erotic films to the battle space, the age of imagology is deterritorialised and networked. For example, in Abu Ghraib prison during 2004, we saw a hybrid of reality television and the military-scientific complex as Iraq prisoners and United States soldiers perform for the camera, with the smiling captors having their pictures taken with humiliated men forced to perform a variety of sexual acts (the proliferation of the 'camp' to manage human 'waste' in the twenty-first century would most likely not surprise them). Barbarity circulates through the most complex military machine humanity has ever produced and across the informational networks of the planetary order that symbolises the progress and cosmopolitanism of the age of enlightenment. For Susan Sontag, there seems 'no reversing for the moment America's commitment to self-justification, and the condoning of its increasing out-of-control culture of violence . . . What is revealed by these photographs is as much the culture of shamelessness as the reigning admiration for unapologetic brutality' (Sontag 2004). Aesthetic barbarity can be found in the increasingly 'real' video games played in living rooms across the planet, normalising barbarity in the centres of rationality and progress (one can watch the movie of *Black Hawk Down* and then play the video game); barbarity can be found in Big Brother-style reality shows where humiliation of participants becomes the spectacle; in a website where the owner of an apartment in New York allows impoverished female visitors to his city to stay free of charge as long as they agree to engage in sexual acts that can be viewed on his internet diary. The fully Enlightened earth radiates disaster triumphant. But is it possible to think beyond the pessimistic vision offered by Adorno and Horkheimer?

The system is leaking

Intellectuals such as Adorno, Horkheimer, Virilio and Foucault are writing against those – such as Francis Fukayama, Bill Clinton and Tony Blair – who rejoice in the security and progress promised by the age of Enlightenment. This optimistic perspective is now articulated by the prophets of neoliberalism who argue that a de-regulated and 'free market' global economy will lead to progress in all aspects of human existence across the planet. For the optimists of the (neo)liberal democratic planet the type of issues raised by intellectuals such as Adorno are problems that can be overcome. Disaster triumphant can be overcome by more efficient forms of capitalism, better forms of global governance, an open information society that circulates awareness of the 'accidents' that will inevitably occur. Enron-style corporate corruption, human rights abuses in Abu Ghraib, ecological degradation resulting from SUV culture: these are all problems that can be corrected in an information society. For some neoliberal optimists (such as those engaged in the 'culture wars' in the United States) the pessimism created by Adorno and others is dangerous for the cosmopolitan age of Enlightenment because it creates a fear and cynicism on developments that are improving human existence.

The liberal democratic planetary order deterritorialises human and non-human existence through the desire to create increasingly 'efficient' forms of economic life. From uprooting communities in order to absorb them into the labour market, through to the building of transportation and information networks that facilitate the movement of bodies, goods, policing forces, and knowledge with increasing speed through to the circulation of desire through the strategies of imagology, the marketing and public relations campaigns that become inescapable in urban and informational environments, the deterritorialisation that makes liberal democracy possible and dynamic depends on facilitating mobility across geopolitical/cultural borders and (bio)regions. Without the creation of such a mobile and deterriorialised society, where all limits (traditions, classes, geographical) can be overcome and erased, the dynamism of this planetary order would be impossible: liberal democracy is deterritorialisation. In order to create a society of free consumers and producers, with desire for goods '(in)securing' identities, it is necessary to make mobility fundamental: physical mobility to seek the better life, psychological mobility to tailor identity to the universe of goods on offer and new work cultures, mobility to enable flows of capital/images/ideas across cyberspace. To make the most of the deterritorialised planetary order one must be willing to adapt to new ideas, work practices, strangers, with speed and efficiency.

For the optimists of liberal democracy this emerging planetary order is a continuation of the Enlightenment project of historical progress, where technology, democracy, free markets and the deterriorialising dynamics they make possible lead to a cosmopolitan planet where traditional identities and practices lose significance. Nationalism, the anti-Enlightenment tendency that haunts the modern world, can be overcome, leading to a world where states have no desire to fight one another; economic practices that impede the flow of goods, capital and bodies are replaced with drives for 'efficiency'. The networked information environments create the possibility for new forms of communication, making citizens aware of 'problems' both in their own states and in distant communities: problems – such as corruption, environmental degradation, return to 'pre-modern' ethnic conflict – can lead to improvement in the *design* of liberal democracy, creating the possibility for reflexivity about the dangers that emerge.

Even the most optimistic liberals acknowledge problems and accidents – but not only can these problems and accidents be managed they can lead to even greater levels of cosmo-politics and global governance. Richard Rorty comments that these 'last two centuries are most easily understood not as a period of deepening understanding of the nature of rationality or of morality, but rather as one in which there occurred an astonishingly rapid progress of sentiments, in which it has become much easier for us to be moved to action by sad and sentimental stories' (Rorty 1998: 185). From Rorty's perspective, philosophers may not have made progress on the question of what it means to act with moral responsibility but a 'human rights culture' has emerged where we can consume stories/news reports of the suffering of distant strangers. Rorty argues that an important intellectual advance that has been made here concerns a declining interest in the question of 'what we are really like': 'There is a growing willingness to neglect the question "What is our nature?" and to substitute with "What can we make of ourselves?"' (Rorty 1998: 169). The moral proximity enabled by books, films, poems, paintings creates an empathy between us ('the rich, safe, powerful people') and those who suffer, the powerless people, the people 'whose appearance or habits at first seemed an insult to our moral identity, our sense of the limits of permissible variation' (Rorty 1998: 185). Through the enlargement of planetary liberal democracy we can make ourselves into something *different*.

Like Zygmunt Bauman, a sociologist who has produced a number of studies exploring the social production of moral distance and indifference, Rorty is arguing that the possibility of moral proximity through images and stories can be disruptive (which is why – as some of the essays here show – moral distance and proximity has to be regulated and controlled), creating a moral self, a self that questions moral responsibility to distant strangers: as Bauman comments one recognises morality 'by its gnawing sense of unfulfilledness, by its endemic dissatisfaction with itself' (Bauman 1992: 183). This is not a 'tidy' solution for those seeking a 'rulebook', the dream of secure moral foundations. But for Rorty, the fact that we can see films like *City of God* and *Schindlers List*, read the Baghdad Blog or a 'political' comic book like those created by Joe Sacco in *The Fixer* and *Safe Haven Gorazde* is a form of progress.

At the same time, there are those such as Jean Baudrillard who would raise questions about this form of moral progress: In the New Sentimental Order, the affluent become consumers of the 'ever more delightful spectacles and catastrophe, and of the moving spectacle of our own attempts to alleviate it' (Baudrillard 1992: 67). Similarly Bauman is aware of the problems of proximity in informational society: Bauman argues that the affluent exist in a tele-city where strangers can be 'gazed at openly, without fear- much as lions in the zoo . . . They are infinitely close as objects; but doomed to remain, happily, infinitely remote as subjects of action' (Bauman 1992: 178).

So just as the internet becomes a space of moral proximity it can also become a digital *atrocity exhibition*, a networked *videodrome*, from images of torture in Iraq through to the exploitation of women and men who sell sexual performance for money or a place to stay.

But for Rorty our networked and deterritorialised society enables moral progress: 'Producing generations of nice, tolerant, well-off, secure, other-respecting students of this sort in all parts of the world is just what is needed – indeed, *all* that is needed – to achieve an Enlightenment utopia' (Rorty 1998: 179). But does this vision not only fail to grasp the points Baudrillard and Bauman are raising but also fail to understand the dynamics of neoliberal capitalism? Capitalism needs inequality – it has no need to create whole populations of well-off, other-respecting citizens. Those who do not make it to the Enlightenment utopia can have their 'alienation' and exclusion satisfied with spectacles that provide them with an Other to blame for their lack of opportunities (the asylum seeker, for example). And the politics of fear, as Adorno and Horkheimer argued (and as Michael Moore's *Fahrenheit 9/11* suggested), plays an important role in the political economy of security, with dangerous others needed to sustain the costs of the military-scientific-policing complex.

The counter-point to the liberal optimists of an Enlightenment utopia are those, like the political philosopher John Gray, who do not believe that the planetary management unfolding through liberal democracy and neoliberal economics can deliver the 'good life'. In the 1980s Gray was a defender of Friedrich Hayek, a thinker central to the project of the neoliberal economy. In the 1990s Gray began to question the laissez-faire ethos of neoliberalism in books such as *False Dawn: The Delusions of Global Capitalism, Straw Dogs: Thoughts on Humans and Other Animals* and *Heresies: Against Progress and Other Illusions*. Gray argues that like most Enlightenment ideologies, communism and neoliberalism are 'obsessively secular'. Yet he argues that they are deeply shaped by religion, based on a faith that humanity can be united in a single way of life: 'Marxism and the cult of the free market are only the latest in a succession of Enlightenment faiths, in which the Christian promise of universal salvation reappears as a political project of universal emancipation' (Gray 2004: 2). The liberal democratic order rests on a *faith* in technology that promises the realisation of the good life for everyone and 'technical fixes' for all the problems and accidents that result from the search for a better world. For Gray, the optimists 'believe this not from real conviction but from fear of the void that looms if the hope of a better future is given up. Belief in progress is the Prozac of the thinking classes' (Gray 2004: 3).

In its most virulent strain, neo-liberalism rests on what Virilio describes as a technical fundamentalism where there can be a technical fix for all the problems that emerge from the march of progress. So, for example, in the case of human-generated climate change, for example, technological solutions will overcome and master any 'distant' dangers that emerge: as George W. Bush argued in presidential debate in 2004, 'Now, I'm going to tell you what I really think is going to happen over time is technology is going to change the way we live for the good for the environment.' Those writing from an alternative perspective will criticise the 'prophets' of the liberal order for ignoring the 'real-time' suffering that occurs from free-markets, financial instability, structural adjustments. But for the liberal optimist this is the route to a more efficient and safe global order: it is the *promise* of a better tomorrow. We need to take our medicine, enforce the regime of health, in order to secure a better tomorrow.

But what if the suffering is for nothing? What if the insecurity and suffering will not lead to a more secure, networked society? What if the dream of a 'perfect market' (see Sum's chapter here), far from ameliorating the insecurity and uncertainty of global existence, will it create new contradictions, forms of inequality and insecurity? What if the technical 'fixes' designed to deliver us from insecurity do not work? This is the 'moral anxiety' that drives the essays collected in this volume.

While many of the authors in this collection share the Frankfurt schools' pessimistic view of the modern world, they are also attuned to the conditions of possibility that the information society creates. Indeed, intellectuals that were concerned with re-thinking the Frankfurt Schools critique – such as Jürgen Habermas – have been concerned to uncover new democratic possibilities in the public sphere.

Now as it has already been suggested, global liberal society depends on the deterritorialisation of bodies, ideas, money, technology, images. As Gilles Deleuze argues:

> Capitalism is founded on a generalised decoding of every flow: flows of wealth, flows of labour, flows of language, flows of art, etc. It did not create any code, it created a kind of accounting, an axiomatics of decoded flows, as the basis of its economy. It ligatures the points of escape and moves ahead. It is always expanding its own borders, pushing them back once more. It has resolved none of its fundamental problems. It can't even foresee the monetary increase in a country over a year. It is endlessly crossing its own limits which keep reappearing farther out. It puts itself in alarming situations with respect to its own production, its social life, its demographics, its periphery in the Third World, its interior regions, etc. The system is leaking all over the place. (Deleuze 2003: 270)

Just as Foucault argued that the modern world was confronted with an excess of biopower, developments that emerge from the 'civilizing process' yet exceed the ability of societies to manage them, it also makes sense to talk of an *excess of information*. Excess in both the sense that information society circulates excessive images, information and ideas (pictures of torture in Abu Graib, beheadings on the internet, pleas from aid workers and contractors in

Iraq begging the global community to help them, the circulation of money across financial markets) but also excess in terms of the images/information/capital that exceed the ability of the organs of the state to control and manage. This excess of information creates alternative conditions of possibility: so, for example, the Baghdad Blog (see Allan's chapter) makes possible new forms of moral proximity, exceeding attempts to manage the official narratives of war and security that circulate under the control of the military-industrial-media-entertainment-network (see Der Derian 2001). In the flow of information, possibilities for communication emerge that exist beyond the ability of the state to code and control them: the system is leaking!

Vanity Fair, as we argued earlier, worked to legitimate the Bush administration's expertise to manage a War on Terror: yet as the administration's intentions in Iraq grew clearer the magazine began to include compelling critiques of their agenda, culminating in a book entitled *What We've Lost* written by the magazine's editor, Graydon Carter. The release of new books by Michael Moore in October 2004, whose film *Fahrenheit 9/11* enraged supporters of Bush (who perhaps contributed to the film receiving an 'R' rating in the United States, a move that attempted to limit the circulation of the film), was countered with the release of *Faith in the White House*, an unofficial documentary on the Christian values of George W. Bush (free copies of the documentary were distributed to churches around the United States). *Fahrenheit 9/11* also provoked *Celsius 41.11: The Temperature At Which The Brain Begins to Die*, an anti-Michael Moore documentary that the *Washington Post* described as a 'cinematic counterstrike' launched by conservatives; attempts to criticise the warrior identity of John Kerry during election campaigning in 2004 were countered by *Going Upriver: The Long War of John Kerry*, a film whose tagline is 'Some men are changed by history. Others Make it'.

The excess of information leads to strategies of re-territorialisation to attempt to contain this excess, new strategies of information war or economic policy to control the excess (see chapters by Compton, David and Kirkhope, Sum and Beder here). This is where the authors differ from the perspective articulated by an intellectual such as Rorty. The chapters in this book are attuned to this excess of information, rejecting both the pessimist visions articulated by Adorno and Horkheimer and the optimistic liberal visions of the global 'open society' leading to a more responsible planetary order.

The chapters in this book reject the heroic narrative in which citizens simply discover the 'truth' or achieve 'moral proximity' and open up the possibility of a more enlightened planetary order, the type of narrative that Gray would argue is the Prozac of the thinking classes. The essays collected here are attuned to the processes of re-territorialisation, the seductive/technical strategies that attempt to (re)code contemporary economic and military developments as the route to freedom and enlightenment. At the same time, there is no consensus or blueprint on how to overcome the deterritorialised problems we confront. Faced with an excess of biopower and information, a plurality of perspectives are contesting the projects for security and efficiency, exploring new conditions of possibility for resistance. It is this excess of perspectives that needs to be cultivated in a period where attempts are made to reduce solutions to the excess of global existence to either/or, us versus them, neoliberalism or disorder.

Chapter outline

The book begins with 'Developing a new speech for global security: exploring the rhetoric of evil in the Bush administration response to 9.11.01' by Timothy Luke. The chapter uses five presidential speeches to explore how the Bush administration has attempted to articulate a new vision of global security shaped by the War on Terror and the emergence of an Axis of Evil. To frame the article in the terms of this introduction: confronted with an excess of biopower, a condition where the enlightened earth radiates disaster triumphant, there are a multitude of (in)security politics that can be selected to provide protection for the citizenry. There is nothing inevitable about the projects that come to define legitimate security politics; and there is no certainty that the legitimate security politics will deliver us from fear. On the contrary, although this security politics sets itself against the 'end of history' optimism of a liberal world order, the vision of security articulated by the Bush administration still rests on an optimism that territories (such as Iraq) can be reshaped into spaces of democracy and order, with dangers such as climate change coded as illegitimate dangers, dangers we need not worry about because a technological 'fix' will protect us. As Paul Virilio argues, there is a 'campaign of civil fear' to prepare populations 'psychologically, pedagogically and morally in the belief in these measures' (Virilio 1990: 39).

Luke's chapter, as well as being a useful introduction into the politics of language developed by Pierre Bourdieu, explores this contemporary campaign of 'civil fear': as Luke informs us, in the absence of a George Marshall or Henry Kissinger to listen to, we must pay attention to the utterances of President Bush because they provide us with indications about where the United States is heading in the twenty-first century. The terms developed by the administration work to normalise (in)security politics through their circulation in political rhetorics, economic arguments and cultural controversies, providing 'key strategic assets for anyone intent upon ruling, and then prevailing globally in struggles over what is real in world politics'. These speeches attempt to legitimate the power of the state in an age confronted with an excess of biopower and an excess of information, re-territorialising the state and its military-scientific complex as the actor that can deliver us from insecurity based on the location of danger outside the space of the 'civilised'.

For an intellectual such as Rorty the excess of information provides the route to a global society where images of suffering can create empathy and the possibility of resistance: images and stories can circulate around the planet beyond the control of nation states, challenging the type of strategies outlined by Luke on the control of the meaning of (in)security politics, strategies that legitimate the division of insiders and outsiders, the civilised and the uncivilised, 'valuable' humans and human waste. In 'Shocked and awed: the convergence of military and media discourse' James Compton looks at how the media became a symbiotic collaborator with the Bush administration, providing *militainment*: the chapter explores a number of spaces where the war in Iraq became dramatised as a spectacle (such as the Saving Private Lynch episode). Compton's chapter raises a sense of caution on the type of perspective articulated by an intellectual such as Rorty, showing how war-as-spectacle reduces moral proximity. But Compton's position also complicates the view that the state (and military-scientific complex) enforces its vision of war on the media to limit and control the excess of information: Compton rejects the 'top-down form of domination' to show examples of the 'willing, and I might add eager, integration of military propaganda, organisational work routines, and the commercial interests of converged-media conglomerates, and other social actors'. In a period where the aestheticisation of politics reaches new levels, we consume and desire spectacles of power, a development which, if managed correctly, provides a 'comfortable' viewing experience; and in a vicious branding war TV channels compete on who is the most patriotic. Dialogue and critical discussion is reduced to a search for spectacle and the type of codings on the 'reality' of (in)security politics mapped out by Luke. And as Compton observes: 'If Disneyland exists, as Baudrillard suggests, to make the rest of the United States appear real, then 'Comical Ali's' outbursts – "We defeated them yesterday. God Willing, I will provide you with more information" – marked the sophisticated American and British Propaganda as truth.'

'Digital divisions: online reporting and the network society' by Stuart Allan sets out to explore online journalism in the context of the informational politics of 9/11 and the war in Iraq in 2003, providing a broad overview of the non-official lines of communication that have opened up. Taking Manuel Castell's work on the 'digital divide' of the network society as his point of departure, Allan argues that a struggle is occurring over the power of news media to shape 'democratic deliberation and debate across what are ever more globalised public spheres'. Allan sees new possibilities for resistance and moral proximity emerging from the new terrain of informational politics: in particular, he points our attention to the emergence of 'blogging' on the internet and the online writings of Salam Pax (now compiled into a more traditional book format). Pax, angered by the activities of both Saddam Hussein and George W. Bush, gave readers an insight into what it felt to live through clean, network-centric war. But more than that, Pax's writings, in their observations on his everyday existence as a young man in Iraq, allowed for the possibility of moral proximity, to give a 'face' to those who seemed Other, beyond our understanding, reduced to statistics and stereotype: 'To the extent', Allan argues, ' that online reporting fosters points of connection at a distance, and in so doing establishes new principles of trust and responsibility, it will help counter the forms of social exclusion endemic to the digital divide.' In a move that develops further the themes we have begun to pursue in this introduction, Allan points us to the strategies that were deployed during the war to contain and control this excess of information: attempts by hackers, for example, to lead an 'electronic onslaught' on al-Jazeera (even to the point where pro-war hackers led viewers to different 'patriotic' sites).

One of the key points in Allan's chapter is that the flexibility of informational capitalism creates unintended consequences as the imperatives of time, space and distance are being re-organised around the planet. This theme is developed further in Matthew David and Jamieson Kirkhope's exploration of the excess of information in the context of intellectual property rights and the deterritorialisation of informational goods (Chapter 4). The authors ground their essay in a discussion of the attempts by corporate interests to maintain profitability in a moment when the system is leaking: due to transformations in informational technology, music and film become deterritorialised in the same manner that war images become deterritorialised, escaping the control of 'legitimate' forms of state and corporate power. Sensitive to the claim that neoliberal 'globalisation' is not simply the move to unorganised deregulation – rather, attempts are made to create new forms of regulation at different scales – David and Kirkhope explore the strategies of re-territorialisation that have been employed to control flows of informational consumer goods. Yet the 'schizophrenic character of technology' means that attempts to control and code flows of information are highly problematic: 'Contemporary encryption software is not without its fallibilities, as algebraic mathematical codes designed to prevent unauthorised access always has the potential to be broken and/or leaked through cyberspace.' With attempts at technical security failing to control flows of informational goods, the authors explore how a more 'traditional' politics of fear has been deployed to construct 'Napster' culture as unpatriotic and deviant. In this discourse a link is made between illegally obtaining informational goods and financing of terror networks, a claim they argue is highly problematic. Attempts to control the excess of information made possible by information communication technology will, the authors conclude, prove futile, leading to a variety of unintended consequences.

The connection between the construction of 'commonsensical codes' that circulate in the public sphere and the (re)construction of financial hegemony is developed further in Ngai-Ling Sum's chapter on 'Global financial markets and the ICT revolution: perfect market or (im-)perfect domination?'

The chapter gives us an overview of the material processes that have deterritorialised global capitalism in the last few decades, concentrating on how transformation in informational and communication technologies have altered the conditions of possibility for global finance. Developing what she describes as a 'neo-Gramscian cultural international political economy approach', Sum is sensitive to the way that processes of neoliberal deterritorialisation were presented in terms of the discourse of the 'perfect market'. The idea of the perfect market is the optimistic dream of the liberal world order: the promise of an efficient global economy that will deliver a better tomorrow. Yet Sum illustrates how the dream of the perfect market is spreading 'structural contradictions, major-crisis tendencies, and strategic dilemmas on a global scale'. Concomitant with policies intended to deterritorialise (and reterritorialise) a global cyber-financial order, a system dominated by those seeking to discipline and normalise the market, is a move to increasingly sophisticated webs of surveillance and discipline (such as credit-rating agencies) that seek to make sure that those who enter the space of cyber-financial flows conform to certain standards of control and discipline: along with the conglomeration of the financial sectors, these processes have led to a disproportionate gain of rentier income by financial actors.

It is difficult to discern whether the strategies of informational politics are outcomes of propaganda techniques developed for war or whether corporate public relations exercises are shaping contemporary war management: what is clear is that the language of neoliberal capitalist culture and network-centric war are increasingly similar (such as the multiple use of the term 'flexibility') and often driven by the same 'advances' in technology (as Sum's chapter illustrated). What Sharon Beder sets out in her chapter on 'Corporate propaganda and global capitalism: selling free enterprise?' is an overview of the connections between corporate activity and public relations, giving us both an insight into why this fusion occurred and the strategies deployed to make neoliberal capitalism appear as 'accepted wisdom in policy circles' (the dream of the 'perfect market') and in society more broadly. For Beder, new formations of propaganda technique emerged as a reaction to the counter-cultural response to social and environmental problems that intensified in the 1960s. Beder then sets out to describe the strategies devised to contain this excess of information, pointing to the rise of neo-conservative think tanks and 'public affairs' departments. Beder observes that for corporate interests feeling threatened by the excess of information the only strategy was to mirror counter cultural strategies: 'Corporations began to adopt the strategies that public-interest activists had used so effectively against them, grass-roots organizing and coalition building, telephone and letter-writing campaigns, using the media, research reports and testifying at hearings.' An important component in the democratisation of information technology, as other chapters have illustrated, is that new developments often create unintended consequences: networks of resistance are often able to use informational technology produced by technocratic elites as a critical tool – and then the strategies of resistance become absorbed by state and corporate interests (although as David and Kirkhope argue, technical security is often impossible. . .). In this chapter we get an overview of the multitude of strategies that are deployed to limit critical thought on the excesses of globalisation.

Up to this point, the chapters have focused on the strategies of control and resistance in the context of war and informational capitalism in the 'developed' world (although the implications of these developments are deterritorialised, exceeding the limits of national territory). 'The revolution will now be televised: strategies of communication and class conflict in Brazil' by Peter Wilkin and Danielle Beswick focuses on the politics of communication between the Workers' Party, President Lula da Silva and the dominant media institution in Brazil, the Globo network. So far the chapters have focused on the problems of the excess of information for liberal democracies; this chapter explores the problem of the excess of information from a different perspective. Simply put, the Globo network became a dominant actor in Brazilian society through its support for a regime that terrorised large sections of the citizenry. The network has adopted flexible strategies to maintain its position of power, patrolling 'the boundaries of Brazil's newly re-emerging democratic political culture by attacking those that went beyond the limit's of what Brazil's ruling classes saw as legitimate policies'. President Lula faces a problem in this context: does he pursue a progressive agenda or develop a neoliberal project? The outcome is not inevitable as da Silva could, the authors argue, work with the Workers' Party, drawing on their organic and far-reaching social forces. What the chapter does is explore complications of the excess of information for a state emerging from being a 'control society' to something not yet decided: President Lula used neoliberal principles to deny Globo access to state funds, a move that can create more diverse networks of communication. However, creating the conditions of possibility for an excess of information means that there are grave dangers for his more progressive agenda.

The next chapter – 'Global solidarity and the communications revolution: resisting state and capital' by John Boyle and Peter Wilkin – broadens the discussion to look at the emergence of the anti-globalisation movement and Indymedia. The chapter explores how information technology has enabled a diverse and pluralistic network of interests concerned with social justice to organise globally. Challenging the view that the anti-globalisation movement is dominated by the affluent and secure, the authors argue that problems of injustice and suffering in the global south were an important driving force in the formation of this decentralised and deterritorialised movement. Indeed, Movements for Global Social Justice took inspiration from the strategies developed by the Zapatistas in Chiapas, Mexico to promote their cause on a global scale, driven also by movements in the South concerned about attempts to dominate agriculture through intellectual property rights, an attempt to contain the excess of genetic information. Boyle and Wilkin also draw attention to the sense of disillusionment felt by many across the globe on the view that organisations like Greenpeace were too intimately connected to the system that they sought to challenge. What becomes clear as the chapter unfolds is that the rise of an alternative media network – Indymedia – to articulate this global agenda stems from a direct awareness of the strategies that state and capital can use to control the excess of information. So the 'low-fi' approach to news circulation, enabled by decentralised networks of local movements, can develop a large following without compromising its concern with social justice. What is more, its decentralised and deterritorialised form means that it appears to avoid the type of 'electronic onslaught' that Allan discussed earlier. While the authors see Indymedia as a work-in-progress they see in its organisation an attempt to evade control . . . the system continues to leak.

In keeping with the lines of thought pursued through the volume, the book concludes with 'The global public sphere: fourth estate or new world information disorder?' by Brian McNair, a chapter that offers a note of caution about the ability of the 'fourth estate' to contribute to the evolution of a global democratic politics. Providing us with a useful survey of the different perspectives on media and communication studies, the chapter is a reminder that – as many of the other chapters have illustrated – the 'progressive impact of these new media cannot be taken for granted, and cannot be predicted in isolation from consideration of the local political, economic and cultural factors which constrain or encourage their adoption, and which shape their use'. For McNair we have to be aware of the dangers of living in a *society of the spectacle* where instantaneous information circulation can evade the types of control discussed in many of the chapters here but that can also lead to a concern with scandal and real-time trivia. As Zygmunt Bauman has observed in a discussion of scandal and politicians, it is 'their own personal morality, not the ethics they promote or fail to promote – the personally corrupting, not socially devastating, effects of political power – the moral integrity of the politicians, not the morality of the world they promote or perpetuate – which seem to exhaust or nearly exhaust the morality-and-politics agenda' (Bauman 1992: 245). What the chapters collected here illustrate is while there are many dangers in informational politics, dangers that risk to exhaust the morality-and-politics agenda and control the excess of information, the system *is* leaking and hierarchies of good/bad or optimism/pessimism fail to capture the complexities of global politics in an information age.

1 | Timothy W. Luke

Developing a new speech for global security: exploring the rhetoric of evil in the Bush administration response to 9.11.01

Overview

The greatest challenges to global security prior to 9.11.01 still were tied largely to the aftershocks of 12.25.91, or, more specifically, the final collapse of the Soviet Union. While the USA welcomed this development in Moscow, the first Bush administration under George H. W. Bush really did very little to lay out any new discourses for global security on the level of the Cold War's experiments with containment, rollback, coexistence or detente. For nearly a decade, the larger world system experienced a series of mostly disconnected, and usually minor, disruptions in the liberal democratic peace – ranging from Somalia, Bosnia, Haiti to Rwanda, Chechnya, Afghanistan – that many believed would crop up occasionally from the New World order forged in the Gulf War of 1991 (Rosenau 1990; Kaplan 1996; and Luke 1996). While it was itself another instance of minor fallout from the unravelling of the old Soviet bloc, the Gulf War in Kuwait, however, created many of the dangerous preconditions for 9.11.01.

9.11.01 seems to have transformed the ambiguous terrains of the post-Cold War era as the US and its allies in the multi-form and varying 'coalition of the willing' have seized upon the struggle against 'global terrorism' to anchor a new global security regime, which is tied neither to the Cold War nor the post-Cold War eras. Defining and developing such a regime requires a new security discourse, and this discourse has, in far too many ways, yet to be effectively articulated. This analysis, then, will examine a few of President George W. Bush's pronouncements about 'the war on terror' for insights into this process, which seem to have been revealed most clearly in five different presidential speeches made during his first administration in 2001–2002. Clearly, the themes developed more fully in these major addresses also surface repeatedly in President Bush's daily comments on public affairs, but the Address to a Joint Session of Congress and the American People on 20 September, 2001, the 'Get on Board' speech at O'Hare International Airport on 27 September, 2001, the Address to the

Nation on 7 October, 2001 announcing attacks on Afghanistan, the State of the Union Address on 29 January, 2002 and the Graduation Speech at West Point on 1 June, 2002 are where the essence of the Bush administration's agendas were first most clearly articulated.

More concretely, this study also will ask how a curious rhetorical figure introduced by President Bush in the 2002 State of the Union speech, namely, the so-called 'axis of evil states', provides insights into how this new security regime is evolving. The Bush administration's effort to conjure up an 'axis of evil' appears aimed at defining a new absolute enemy whose nefarious fifth columns at home and invidious sneak attacks abroad constitute a pretext that more than justifies an aggressive interventionist foreign policy on the behalf of the USA and its allies. While the 9.11.01 events truly were terrible, it is also clear that they were not the worst possible assault on the USA ever perpetrated by any enemy foreign or domestic. Yet, because of the powerful images taken during this violence, President George W. Bush is now working hard to create a vision of an enemy so evil, so widespread, and so threatening that everything in the nation's foreign, military and security affairs must change radically to defeat it.

A world's sole remaining superpower needs a worthy adversary, if not an absolute enemy, to ground its strategic efforts, and the US clearly drifted during the 1990s without any readily defensible opposition (Kennedy 1993). Despite all the talk about Iraq since 1991, Baghdad alone plainly lacked the heft to constitute a credible enemy in and of itself – as its invasion in March 2003 and occupation since May 2004 have shown. An axis of evil, however, which allegedly counts Iraq, Iran, or North Korea among its ranks, is far more threatening prospect, even if the plausibility of such a coalition is hard to defend. Nonetheless, saying something is so, often moves it towards becoming so. To imagine a new community of allies, it also therefore helps to have a very clearly defined enemy (Anderson 1991). Consequently, the Bush administration's construction of Iraq as the pivotal directing point for an axis of evil – first as a state with real but hidden 'weapons of mass destruction' (WMD) and then as the worlds' biggest new terrorist haven – continues to be an essential ingredient in Washington's strategies for coping with the post-Cold War, and now what comes after in 'the post-post-Cold War' world order.

A study like this one is difficult to conduct, because the President George W. Bush plainly is not running one of the more rhetorically adept regimes that have ever occupied the White House. In contrast to Presidents Clinton or Reagan before him, President George W. Bush also is not an effective speechmaker. Instead he relies a great deal, like his father and President Reagan, upon a cadre of speechwriters whose words he then often struggles to deliver correctly. Even so, this speech writing has become a discursive space where the USA's leadership is developing new figures of speech to define 'security' in the twenty-first century. Likewise, there has not been a great architect for this conceptual transition at work either in the White House or the State Department. Secretary of State Colin Powell has been a low-key figure since 2000, and he is resigning at the end of the president's first term. Likewise, his successor, National Security Advisor, Condoleezza Rice, also is not given to making big, bold public assessments of world affairs. Without a George Marshall, a Henry Kissinger or even a George Schultz to listen to, one must then pay more attention to the declarations and utterances of President Bush. His remarks on foreign and domestic affairs since 9.11.01, however, do provide a tremendous source of material to consider larger questions about where the USA is headed in the twenty-first century as well as where Washington now draws its lines between a friendly 'inside' and threatening 'outside' (Walker 1993).

The politics of speech: speech wrights and speech writs

Anyone who still abides by an instrumental understanding of language in which words are assumed to have certain meanings, follow permissible uses, and abide by correct constructions will be disappointed by this analysis. Such approaches to language are all too often unsophisticated, presumptuous and confused. Instead, this investigation will go along with Bourdieu (1990: 54), who observes that 'when dealing with the social world, the ordinary use of ordinary language makes metaphysicians of us'. Diplomatic communiqués, official pronouncements and executive declarations all rely upon using words in quite artful performances whose power and knowledge effects can be profound and pervasive precisely because of their metaphysical import. Language is action, and the word-making moves of world statesmen often have world-making outcomes for the states that hang upon such words (Burke 1954; Greimas 1987; and Bourdieu 1990). 'Speech writing', then, produces 'speech writs'. Once such writs are issued, the speech wrights in government often work towards rewriting the world to fit their words or fulfil their writs.

'Writ' comes into modern English from Old Norwegian, Old High German, Old Icelandic, and Old English where it first meant 'a pen stroke, a character', or 'a drawing'. In many ways, the rhetorical writs spun up by speech writing today are efforts aimed at drawing and redrawing the characteristics of the world's geopolitical terrain. From strokes of rhetoric, the Bush administration has struggled after 9.11.01 to propound a series of new national security writs about the nature of conflict and cooperation in the twenty-first century as 'a war on terror'. Because most of the chaos of the immediate post-Cold War period made so little sense to people inured to the more clear-cut antagonisms the Cold War, this post-9.11 task is doubly demanding.

The last vestiges of Cold War struggle with the USSR have been erased by Washington's many friendly dealings with Moscow under Yeltsin and Putin, but the complexities of the New World Order declared by President George H. W. Bush during the Gulf War never substantially shifted most of the USA's diplomatic or military practices. The Clinton administration's celebration of 'globalisation' only echoed the corporate ideologies of the 1990s, and this administration never came completely to grips with the radical Islamic terrorist strikes around the world from 1993 to 2000. The audacity and effectiveness of the Al Qaeda terrorists on 9.11.01, however, have provided the administration of President George W. Bush with a remarkable opportunity to reframe the nation's domestic and foreign strategies of governance to suit what it imagines to be new twenty-first century realities. Consequently, the formal speech writing of this administration should be read more attentively to observe how this regime is redrawing world geopolitical realities as well as the USA's engagement with many new enemies and friends in this global environment.

In this respect, Bourdieu also usefully notes that 'the social world is the locus of struggles over words which owe their seriousness–and sometimes their violence–to the fact that words to a great extent make things, and that changing words, and, more generally, representations (for example, pictorial representation, like Manet), is already a way of changing things. Politics is, essentially, a matter of words' (1990: 54). This observation is true inasmuch as individuals and groups tussle over words, with language, and in deeds, for greater symbolic power. And, the metaphysical act of naming things, and thereby bringing them into being out of nothingness, is, as Bourdieu asserts, 'the most typical demonstration' (Bourdieu 1990: 55) of such power-in-action. Speech is a series of strokes, whose characters draw and redraw realities in new writs of action.

Political rhetorics, therefore, roll up together many versal possibilities as they become entangled in the politics of actualising their more complete realisation in practice. At the same time, experts can opine about these emerging rhetorics, while lay persons may believe wholeheartedly those opinions, which begins the confirmation of the new *doxa* expressed by these discourses (Bourdieu 1998a: 39–63). Such speech then extrudes elements of 'what is' out of what it refers to. Out of all the debates exploring what the subjects under discussion could be, speech writing often writes what will be. By presuming to suggest what such changes should be, the exponents of this or that speech often cause parallel events and processes to come into effect, which tests, in turn, what they should and should not be. The hesitant multiversal qualities of these transformations can become much more definitive and universal, because speaking about them anchors the practical invention of their referents (Peirce 1955). President Bush's axis of evil could be many different things, but its rhetorical construction now requires very specific forms of completion, definition, and execution in American policy. Whatever the axis of evil might be, it is so because of how it has been imagined by the White House's rhetoric's that discover, define and then describe such terms in political debates (Connolly 1992 and Halton 1995).

Terms, like 'the axis of evil', 'enduring freedom', 'evildoers' or 'struggle of freedom and fear', are the creations of speech writers intent on rewriting the unspoken and spoken understandings of fully mediatised and highly educated publics. Such audiences often accept, as Bourdieu claims, 'the vague debates of a political philosophy without technical content, a social science reduced to journalistic commentary for election nights, and uncritical glossing of unscientific opinion polls' (Bourdieu 1998b: 7). Because they openly trade into and out all of the ordinary opinions that are so dearly embraced by some simply because they have already been accepted by many, such speech writers now act as doxosophers. These mediated doxosophies then frequently anchor the basic ideas and ethics that 'the voting public' relies upon in its processes of self-governance. Not surprisingly, such speech writers, as Bourdieu indicates, often see themselves as 'technicians of opinion who think themselves wise', and their patterns of speech writing usually 'pose the problems of politics in the very same terms in which they are posed by businessmen, politicians, and political journalists (in other words the very people who can afford to commission surveys . . .)' (Bourdieu 1998b: 7). As lovers of opinion, they continue propounding new doxa from their work in speech writs.

Speech writing, then, is decisively important here. When successful, it flows into the larger cultural habitus shared by major corporate, governmental and professional authorities. Allusions to alikeness and definitions of difference in such rhetorical constructs can be easily expressed through diplomatic actions when political agents share such outlooks. As Bourdieu maintains, 'the habitus fulfils a function which another philosophy consigns to a transcendental conscience: it is a socialized body, a structured body, a body which has incorporated the immanent structures of a world or of a particular sector of that world–a field–and which structures the perception of that world as well as action in that world' (Bourdieu 1998a: 39–63).

Ideas of necessity, desirability, and universality implied by speech writing are imparted to institutions and interjected into other ideas through habitus as the speech wright 'retranslates the intrinsic and relational characteristics of a position' in the world with its many styles of living into 'a unitary set of choices of persons, goods, practices' (Bourdieu 1998a: 8). Once these doxic effects begin to shape the fields of action and decision, those results are easily integrated into the shared habitus. Inside of such doxological systems of valorisation, speech wrights help make 'distinctions between what is good and what is bad, between what is right and what is wrong, between what is distinguished and what is vulgar' (Bourdieu 1998a: 8), as the constructs of the world carried by words push and pull everyone toward world constructions that match the wordings that have been tested by rhetoric in diplomatic discourses.

Shared speech bolsters the symbolic order of society to the extent that its terms are, first, systematic and coherent as discursive frameworks, and, second, consistent and agreeable with objective conditions in the institutional structures of society. With these dispositions, speech writing ensures popular belief in the established order as well as coordinates the actions and thoughts of the larger publics with ruling/owning/controlling elites by finding the right relations of '*doxic submission* which attaches us to the established order with all the ties of the unconscious' (Bourdieu 1998a: 55). The work of speech writers as political speech wrights has become even more intriguing in the aftermath of the Cold War. Having won the long twilight struggle against communist totalitarianism, the United States is governed by conservative Republican leaders who now believe this nation incarnates what is best in the human spirit (Reich 1991; Barber 1995). Consequently, a genuine world politics, whose key issues range from global peace to individual freedom to political justice, are getting greater consideration in the pronouncements of the White House as America's presidents wend their ways through the politics of the post-Cold War era.

Spinning up the axis of evil

On one level, it is possible to claim there is very little evidence substantiating the existence of 'an axis of evil' either out on the ground or back in the farthest corners of the world system. Yet, this is just the point. The Bush administration has promised to not waver, to not falter, and to not fail in carrying this battle to the enemy. Therefore, it needs a pretext for conveying this coercive intent whenever, wherever and to whomever it must. Asserting that an indefinite axis of evil exists, and then doing everything it can to generate evidence to support its case, is an expression of the new speech needed to delimit, detail and defend its vision of twenty-first century world affairs.

While the ferocity of 9.11.01 was not unprecedented, and recent revelations from the CIA, FBI, NSA and the National 9/11 Commission suggest that these attacks were even widely anticipated by the USA prior to 9.11.01, the audacity and lethality of the assaults on the Pentagon and World Trade Center underscore the need for a new security discourse. By happening in Year One of the twenty-first century, 9.11.01 has enabled the Bush Administration to junk most of the nation's old Cold War rhetoric as well as much of its never widely embraced post-Cold War terms of speech. President Bush remains, at best, a mediocre communicator, but his trusted advisors, expert pollsters and gifted writers are working with him in a joint effort to rewrite the figure and tenor of political speech in the USA for the twenty-first century.

Many of the better indicators of this rhetorical reformation are the organic connection between President Bush's State of the Union speech in January 2002 and his West Point commencement speech in June 2002. His declaration of war against an 'axis of evil' in January is matched in June by a new aggressive foreign policy whose prime predicate is 'no neutrality' in waging another long twilight struggle between right and wrong, good and evil, light and darkness. Repudiating any traditional notions of simple containment or mere deterrence, Bush pledged the nation to an activist policy of pre-emption, promising its terrorist foes that the American armed forces would be readied 'to strike at a moment's notice in any dark corner of the world'.

From the first day after the attacks of 9.11.01, President Bush has worked to transform the hunt for individuals who commit acts of terrorist violence into a new kind of war. In a world where 'soft power' attracts intense attacks by non-state actors, a strategy tied to resisting the 'hard power' of states simply will not work. As he explained in the Cabinet Room of the White House during a 9.12.01 meeting with his national security team, the events of 9.11 were something different from terrorist violence: 'The deliberate and deadly attacks which were carried out yesterday against our country were more than acts of terror. They were acts of war' (www.whitehouse.gov /news/releases/2001/09/20010912–4.html).

Finding himself in a new war, or the first war of the twenty-first century, President Bush finds a new national imperative of action for all Americans as well as the profile of a new enemy that is stateless, furtive, and unprincipled:

> The American people need to know that we're facing a different enemy than we have ever faced. This enemy hides in shadows, and has no regard for human life. This is an enemy who preys on innocent and unsuspecting people, then runs for cover. But it won't be able to run for cover forever. This is an enemy that tries to hide. But it won't be able to hide forever. This is an enemy that thinks its harbours are safe. But they won't be safe forever.

Having labelled the terrorists as cowardly, unscrupulous, and vicious in their globally dispersed dispositions, President Bush also correctly cast their attacks as an assault on the globalising world, only one that was focused first on the USA.

Ultimately, this new alliance of America and 'the freedom-loving nations of the world stand[ing] by our side' will, in turn, now be engaged in 'a monumental struggle of good versus evil'. Therefore, Mr. Bush asserted 'the war on terror' is truly a global war for the USA with global allies and enemies.

> This enemy attacked not just one people, but all freedom-loving people everywhere in the world. The United States of America will use all our resources to conquer this enemy. We will rally the world. We will be patient, we will be focused, and we will be steadfast in our determination. (www.whitehouse.gov /news/releases/2001/09/20010912–4.html)

President Bush claims that he realised the USA was under some new sort of attack on 9.11.01, but he did not know why, how or by whom. The events of the first week soon gave him answers to these questions, and the President quickly defined this attacking enemy as a host of 'evil ones' or 'evil-doers'. On 9.13.01, as he declared Friday, 9.14.01 a national day of prayer and remembrance, the President was clear about his intent to hunt down and destroy these opponents: 'Civilized people around the world denounce the evil-doers who devised and executed these terrible attacks. Justice demands that those who helped or harboured the terrorists be punished–and punished severely. The enormity of their evil demands it.'

After nearly a week of national paralysis and anticipation, President Bush on Sunday, 9.16.01 called on the nation in remarks made on the South Lawn at the White House to return to work, but know also that they were returning to their daily tasks in a brand new world – one where 'evil-doers' lurked in their midst, plotting more outrages. As President Bush observed in his prepared remarks and Q-and-A with the press,

> and tomorrow the good people of America go back to their shops, their fields, American factories, and go back to work.
>
> Our nation was horrified, but it's not going to be terrorized . . . we're a nation that can't be cowed by evil-doers . . . but we've been warned. We've been warned there are evil people in this world. (www.whitehouse.gov/news /releases/2001/09/20010916–2.html)

Thus, the nation challenged by evil-doers will wage war in return against this 'new kind of enemy', or, some people so barbaric that they would fly airplanes into buildings full of innocent people. And, therefore, we have to be alert in America,

> We need to go back to work tomorrow and we will. But we need to be alert to the fact that these evil-doers still exist. We haven't seen this kind of barbarism in a long period of time. No one could have conceivably imagined suicide bombers burrowing into our society and then emerging all in the same day to fly their aircraft–fly US aircraft into buildings full of innocent people–and show no remorse. This is a new kind–a new kind of evil and we understand. And the American people are beginning to understand. This crusade, this war on terrorism is going to take a while. It is time for us to win the first war of the twenty-first century decisively, so that our children and our grandchildren can live peacefully into the twenty-first century. (www.whitehouse.gov/news/ releases/2001/09/20010916–2.html)

Because the war at hand is uncertain, undeclared, and undefined by traditional standards, President Bush warned the nation that the USA would go anywhere and fight with any ally to rid the world of this new foe.

Seeing Al Qaeda and Osama Bin Laden allied with the Taliban in Afghanistan as the nation's enemies, the President quickly won the support of Pakistan's President Mushsaraf whom ironically the President could not name or place during his 2000 election campaign, to help the USA 'to hunt down, to find, to smoke out of their holes the terrorist organization that is the prime suspect', which would be a difficult task given how 'this American people are used to a conflict where there was a beach head or a desert to cross or known military targets. That may occur but right now we're facing a people who hit and run. They hide in caves' (www.whitehouse.gov/news /releases/2001/09/20010916–2.html).

President Bush's speechwriters in these utterances are seeking to rewrite the world around justice and injustice; and, as a just hyperpower, the USA must root out and eradicate terrorism wherever it operates. In the State of the Union address, he claims,

> Our cause is just, and it continues. Our discoveries in Afghanistan confirmed our worst fears, and showed us the true scope of the task ahead. We have seen the depth of our enemies' hatred in videos, where they laugh about the loss of innocent life. And the depth of their hatred is equalled by the madness of the destruction they design. We have found diagrams of American nuclear power plants and public water facilities, detailed instructions for making chemical weapons, surveillance maps of American cities, and thorough descriptions of landmarks in America and throughout the world.
>
> What we have found in Afghanistan confirms that, far from ending there, our war against terror is only beginning. Most of the 19 men who hijacked planes on September the 11th were trained in Afghanistan's camps, and so were tens of thousands of others. Thousands of dangerous killers, schooled in the methods of murder, often supported by outlaw regimes, are now spread throughout the world like ticking time bombs, set to go off without warning.
>
> Thanks to the work of our law enforcement officials and coalition partners, hundreds of terrorists have been arrested. Yet, tens of thousands of trained terrorists are still at large. These enemies view the entire world as a battlefield, and we must pursue them wherever they are. So long as training camps operate, so long as nations harbour terrorists, freedom is at risk. And America and our allies must not, and will not, allow it. (www.whitehouse.gov/news /releases/2002/01/20020129–11.html)

Getting these terrorists, however, is only the USA's first goal. Its second objective is destroying an 'axis of evil states' that aid and abet the world's alleged terrorist network. The writs of twenty-first century security speech demand that the USA face down and then dismantle every threat to its security from stateless and state-sponsored terrorism (Luke and Tuathail, 1997; Friedman 1999). With regard to terrorist states, President Bush is very clear:

> Our second goal is to prevent regimes that sponsor terror from threatening America or our friends and allies with weapons of mass destruction. Some of these regimes have been pretty quiet since September the 11th. But we know their true nature. North Korea is a regime arming with missiles and weapons of mass destruction, while starving its citizens.
>
> Iran aggressively pursues these weapons and exports terror, while an unelected few repress the Iranian people's hope for freedom.
>
> Iraq continues to flaunt its hostility toward America and to support terror. The Iraqi regime has plotted to develop anthrax, and nerve gas, and nuclear weapons for over a decade. This is a regime that has already used poison gas to murder thousands of its own citizens – leaving the bodies of mothers huddled over their dead children. This is a regime that agreed to international inspections – then kicked out the inspectors. This is a regime that has something to hide from the civilized world.

States like these, and their terrorist allies, constitute an axis of evil, arming
to threaten the peace of the world. By seeking weapons of mass destruction,
these regimes pose a grave and growing danger. They could provide these arms
to terrorists, giving them the means to match their hatred. They could attack
our allies or attempt to blackmail the United States. In any of these cases, the
price of indifference would be catastrophic.

We will work closely with our coalition to deny terrorists and their state
sponsors the materials, technology, and expertise to make and deliver weapons
of mass destruction. We will develop and deploy effective missile defences to
protect America and our allies from sudden attack. And all nations should
know: America will do what is necessary to ensure our nation's security.

We'll be deliberate, yet time is not on our side. I will not wait on events,
while dangers gather. I will not stand by, as peril draws closer and closer. The
United States of America will not permit the world's most dangerous regimes
to threaten us with the world's most destructive weapons. (www.whitehouse
.gov/news/releases/2002/01/20020129–11.html)

By not allowing 'the world's most dangerous regimes to threaten us with the
world's most destructive weapons', President Bush is seeking to guarantee
the USA's 'national security' and 'homeland security'. Still, the other corner-
stone of his plan for the USA is an equally spirited defence of its 'economic
security'.

Such rhetoric cannot be ignored. To claim such an axis exists, and that it
is evil, is to dip into a river of discursive traditions whose flow is very familiar to most listeners for whom this rhetoric is created. Saying something is
so begins to make it so, if only because these claims will bob along in the
streams of prevailing discursive practice (Deibert 1997). 'Discursive practices', as Foucault asserts, 'are characterized by the demarcation of a field
of objects, by the definition of a legitimate perspective for a subject of
knowledge, by the setting of norms for elaborating concepts and theories.
Hence, each of them presupposes a play of prescriptions that govern exclu-
sions and selections' (quoted in Deibert 1997: 11). President Bush always
struggles to communicate articulately, and he must succeed to ply the cur-
rents of communicative interactions that signal the USA's goals, intentions
and strategies in world affairs. The discursive practices of America's
national leadership as well as the historical knowledge of North Atlantic
publics make it possible for him to utter a phrase like 'an axis of evil'.
Having said it, however, makes it necessary for him to demarcate, stabilise
and legitimate this field of objects in an effective fashion, which the speech
writing and staff work of the Bush administration has been at pains to do
since January 2002.

President Bush prepared the ground for his 'axis of evil' rhetoric on
September 20 in his address to a Joint Session of Congress. This speech characterised global terrorism and its followers as the 'heirs to all the murderous
ideologies of the twentieth century. By sacrificing human life to serve their
radical visions – by abandoning every value except the will to power –

they follow in the path of fascism, and Nazism, and totalitarianism'
(www.whitehouse.gov/news/releases/2001/09/20010920–8.html).

The terrorists' having declared war on the USA, the USA will, in turn,
declare war on global terrorism in a battle that will be like no others the
nation has waged. Instead, this conflict will require

> far more than instant retaliation and isolated strokes. Americans should not
> expect one battle, but a lengthy campaign, unlike any other we have ever seen.
> It may include dramatic strikes, visible on TV, and covert operations, secret
> even in success. We will starve terrorists of funding, turn them one against
> another, drive them from place to place, until there is no refuge or rest. And we
> will pursue nations that provide aid or safe haven to terrorism. Every nation,
> in every region, now has a decision to make. Either you are with us, or you are
> with the terrorists. From this day forward, any nation that continues to harbor
> or support terrorism will be regarded by the United States as a hostile regime.

With these words, the USA left behind both the Cold War, and the post-Cold
War era, and pushed ahead into a new security environment.

At home, the attack on civilians on American territory moved the White
House to create a new Office of Homeland Security to increase the active and
passive defence of the nation everywhere 24/7. Abroad, President Bush
declared that battle must involve all of the world's nations in a struggle
against extremism, radicalism and terrorism. Hence, the White House also
made it clear that this fight is not America's alone. As he recounted in his
remarks, the citizens of 80 other countries were killed at the World Trade
Center with scores of citizens killed from the nations of Pakistan, Israel,
India, Mexico, Japan, Iran, and Canada as well as hundreds from the United
Kingdom. Consequently, Bush asserted,

> This is civilization's fight. Thus the fight of all who believe in progress and plu-
> ralism, tolerance and freedom.
>   We ask every nation to join us. We will ask, and we will need, the help of
> police forces, intelligence services, and baking systems around the world. The
> United States is grateful that many nations and many international organiza-
> tions have already responded – with sympathy and with support. Nations from
> Latin America, to Asia, to Africa, to Europe, to the Islamic world. Perhaps the
> NATO charter reflects best the attitude of the world: An attack on one is an
> attack on all. (www.whitehouse.gov/news/releases/2001/09/20010920–8.html)

Thus, the USA became engaged in a new titanic struggle, which President Bush
also sees a call to redefine both himself as a leader and the USA as a nation.

Noting that great harm has been done to the USA, and that it has suffered
great harm, President Bush's speech writers on September 20, 2001 rewrote
the realities of American hyperpower. That is,

> in our grief and anger we have found our mission and our moment. Freedom
> and fear are at war. The advance of human freedom – the great achievement
> of our time, and the great hope of everytime – now depends on us. Our nation

– this generation – will lift a dark threat or violence from our people and our future. We will rally the world to this cause by our efforts, by our courage we will not tire, we will not falter, and we will not fail.

And, more importantly, President Bush also found his personal mission and moment in 9.11. Recounting how he would carry the badge of a NYPD officer, who fell at the WTC, the President maintained that he too would not 'forget the wound or those who inflicted it. I will not yield; I will not rest; I will not relent in waging this struggle for freedom and security for the American people' (www.whitehouse.gov/news/releases/2001/09/20010920–8.html).

Even though its allies and antagonists see the US as a hyperpower, few domestic interest groups anywhere in the USA are enthusiastic about embracing the putative obligations of wielding such power. Therefore, the President must spin up this rhetoric, and do it very effectively, if he is to succeed at redrawing the world to suit these structures of significance.

Winning the war between 'freedom' and 'fear'

The axis of evil trope plainly serves a useful purpose as a standing writ of authority for the USA to intrude upon, inspect and ultimately interrupt the domestic affairs of any nation touched by Al Qaeda's transnational operations. Nonetheless, it also helps anchor the Bush administration's oddly conservative, but also strangely neoliberal, commitment to 'freedom'. Here too one sees the writs of speech writing redrawing the meanings of key political concepts and concerns. Freedom at the White House today is essentially a bundle of negative freedoms, and it has a national security tinge to its sense of positive freedoms.

This interventionist impulse was writ quite large in the West Point graduation speech. There President Bush was very explicit:

> The work ahead is difficult. The choices we will face are complex. We must uncover terror cells in 60 or more countries, using every tool of finance, intelligence and law enforcement. Along with our friends and allies, we must oppose proliferation and confront regimes that sponsor terror, as each case requires. Some nations need military training to fight terror, and we'll provide it. Other nations oppose terror, but tolerate the hatred that leads to terror – and that must change. We will send diplomats where they are needed, and we will send you, our soldiers, where you're needed.
>
> All nations that decide for aggression and terror will pay a price. We will not leave the safety of America and the peace of the planet at the mercy of a few mad terrorists and tyrants. We will lift this dark threat from our country and from the world.

Such activist plans for global intervention are, in turn, all the more necessary to President Bush because these opponents are every bit as evil as those the nation once faced in the twentieth century. Like the Cold War and World

War II before it, the White House sees moral purpose behind its plans in this war:

> Because the war on terror will require resolve and patience, it will also require firm moral purpose. In this way our struggle is similar to the Cold War. Now, as then, our enemies are totalitarians, holding a creed of power with no place for human dignity. Now, as then, they seek to impose a joyless conformity, to control every life and all of life.
>
> America confronted imperial communism in many different ways – diplomatic, economic, and military. Yet moral clarity was essential to our victory in the Cold War. When leaders like John F. Kennedy and Ronald Reagan refused to gloss over the brutality of tyrants, they gave hope to prisoners and dissidents and exiles, and rallied free nations to a great cause. (www/whitehouse.gov /news/releases/2002/06/20020601-3.html)

To stand for right and good, President Bush issues the writs to define these beliefs. Again, at West Point he asserts:

> Some worry that it is somehow undiplomatic or impolite to speak the language of right and wrong. I disagree. Different circumstances require different methods, but not different moralities. Moral truth is the same in every culture, in every time, and in every place. Targeting innocent civilians for murder is always and everywhere wrong. Brutality against women is always and everywhere wrong. There can be no neutrality between justice and cruelty, between the innocent and the guilty. We are in a conflict between good and evil, and America will call evil by its name. By confronting evil and lawless regimes, we do not create a problem, we reveal a problem. And we will lead the world in opposing it. (www.whitehouse.gov/news/releases/2002/20020601-3.html)

The vague ideal of freedom is, at the same time, thrown forth as the other great writ of authority that the USA is guaranteeing for the world (Ohmae, 1990; Reich, 1991; and, Greider, 1997). 9.11.01 is unifying the great and good allegedly 'for freedom' and 'against fear' in a new global alliance:

> Today the great powers are also increasingly united by common values, instead of divided by conflicting ideologies. The United States, Japan and our Pacific friends, and now all of Europe, share a deep commitment to human freedom, embodied in strong alliances such as NATO. And the tide of liberty is rising in many other nations.
>
> Generations of West Point officers planned and practiced for battles with Soviet Russia. I've just returned from a new Russia, now a country reaching toward democracy, and our partner in the war against terror. Even in China, leaders are discovering that economic freedom is the only lasting source of national wealth. In time, they will find that social and political freedom is the only true source of national greatness.
>
> When the great powers share common values, we are better able to confront serious regional conflicts together, better able to cooperate in preventing the spread of violence or economic chaos. In the past, great power rivals took sides in difficult regional problems, making divisions deeper and more complicated.

Today, from the Middle East to South Asia, we are gathering broad international coalitions to increase the pressure for peace. We must build strong and great power relations when times are good; to help manage crisis when times are bad. America needs partners to preserve the peace, and we will work with every nation that shares this noble goal. (www.whitehouse.gov/news/releases/2002/06/20020601–3.html)

In the fight of 'freedom' with 'fear', the President's speech writers are promulgating writs of authority for Washington to rewrite the world's geopolitical terrains with its hyperpower. Destroying Al Qaeda and the Taliban in Afghanistan, and then Saddam Hussein and the Ba'athists in Iraq, are simply necessary stops on the road to more complete freedom. Hence, President Bush proclaims:

> I am certain of this: Wherever we carry it, the American flag will stand not only for our power, but for freedom. Our nation's cause has always been larger than our nation's defence. We fight, as we always fight, for a just peace – a peace that favors human liberty. We will defend the peace against threats from terrorists and tyrants. We will preserve the peace by building good relations among the great powers. And we will extend the peace by encouraging free and open societies on every continent.
>
> Building this just peace is America's opportunity, and America's duty. From this day forward, it is your challenge, as well, and we will meet this challenge together. You will wear the uniform of a great and unique country. America has no empire to extend or utopia to establish. We wish for others only what we wish for ourselves – safety from violence, the rewards of liberty, and the hope for a better life. (www.whitehouse.gov/news/releases/2002/06/20020601–3.html)

Working as the guarantor of freedom working to rid the world of 'evil-doers' who cause fear, the USA again has mission to serve.

Still, convincing 'the Arab street' about the sincerity of the USA's commitment to safety, liberty, and a better life for Iraq, as expressed in the last line, is harder and harder with each passing month of Iraq's occupation after Abu Ghraib, the battles for Fallujah, rising malnutrition levels across the country in 2004, and the counterinsurgency campaigns leading up to the planned Iraqi national elections in 2005.

As a former superpower matched against an absolute enemy, first, with fascism, and then later with communism, the USA almost requires such demonic opponents to focus its attention and energy. For a decade in the 1990s, America's elites and masses lack such counterparts, and the post-Cold War era was largely one of distraction and drift at home and abroad. Neither radical Islam nor rogue dictatorships on their own constitute a new absolute enemy with serious hyperpower potential as such. Still, all of these forces together can be recast as a more credible extensive threat, and the Bush administration has spent years burnishing Osama bin Laden, Al Qaeda, Saddam Hussein, the Taliban, and all radical Islamicists into the threat that no nation can deny. While this threat is not quite an evil empire, and it is not really an axis of totalitarian powers, the Bush administration has crafted a style of speech that twists what does exist into an axis of evil worthy of mounting a permanent mobilization of the republic's citizens and soldiers by likening them to the twentieth century's fascist and communist totalitarians.

Yet, it is unclear how much traction the axis of evil rhetoric actually has generated for the Bush administration. A lack of unquestionable evidence in the file of each of these states, at least in the public domain, makes it difficult to prove allegations of evil doing. Past histories, hearsay accounts, and circumstantial indications all can be trundled out to provide backing, but it is not clear that the public at home or overseas is actually listening. Moreover, the fascist analogy can be overplayed. President Bush's father, after all was said and done, spent months calling Saddam Hussein 'a new Hitler', and then left this new Hitler in power after the Western coalition secured Kuwait's oil for the West. He also failed to back the anti-Saddam uprisings inside Iraq after the war. Many doubt the sincerity of his son's use of comparable rhetoric today, especially after the realization that Iraq actually had no WMD after the coalition of the willing invaded and occupied the country in 2003. Foreign publics, ironically, follow the axis of evil rhetoric, more closely, but this rhetoric is received more incredulously, or even light-heartedly, among them as another sign of America's disconnection from the rest of the world.

President Bush was not elected in 2000 to reshape the USA's place in the world with a new foreign policy. Indeed, the contestedness of his electoral victory as well as the patently domestic slant to his campaign was not a solid foundation to build a new departure for American foreign policy. President Bush's first big foreign policy address in the 2000 campaign only raised the vague prospect of 'realism in the service of American ideals', and it dwelt on the challenges of living in a world with no major enemies. In President Bush's playbook, 'American ideals' since 9.11.01 also have been all too often rearticulated as the liberty to spend at the mall, fly to the Caribbean on vacation or accumulate property without any estate tax. This pedestrian construction of republican ideals for the USA did little to express the bigger picture behind the American experiment for a war on global terrorism. 9.11.01, nevertheless, changed this rhetorical terrain considerably, and President Bush was re-elected during 2004, in large part, to continue his aggressive foreign policy agenda. Having derided President Clinton's more mediagenic idealism and half-hearted efforts at nation-building, the Bush administration has instead seized upon one of the most polydimensional, conflicted, and questioned ideas in America's political lexicon, namely, 'freedom' to anchor its conduct of the war on global terrorism.

For President Bush, the battle against Al Qaeda and global terrorism is one between good and evil, freedom and fear. As he announced the USA's first attacks against the Taliban on October 7, 2001, he was quite clear about this struggle: 'the name of today's military operation is Enduring Freedom. We defend not only our precious freedoms, but also the freedom of people everywhere to live and raise their children free from fear' (www.whitehouse .gov/news/releases/2001/09/20011007–8.html). Freedom is, of course, an elusive quality, but fear is made fairly concrete. It is a general apprehension about airplanes being highjacked, anthrax attacks, bombing big buildings and major economic disruptions.

At his West Point graduation day speech, President Bush argued that the war on terror was not unlike the twentieth century's wars on totalitarianism: 'In this way our struggle is similar to the Cold War. Now, as then, our enemies are totalitarianism, holding a creed of power with no place for human dignity. Now, as then, they seek to impose a joyless conformity, to control every life and all of life.' Freedom, and the fight to realise its bene-fits, are what the new security writs are all about. In the West Point speech, President Bush's speechwriters issued their clearest writs on what the world's new security environment should produce. While eschewing clash of civil-isation talk, the President now largely draws a universalising, and fairly Westernised, vision of 'freedom' for the twenty-first century.

As a liberal democratic republic, the USA also rests upon neoliberal cor-porate economy (Jameson 1991; Reich 1991; and Greider 1997). By stand-ing allegedly for something more than the absence of war, the USA has pledged that it aggressively will back its special cultural freedoms, economic liberties, and personal choices. Although it is thin, this is its 'greater objec-tive' beyond all of the nation's efforts to control the threat of terrorism. At West Point, the President enjoined the US Army's newest cohort of military officers to begin 'a life of service' with a very clear purpose as this writ for the New World Order suggests:

> We have a great opportunity to extend a just peace, by replacing poverty, repression, and resentment around the world with hope of a better day. Through most of history, poverty was persistent, inescapable, and almost uni-versal. In the last few decades, we've seen nations from Chile to South Korea build modern economies and freer societies, lifting millions of people out of despair and want. And there's no mystery to this achievement.
>
> The 20th century ended with a single surviving model of human progress, based on non-negotiable demands of human dignity, the rule of law, limits on the power of the state, respect for women and private property and free speech and equal justice and religious tolerance. America cannot impose this vision – yet we can support and reward governments that make the right choices for their own people. In our development aid, in our diplomatic efforts, in our international broadcasting, and in our educational assistance, the United States will promote moderation and tolerance and human rights. And we will defend the peace that makes all progress possible.
>
> When it comes to the common rights and needs of men and women, there is no clash of civilizations. The requirements of freedom apply fully to Africa and Latin America and the entire Islamic world. The peoples of the Islamic

nations want and deserve the same freedoms and opportunities as people in every nation. And their governments should listen to their hopes.

A truly strong nation will permit legal avenues of dissent for all groups that pursue their aspirations without violence. An advancing nation will pursue economic reform, to unleash the great entrepreneurial energy of its people. A thriving nation will respect the rights of women, because no society can prosper while denying opportunity to half its citizens. Mothers and fathers and children across the Islamic world, and all the world, share the same fears and aspirations. In poverty, they struggle. In tyranny, they suffer. And as we saw in Afghanistan, in liberation they celebrate.

America has a greater objective than controlling threats and containing resentment. We will work for a just and peaceful world beyond the war on terror.

Speech writing here restates the standing writs of American superpower from the Cold War and immediate post-Cold War eras, but it goes beyond those positions. Even though the Bush team derided the Clinton administration for various experiments in 'nation-building', it essentially declares that it must go beyond those efforts one better. Here one sees the writs of hyperpower in the White House outlining an American-led program for 'world-building', if not a 'civilisational struggle', on a scale not seen for quite some time as the USA resolves to strike pre-emptively anywhere and anytime to construct what conservative Republican partisans regard as 'a just and peaceful world'.

Closing

This preliminary analysis of President Bush's rhetoric in the wake of 9.11.01 is meant to find a larger purpose in the USA's reactions to the terrorist attacks. In addition, it seeks to show how speech writing is more than just daily diplomatic discourse. State authority is staked out and sustained with speech writing, and these world events show how closely these connections operate in the coercive constructivism of the Bush administration's campaigns in the Mideast.

This study also suggests that political speech continuously spins up the rhetoric required to serve as the key containers for carrying forward the processes of statecraft. Rhetoric and myth create belief; and, in being believed, such writs of action can become the tools to redraw reality in the on-going tussles of social forces. By being believed, for those whose deeds actuate and affirm their content, speech writs cannot be ignored. Within many established institutional sites, these kinds of speech writs also serve as powerful screens whose discursive expanses can be dominated by activist public intellectuals, mass media outlets, and vested social interests to further a ruling regime's policy agendas.

Rather than occluding reality, rhetorical writs give greater focus to action through the frames suggested by such polysemic figuration. Speech writing, and its speech writs, outline more determinate visions of what can be, should be, and will be done. For many people, believing in the global terms and conditions derived from such speech writs, following the programmatic designs of speech wrights who propound such beliefs, and then accepting their doxic effects in thought and action, all lead somehow to even more of the same being done (Agger 1989; Luke 1996). Speech writs, therefore, can be a tool of psychosocial determination as well as the means for ontopolitical interpretation. Once an axis of evil is discovered, Iraq can be invaded, Libya pressured in to submission, Iran harassed by transnational inspectors, and North Korea subjected to additional monitoring, or even meddling, from the outside world. The doxic constructs of speech writs plough open the fields of interpretative interaction where ideas link up with institutions. As institutions unfold their activities in daily practice, they remediate ideas so fully that the symbolic order actuates and affirms them in many other realms of psychological and social behaviour.

Looked at as such, speech writs very often seem quite colourless. When one hears such 'ready-made phrases all day', as Bourdieu concludes, they can become a doxosophy, or 'a whole philosophy and a whole worldview which engender fatalism and submission'. Few things, then, are more pressing than the disposition of the world in such speech writing, because its writs circulate widely in political rhetorics, economic arguments and cultural controversies. Words that engender fatalism also can spark resistance, if and when rhetorical writs are not followed in practice. This fact alone turns them into key strategic assets for anyone who is intent upon ruling, and then prevailing globally in struggles over what is real in world politics. The Bush administration is discovering this difficult truth daily on the ground in Iraq and Afghanistan. When the White House launches wars on rhetorical claims to find WMDs, advance freedom and create prosperity, and then finds no such weapons, facilitates the spread of violent anarchy, and fails to generate jobs, feed people or rebuild economies, then its doxosophers will be doubted. The strategic effects of speech writing, therefore, must never be discounted.

Shocked and awed: the convergence of military and media discourse

More than one year after the United States military occupation of Iraq there still is no credible evidence linking Saddam Hussein to the Al Qaeda terrorist network, nor is there any trace of the Middle Eastern dictator's ballyhooed Weapons of Mass Destruction (WMD) programme. These stubborn facts notwithstanding, and in the face of opinion polls that indicate public support for the US-led invasion of Iraq had slipped, US President George W. Bush and other members of his administration continued to reassert the same dubious claims that helped them win over American public opinion in the lead-up to the 2003 invasion. 'The reason I keep insisting that there was a relationship between Iraq and Saddam and Al Qaeda: because there was a relationship between Iraq and Al Qaeda', Bush said after a cabinet meeting of 17 June (Milbank 2004).

In a *New York Times*/CBS News poll, conducted over the weeks leading up to the invasion, 45 per cent of respondents said Saddam Hussein was directly involved in the attacks. A second poll, conducted before the second anniversary of the September 11 attacks, found the number had increased. The *Washington Post* poll reported that nearly 7 in 10 respondents thought Hussein was involved in the attacks – a troublesome figure considering there is no evidence to support the opinion. A Knight Ridder poll reported that 44 per cent of respondents believed that some of the September 11 highjackers were Iraqi citizens (Feldmann 2003; Milbank and Deane 2003; Nagourney and Elder 2003). No Iraqis were involved. Moreover, staff reports of the bipartisan commission investigating the September 11 attacks flatly contradicted one of President Bush's central justifications for the invasion, saying that there did not appear to be any 'collaborative relationship' between Hussein and Al Qaeda (Shenon and Marquis 2004). And in January 2004 David Kay, the man who led the CIA's efforts to locate WMD in the months following the occupation, told the Senate Armed Services Committee that 'we were almost all wrong' about Iraq's WMD programme. Information used to build support for war would be exposed as misleading, but only after the window of opportunity to intervene in policy implementation had passed. 'While few shed tears for the exit of the murderous Saddam Hussein', wrote *Editor and Publisher* reporter Joe Strupp in June 2003, 'the press needs to remind the public that the war was sold to them not on the basis of 'regime change' but on the personal threat to Americans posed by Saddam's so-far-missing weapons' (Strupp 2003).

What was behind the success of the US government's media and public relations campaign? Scholarship investigating the relationship between the media and the US military has chronicled how US news media have largely downplayed critical perspectives on military actions (Herman and Chomsky 1988; Kellner 1992; Mowlana et al. 1992; Mermin 1999). Jonathan Mermin, in his work investigating media coverage of post-Vietnam US military interventions, has found evidence to support W. Lance Bennett's (1990) indexing thesis that predicts news coverage will reflect the degree of policy debate and disagreement that exists among elite government officials. Richard Ericson (Ericson et al. 1989) and Mark Fishman (Fishman 1980) have also argued that journalism's heavy reliance on official government sources is a crucial influence on journalistic content. Susan Moeller's extensive study of US media's coverage of WMD came to a similar conclusion. 'Most journalists', she writes, 'accepted the Bush administration's formulation of the "War on Terror" as a campaign against WMD.' And in so doing, 'Many stories stenographically reported the incumbent administration's perspective on WMD' (Moeller 2004: 3). That is not to say that all news media dutifully filed the same reports. A detailed survey conducted by researchers at the University of Maryland found that audience misperceptions about Iraq-al Qaeda links varied significantly depending on their source of news. Americans 'who receive most of their news from Fox News are more likely than average to have misperceptions. Those who receive most of their news from NPR or PBS are less likely to have misperceptions' (Kull 2003: 12). Virtually all major US newspapers backed Bush's decision to attack Iraq in their editorial pages.

These opinion polls are consistent with research conducted by Daya Kishan Thussu (2002) who argues that 'media-savvy governments' have become particularly adept at selling military actions by using the resources made available to them in a globally networked 24-hour news environment. It is this point that I wish to develop further. This chapter builds on the above research in order to delve into the symbiotic relationship that exists between the media and the military. It argues that the US government exploited a convergence of media and military discourse that is constitutive of the political field. As Paul Rutherford argues, 'what contributed to the success of this propaganda was that it used the news media, a more trusted source, and not the normal ad media, often discounted by consumers, to promote the Bush agenda' (Rutherford 2004: 33). I argue that spectacular narrative forms deployed by the US military, such as 'Shock and Awe', and the 'Saving of Pvt. Jessica Lynch', are constitutive of the mediated political field. That is to say, that these narratives are fully integrated into military and corporate public-relations campaigns along with the daily production regimes of 24-hour cable news channels. I view spectacular media events – such as the invasion of Iraq – as '*hog fuel*' for 24-hour news channels and websites. In particular, I believe they are well suited to a global trend toward '*high-volume flexible production systems*' characterised by *flexible forms of management, labour performance* and *increased intensity* in the speed of production and turnover time (Castells 2000; Harvey 1989).

I am not suggesting a strictly top-down form of domination in which the military imposes its will on a reluctant US media. Instead, I tease out examples of the willing, and I might add eager, integration of military propaganda, organisational work routines, and the commercial interests of converged-media conglomerates, and other social actors. There is no conspiracy. Social actors continue to pursue their own interests independently. My point is that these interests have converged. Following Guy Debord (1995), we can say that these spectacular narrative forms, such as Shock and Awe, do not represent the spectacle in its entirety; instead, spectacular media events are component parts of a much larger integrated promotional system of commodity production, circulation and exchange. For heuristic purposes I call this promotional system the integrated news spectacle. The term is used to refer to the 'constellations' of social forces, new technologies and institutional logics that have converged in unique and contingent ways to produce a highly complex integration of the cultural, economic, social, professional and political realms.

Dramatic narratives and the political field

Dramatic narratives constitute what Pierre Bourdieu (1991) calls the *tools* of 'perception and expression' available to social actors in the political field. The performance of politics and the narratives and cultural texts employed by political actors are part of a struggle to narrate the social. Murray Edelman describes the situation well.

> The spectacle constituted by news reporting continuously constructs and reconstructs social problems, crises, enemies, and leaders and so creates a succession of threats and reassurances. These constructed problems and personalities furnish the content of political journalism and the data for historical and analytic political studies. They also play a central role in winning support and opposition for political causes and policies. (Edelman 1988: 1)

The news spectacle is, in partial form, about the dramatisation of collective life, not its direct experience. It is a dramatic representation of social relations. News narratives, according to Edelman 'objectify', in dramatic form, the hopes and fears of people (96). The news spectacle dramatises a political world beyond the everyday experiences of people while simultaneously offering explanations, admonitions and reassurances for social problems ranging from unemployment and crime to healthcare and abortion. Dramatic storytelling – whether it be tales of political sex scandals or the hagiography of political image making – is constitutive of the process by which cognitive maps are constructed and used by individuals and social groups to assess social life and to make sense of the seeming chaos of the modern world. It is through the news spectacle that social actors are characterized using a binary code of the sacred and profane (Alexander and Jacobs 1998). In politics, actors are viewed as democratic/anti-democratic, trustworthy/deceitful, or populist/elitist, ally/enemy, etc. The news spectacle represents social reality by telling stories about collective life that make it possible to imagine political communities based on class, race and gender, and to mobilise these communities in support or opposition to particular public-policy initiatives, political candidates and the platforms they represent. The meaning of news spectacles, from hotly contested presidential elections to the symbolic excommunication of President Bill Clinton, is always ambiguous because people draw upon different narratives explanations of events. 'It is the ambiguity and the controversy that make developments political in character' (Edelman 1988: 95). The clichéd adage that one group's freedom fighter is another group's terrorist is true. Researchers need to ask which groups possess the ability to define social and political deviance and its legitimate limits. In other words, one must understand which individuals, social groups and institutions have the resources to represent rival groups and their interests as deviant (i.e., undemocratic, unpatriotic, elitist, etc.). This struggle involves the exercise of symbolic power. As Steven Livingston and W. Lance Bennett write 'Understanding who constructs what is political about news events remains one of the most important subjects in political communication' (Livingston and Bennett 2003).

Dramatising politics and the politics of drama

The social relations of power of mediated politics – what form it takes and whose interests are served – must be investigated through a historical analysis of the *use* of dramatic narratives and the social relations of which they are a part. In other words, one must examine how the mediated production of political representation is structured by social relations while simultaneously investigating how the mediated production of symbolic forms, itself, is a structuring process that contributes to the maintenance of social relations. One must refer dramatic narratives back to historically situated interests and the media apparatus in which the struggle to legitimate political agendas is played out. Dramatic narratives used in political struggles over such things as social or fiscal policy reform, and the social norms in whose name this practice is conducted, are the tools of 'perception and expression' offered by the political field; as such, dramatic narratives, contribute to 'the universe of political discourse, and thereby the universe of what is politically thinkable' (Bourdieu 1991: 172). One's ability to play the game of politics, therefore, is linked to one's access to the resources of the political field.

Dramatic narratives fall under the rubric of the integrated system of news production and distribution to the extent that commercial news media remain the primary site through which competing social forces appeal for support within civil society. The logic and structure of what I choose to call the integrated news spectacle is thus a factor in determining which individuals or groups have the resources to fully pursue their agendas, represent their interests, and potentially have them accepted as common sense. It is also responsible, in part, for the style of politics. The organizing mechanism of our image-saturated media culture – and therefore, image politics – is the impersonal network of market exchange. The cultural texts stemming from the promotional packaging of political life have been aestheticised through marketing and advertising in an attempt to bridge the gap between consumers and producers – i.e., the broader public and political professionals. Dramatic narratives – mediated through a particular set of market transactions – have become constitutive of economic competition and the rational organisation of journalistic institutions and political professionals; they have become objects of rational and strategic action by commercial and political interests. Political practice has become reified and susceptible to forms of domination to the extent that: (1) political life is conducted according to the logic and rules of the integrated spectacle; and (2) politics favours particular social actors and dramatic narratives – *those more fully integrated within the promotional logic of the system of production, distribution and exchange.*

Shock and awe

On 21 March 2003, millions of television viewers around the world watched the night sky light up over Baghdad as US and British forces rained close to 1,500 bombs and cruise missiles down on the ancient Iraqi capital. One could be forgiven for thinking the focus of news coverage would be on the plight of civilians frantically taking what shelter they could find from the bombardment. Such was not the case. The aerial attack was the beginning of a much-anticipated military spectacle dubbed 'Shock and Awe'. Reporters, both in Baghdad and those safely tucked in their network studios, were bursting with excitement. 'The sky is lit up, Tom!' shouted veteran war correspondent Peter Arnett to NBC News anchor Tom Brokaw. 'Just like out of an action movie, but this is real, this is real, this is shock and awe, Tom!' Brokaw took his cue. 'The overture is over', he replied. 'This is the main piece' (Rosenthal 2003). Jingoistic US cable leader Fox News would not to be outdone. 'It's fascinating and amazing', enthused conservative host Brit

Hume, 'to see this with the lights on in Baghdad' (Barnhart 2003). CBS took a few minutes before the network broke from its NCAA basketball coverage, but once it had made the switch, channel surfers looking for a sense of the potential human cost of the attack would be similarly frustrated. CBS News anchor Dan Rather did feel the need to comment on what he thought was the 'somewhat historic' nature of waging war 'when we have 24-hours-a-day' media coverage worldwide. In contrast, a less spectacular attack on one of Saddam Hussein's palaces two days earlier – the object of Brokaw's overture remark – received less glowing reviews. 'If You Have to Ask, It's Not "Shock and Awe",' read a graphic on Fox News. 'It could be called "Shock and Pause",' said NBC reporter Jim Miklaszewski (Rosenthal 2003). Dan Rather, known for his over-the-top one-liners, could not contain his own enthusiasm, comparing the air raid with 'the rocket's red glare, and bombs bursting in air' (Houston 2003a). Rather's corny patriotism notwithstanding, the lack of 'awe' generated from the earlier, and much smaller, air raid had left broadcasters with a palpable sense of disappointment. They had been primed for a full-blown spectacle, a performance that, in their view, had not been delivered. So when it finally came, as they had promised viewers it would, they could not contain themselves.

The now-infamous branding slogan first gained public notoriety in January 3003 when CBS News aired a report by correspondent David Martin. The story contained information leaked by unidentified Pentagon sources who confirmed that 'Shock and Awe' was indeed the label given to the attack plans being prepared for the anticipated invasion of Iraq. Alongside a 'Showdown with Saddam' logo that was set against an American flag and a combination gun sight/radar-screen graphic, Martin told viewers that 'Shock and Awe' is predicated on a spectacular, and overwhelming display of military might aimed at destroying an opponent's will to fight. It centres on the psychological intimidation of the enemy and downplays the need for traditional military ground forces. The concept is associated with Harlan Ullman, co-author of the book titled *Shock and Awe: Achieving Rapid Dominance*. Ullman acknowledges his debt to famed military strategists Sun Tzu and Carl von Clausewitz, both of whom wrote about the importance of extinguishing an adversary's will to fight. What makes Ullman's use of the concept unique is its attachment to an integrated information environment that combines high-speed technological surveillance, communication and spectacular display.

> Battlefield awareness requires three information technologies: collection, fusion, and dissemination of real-time actionable information to a shooter. Rapid Dominance requires an unprecedented level of real-time information collection . . . It would be hard to overstate the importance of information dissemination within Rapid Dominance. Administering Shock and Awe requires a spectrum of attacks that the adversary is unable to fathom. (Ullman and Wade 1996)

If successful, Ullman told Martin, there would be no ground war involving large-scale tank battles, as was the case in the 1991 Gulf War, and fewer lives would be lost (CBS News 2003). The aestheticised discourse of 'Shock and Awe' promises the 'surgical' use of 'smart bombs' and other weaponry in order to create a strong psychological effect while minimising the material destruction of military and civilian infrastructure. War without blood. That is to say, viewers at home would not be exposed to blood, especially American blood. The online version of the story contained a personal note from anchor Dan Rather, who reassured the public that the report contained no information that the Defence Department thought could help the Iraqi military.

There were two intended audiences for the discourse: foreign military adversaries and their civilian populations, and domestic citizens. 'Shock and Awe' is designed to strike fear in the enemy, while at the same time reassure those on the home front concerned about the carnage of war. The phrase was quickly added to the popular lexicon. A flood of trademark applications for the term began to appear for products and services ranging from teddy bears and ski boots to men and women's underwear. Sony backed off plans to market a 'Shock and Awe' video game following accusations of war profiteering (BBC News Online 2003a; Harper's 2003).

'Shock and Awe' is simultaneously a battle strategy and an ideological discourse connected to what military strategists call the 'Revolution in Military Affairs' (RMA), or as Kevin Robins and Frank Webster prefer, 'Information Warfare' (1999). Robins and Webster contrast Information Warfare with Industrial Warfare to highlight the heightened importance information and communication technologies play in the rational administration and control of warfare. They admit that the use of information has always been an integral part of warfare. Nonetheless, Robins and Webster argue that important differences exist. First, in the modern industrial period, roughly from the First World War through to the Vietnam War, warfare involved the mobilisation of large elements of the general population with a commitment to total warfare. Since the end of the Vietnam War, citizens have become more apprehensive about sanctioning large-scale human casualties. As a result, it has become more difficult to mobilise an entire society for war – both in terms of shifting industrial production from domestic to military products and in the curtailment of the consumption of everyday goods and luxury items. Meanwhile, a shift has occurred, particularly following the collapse of the Soviet Union, toward what Manuel Castells calls 'Instant Wars'. These are relatively short-lived conflicts that are waged without conscription by professional forces, and that rely upon technological improvements in weaponry and information management to limit public knowledge of the material and human consequences of battle (Robins and Webster 1999: 154–157; Castells 2000: 486). The 1991 Gulf War, it is argued, provided the most fully developed example. Power was in effect operationalised, not simply by brute military force and large-scale industrial production, but through administrative

surveillance – the monitoring of enemy forces and domestic political opposition – and spectacular display. 'Well-trained, well-equipped, full-time, professional armed forces do not require the involvement of the population at large
in the war effort, except for viewing and cheering from their living rooms a
particularly exciting show, punctuated with deep patriotic feelings' (Castells
2000: 486). In a sense, the 'Gulf War did not happen' for most viewers of the
war spectacle – to borrow Baudrillard's well-known line – that is, when compared to women who gained their first work experience in factories during
the Second World War, and who, while waiting for their husbands, sons and
brothers to return from abroad, went without many everyday comforts. The
mediated version of the war was experienced at a distance through self-refe-
rential discourses, such as Shock and Awe.

The use of perception management by nation-states is not, of course, particularly novel. And we must be cautious not to overstate the extent of the
historical shift represented by the so-called RMA. After all, as John Downey
and Graham Murdock remind us, the use of information contained in maps
was integral to the swift movement of Napoleon's forces in the early-19th
century, while 'the stubborn persistence of core features, and failures of
Industrial Warfare' remain (Downey and Murdock 2003: 75). Technology
fails, humans make errors, and people still die in large numbers, particularly
those unfortunate enough to be the target of the world's only superpower.
The Associated Press estimated that 3,240 civilians perished from the war's
beginning 20 March to the end of large-scale military conflict on 20 April
(Bedway 2003). A running tally by the website iraqbodycount.net, which
used a different methodology, more than doubles that estimate. Notwithstanding these warnings, I want to argue that spectacular narrative
forms such as 'Shock and Awe' are constitutive of the political field. These
narratives are fully integrated into military, government, and corporate
public-relations campaigns along with the daily production regimes of mainstream news media, particularly 24-hour cable news channels.

The experience of warfare is, for a majority of Western citizens, limited
to spectacle. Western liberal democracies require the support of public
opinion to wage war. The bulk of the population is mobilised, not as soldiers
and producers of war armaments, but as 'spectators of war', who are sold
on the rightness of battle in the name of sacred universal values. Citizens are
told the so-called War Against Terrorism is undertaken in the name of security, democracy, freedom and human rights, not to secure vital oil interests.
The Manichean struggle between good and evil was engaged, not only on
the battlefield (or in 'battlespace', as proponents of RMA prefer), but also
through the spectacle of dramatic narrative forms. America – a 'target of
hate because of its freedoms' – takes on 'evildoers' in a just global struggle
that will require eternal vigilance and flexibility of response. 'Perception
management', conducted by war-time governments, says Frank Webster,
'must therefore attempt to combine ways of ensuring a continuous stream of

media coverage that is positive and yet ostensibly freely gathered by independent news agencies' (Webster 2003: 64). Governments need to appear to practice what they preach. Perception management of this type is achieved most efficiently by tapping into the resources made available to political actors by the integrated news spectacle. My argument is that the administration of George W. Bush enjoyed an enormous amount of political success packaging and selling the America-led invasion of Iraq under the rubric of the 'War on Terror' narrative by making deft use of those resources.

Branding war

September 11 was a spectacular example of 'mass-mediated terrorism', planned and executed to attract media interest in order to further a political agenda (Nacos 2002). It was also the promotional fulcrum point for a host of major policy initiatives from the Bush administration, including arguments justifying the US invasion of Iraq. From the beginning, the events of September 11 and the declared war on terror were invoked as justification for the Bush doctrine of 'pre-emptive military strikes'. As Douglas Kellner makes clear, the Manichean logic used by Bush, and he correctly adds radical Islamists, rhetorically empowers those who wield it with a flexibility of purpose. 'This amorphous terrorist Enemy . . . allows the crusader for Good to attack any country or group that is supporting terrorism, thus promoting a foundation for a new doctrine of pre-emptive strikes and perennial war' (Kellner 2003a). Part of the appeal of the discourse of terror, among those who would deploy it, is that it trumps international law that explicitly prohibits nation-states from engaging in unprovoked invasions. As one Fox News.com headline put it: 'Why Now? A Better Question Is Why Wait?' (Adelman 2002). To be against the invasion of Iraq, following this logic, is to side with evil. It implies that one is callously willing to put the lives of one's fellow citizens at risk. It, in turn, conveniently brands opponents as unpatriotic.

The Bush administration tapped into America's newfound vulnerability to terror to push through a series of draconian security measures that stripped citizens of civil liberties and awarded powers of surveillance to the state previously thought intolerable. The USA Patriot Act, backed by the bureaucratic muscle of a new secretariat ominously named the Office of Homeland Security, gave the state power to eavesdrop on private phone, e-mail communications and detain citizens without warrants, all in the name of their own security. Colour-coded terror alerts issued by the Homeland office soon became institutionalised, each warning receiving a ritual media response. Reports accusing police of misusing their authority began to accumulate, including abuse of prisoners and the creation of police databases containing names of people arrested during antiwar protests (McCool 2003; Shenon 2003). Bush would eventually cite the 'national emergency' created by September 11 to justify his decision to limit scheduled pay increases for federal workers (King 2003).

The Bush administration was not alone in its desire to tap into the spectacle. Following September 11, Washington lobbyists wasted no time in connecting their pet issue to the tragedy. 'No self-respecting lobbyist', said Democratic Representative Edward J. Markey, has failed to 'repackage his position as a patriotic response to the tragedy.' In one of the more ridiculous examples, the *New York Times* reported that the American Traffic Safety Service Association, whose members make traffic signs, petitioned the federal government for increased funding to instal more signage. The reason offered was that they would prevent potential traffic jams after terror attacks (Rosenbaum 2001). Selling fear made good business sense. The *Guardian* newspaper quoted *PR Week* as offering this bit of advice: 'The trick in 2002, say public affairs and budget experts, will be to redefine your pet issue or product as a matter of homeland security . . . If you can convince Congress that your company's widget will strengthen America's borders, or that funding your client's pet project will make America less dependent on foreign resources, you just might be able to get what you're looking for' (Rampton and Stauber 2003).

Public-relations analysts Sheldon Rampton and John Stauber argue that while the Bush administration failed to convince the UN Security Council and other NATO allies such as Germany, France and Canada to endorse its unilateral attack on Iraq, it enjoyed incredible success at home. 'And a key component has been fear: fear of terrorism and fear of attack' (Rampton and Stauber 2003). Kellner has dubbed the strategy 'Terror War' (Kellner 2003b). Fear, according to Michael Hardt and Antonio Negri, is the glue that holds together the society of the spectacle. 'The society of the spectacle rules by wielding an age-old weapon. Hobbes recognized long ago that for effective domination 'the Passion to be reckoned upon, is Fear'. For Hobbes, fear is what binds and ensures social order, and still today fear is the primary mechanism of control that fills the society of the spectacle' (Hardt and Negri 2000: 323). But the spectacle of war, and its corollary fear, does not simply intimidate and pacify citizens. At the heart of the spectacle is a promise to reunite what has been sundered, to return what is feared to have been lost; and this promise is resolved at the level of myth. Samuel Weber argues that 'the spectacle' of terror and war, 'at least as staged by the mainstream broadcast media, seeks simultaneously to assuage and exacerbate anxieties of all sorts by providing images on which anxieties can be projected, ostensibly comprehended, and above all *removed*' (Weber 2002: 457). That is why, he argues, it is imperative that the object of one's fear must be named and located. 'In the images of catastrophe that dominate broadcast media 'news', the disunity is projected into the image itself, while the desired unity is reserved for the spectator off-scene (and for the media itself as global network)' (455).

There is no centralised 'man behind the screen' whose job it is to manipulate the spectacle, although the spectacle's unity of appearance may give the impression that one exists. The integrated news spectacle is both concentrated and diffuse. It operates through the efforts of disparate social actors, some (governments and corporations) to be sure with more power than others, but each pursuing its own interests. What unifies them is their adaptation and use of the spectacle's logic. As for spectators, one might say, following Debord, that what unites them is the same thing that maintains their separateness from one another – the image of the spectacle.

CBS News reported on 4 September 2002, that Defense Secretary Donald Rumsfeld told aides that he wanted them to draw up plans to attack Iraq a mere five hours after doomed American Airlines Flight 77 crashed into the Pentagon. The report by correspondent David Martin cited notes taken by aides who were with Rumsfeld on September 11. Despite intercepted phone calls, airline passenger manifests, and other information linking the Al Qaeda organisation to the terror attacks, Rumsfeld reportedly insisted that attempts be made to connect Saddam Hussein to the suicide hijacking. 'Go massive', he is said to have written, 'Sweep it all up. Things related or not' (CBS News 2002). Rumsfeld's determination is all the more striking given that reports quoting CIA sources indicate two top-level Al Qaeda leaders had told US interrogators, months prior to the invasion of Iraq, that their organization had no links with Saddam Hussein (Bruce 2003). A leaked British Intelligence Staff report had also cast doubt on any connection, suggesting that Al Qaeda's 'aims are in ideological conflict with present-day Iraq', itself a secular dictatorship (Rangwala and Whitaker 2003). Moreover, hawks within the Bush administration had been pushing for an American military presence in the Persian Gulf region prior to the September 11 attacks in order to secure American strategic interests, including oil supplies. The policy was contained in a well-publicised 2000 report prepared for the Project for a New American Century – a neoconservative think tank whose members include Vice President Dick Cheney, Defense Secretary Donald Rumsfeld and Deputy Secretary of Defense Paul Wolfowitz.[1] The terror attacks in New York and Washington simply provided the administration with a useful promotional hook for a long-standing desire, on the part of senior administration officials, for a military presence in the region via 'regime change' in Iraq.[2]

The dominant media frame following September 11 characterised the attack as an act of war that required a swift military response. The merits of alternative non-violent policy responses were minimised. A study of the structural metaphors used by *NBC Nightly News* in its coverage of the lead up to war shows that stories were framed as part of a countdown to an invasion that was assumed to be inevitable. 'Rather than investigate, analyze, or debate the rationale for war, the broadcast instead offered, through metaphor, a dramatization of war unfolding' (Lule 2004: 187). Discussion of how historical context, including the US military presence in Saudi Arabia, and past American funding of Islamic fundamentalist groups, might have played a role in sowing the seeds of Al Qaeda was discouraged in many media reports and readily condemned as 'blaming the victim'. As Kellner indicates, Fox News led the charge among cable networks. On 13 September, only two days after the tragedy, the host of the network's leading prime-time programme, *The O'Reilly Factor*, admonished the former Clinton administration for security lapses and pinned blame for the actual attack on Saddam Hussein. His Republican guests Jean Kirkpatrick and Newt Gingrich agreed (Kellner 2003b: 59). Credible evidence for either charge was not presented.

The die was cast in 29 January, 2002, when President Bush used the State of the Union address to include Iraq, along with Iran and Stalinist North Korea, as a member of the 'Axis of Evil'. All three 'rogue states', argued Bush, possessed 'weapons of mass destruction' (WMD) and presented a threat to American security. Osama bin Laden and the Al Qaeda movement were not mentioned. The protean quality of 'rogue' states allowed for the construction of an abstract form of secularised evil for which there are no historical 'root causes'. Unlike more civilised nation-states, rogues do not pursue rational interests. As Weber argues, these states and their leaders are defined as pathological, 'whose roguishness consists in their refusal to follow the norms of international behaviour as laid down by the United States government' (Weber 2002: 456). By now international law had been relegated to an arbitrary 'opt-in' status by the US administration. A year later in his 28 January 2003 State of the Union speech, Bush made clear his administration's intentions regarding 'regime change' in Iraq: 'A brutal dictator, with a history of reckless aggression . . . with ties to terrorism . . . with great potential wealth . . . will not be permitted to dominate a vital region and threaten the United States'.

Promoting patriotism

From the beginning, the invasion of Iraq was a cable-TV affair. Significantly, 70 per cent of Americans polled reported they had relied on cable as their main source of news about the conflict. Ratings were superb. Nielson data indicate that the number of average daily viewers had jumped 300 per cent for CNN and MSNBC. Fox enjoyed a 288 – per cent spike (Sharkey 2003). The Pentagon was prepared. It understood the importance of television and contracted a designer who had worked for Disney, MGM, and *Good Morning America* to build a $250,000 studio for the daily media briefings. The first Gulf War made CNN a global leader in 24-hour news. In this conflict the all-news pioneer would not be alone. In addition to Fox and MSNBC, 24-hour competition for scoops came from Qatar-based Al Jazeera, which used the international reputation it first gained reporting on the Afghanistan conflict to pursue plans for an English-language website.

The war commodity is problematic; many sponsors, such as Proctor & Gamble, were worried that their brands could be damaged if associated with body bags (Cassy and Milmo 2003; Chunovic 2003). The US networks had to forgo $77 million in advertising revenue in order to air commercial-free news during the first week of the conflict. The cable-news networks sacrificed roughly 71 per cent of their weekly ad revenue. But after the initial 'awe' had worn off, commercials returned (Beard 2003). Despite obvious financial hurdles, the spectacle of war is in the long-term interests of all-news networks seeking to extend their brand, and expand their audience. China's state-run China Central Television (CCTV) was openly trying to court some of the marketing magic enjoyed by CNN in 1991. CCTV-1, the network's main news channel, ran non-stop coverage on the first day of the war that carried video of advancing US forces. Senior editors talked about the need to adopt Western professional standards of 'objectivity' as a way of attracting and holding audiences in what was becoming an increasingly competitive global commercial-television market (Chang and Hutzler 2003). Military pundits would also do well. The expanded number of 24-hour cable outlets meant there was more need than ever for commentary. Whereas in 1999, retired generals provided opinion without pay, for the most part; by 2003 those same experts were striking lucrative, and exclusive, contracts with networks (Tugend 2003). The crucible of war coverage would also lend much-desired gravitas to ambitious reporters, such as CBS News correspondent Lara Logan – a former model – hoping to boost their careers.

The US news media were in Iraq to cover the invasion, but they were also engaged in a vicious branding war, each network trying to project an image of itself as more patriotic than the competition. CNN and MSNBC were feeling the ratings pinch after watching the aggressively patriotic Fox News grab the top spot. Graphics with fluttering flags were ubiquitous, as were the words 'we' and 'us' when identifying US military personnel. 'The conveying of actual news often seems subsidiary to their mission to out-flag-wave one another and to make their own personnel, rather than the war's antagonists, the leading players in the drama', wrote Frank Rich in the *New York Times* (Rich 2003). Both MSNBC and Fox News branded their news coverage with the US government's logo for the conflict: 'Operation Iraqi Freedom'. Fox allowed soldiers to go on camera and send personal messages to loved ones at home. MSNBC created a video-montage bumper in which still photos of military personnel were overlaid with the motto 'May God bless America. Our hearts go with you' (Sharkey 2003). CNN boasted after its medical correspondent, Sanjay Gupta, performed emergency brain surgery on a mortally injured young Iraqi boy. Gupta, an accomplished neurosurgeon, was travelling as an 'embedded' reporter with a US-military medical unit known as the 'Devil Docs'. What received less attention was how the boy, who didn't survive surgery, was among three people killed by US Marines when they opened fire on a taxi passing through a checkpoint (MacDonald 2003). One of the more sensational moments in the branding war involved rivals MSNBC and Fox News. Both networks broadcast news items and promotional spots that took patriotic digs at each other. The promotions came after Fox's charismatic Geraldo Rivera ran afoul of the US military by revealing troop locations when he drew a map in the sand while on camera. Veteran Peter Arnett, who had been filing reports for NBC, MSNBC and National Geographic Explorer, was fired after granting an interview with Iraqi state TV. He had told the interviewer that President Bush was facing a 'growing challenge' to the 'conduct of the war' at home. At the time, this was factually correct, but by granting an interview that could be used by the Iraqi regime for propaganda purposes, he had opened himself up to attack. After running a story about Rivera's run in with the US military, MSNBC broadcast a spot assuring its audience that it would never 'compromise military security or jeopardize a single American life'. Upset, Fox responded with its own spot that showed a portion of Arnett's Iraqi TV interview. 'He spoke out against America's armed forces', said an announcer, 'he said America's war against terrorism had failed; he even vilified America's leadership. And he worked for MSNBC' (Rutenberg 2003a).

On the morning of 26 March, CNN led newscasts with a report that US forces had killed 200 Iraqis in a large land battle. That same day, at least 15 Iraqi civilians died after an apparent US bombing of a Baghdad marketplace. The marketplace bombing was reported, but attention quickly faded among the US networks. Coverage shifted to President Bush's visit to the MacDill Air Force Base near Tampa, Florida. The trip was billed as a morale booster for troops one week into the war. 'If that rendition of the *Star-Spangled Banner* doesn't stir you, I don't know what will', said CNN's morning anchor Paula Zahn, after Bush was greeted by the singing of the anthem. Zahn would later win her own prime-time show on the strength of her performance during the conflict. Later that day, all the major news channels broadcast live a news briefing from central command's new studio in Qatar. 'OK, so, a lot of negative questions there', said Fox's anchor. 'But let's focus on the positive' (Burkeman et al. 2003).

Anti-war voices that challenged 'Brand America' were hard to find before or during the conflict. Those people who did speak out faced a range of penalties, including threats, job loss, and arrest (Kenna 2003). With the exception of CNN's 'Voices of Dissent', a segment created in the weeks leading up to the war, and later renamed 'Arab Voices' after hostilities started, antiwar voices were largely absent. 'Get the following production pieces in the studio NOW: . . . Patriotic music that makes you cry, salute, get cold chills! Go for the emotion', read a 'War Manual' produced by McVay Media, a Cleveland-based broadcast media consultant. McVay advised clients to downplay protests against the war because they drive away viewers (Farhi 2003). One mass 'die-in' staged by protesters in New York, was mocked by Fox News.

A few blocks away, a message on the news ticker outside Fox's New York headquarters read: 'War protester auditions here today . . . thanks for coming' (Cowen 2003). On another occasion, a Fox anchor referred to war protesters as 'the great unwashed' (Rutenberg 2003b). The pro-war flack emanating from media organisations was extensive. Radio stations owned by Clear Channel Communications, the owner of close to 1,200 stations across the United States, organised rallies that endorsed the US government's position against Iraq (Jones 2003). Country-music stations owned by the corporate giant, along with radio chain Cumulus Media, stopped playing songs by the popular Dixie Chicks after the group's lead singer, Natalie Maines, criticised President Bush while performing in London.

The usual support came from right-wing talk-radio hosts such as Rush Limbaugh; but there was one TV talk show that regularly included antiwar guests along with supporters of the Bush position. Veteran Phil Donahue had his show cancelled by MSNBC in February 2003, as the build up to war intensified. The official reason offered by MSNBC was that the programme trailed Fox's *The O'Reilly Factor* by a wide margin. But while the programme was badly behind in ratings for its time slot, it was still MSNBC's top-rated programme, ahead of *Hardball With Chris Matthews*. A different reason was offered by Rick Ellis, a columnist with *All Your TV* website. Ellis claims he received a leaked internal report from NBC that argued Donahue would be a 'difficult public face for NBC in a time of war' (Ellis 2003). MSNBC soon hired conservative radio talk-show host Michael Savage. His views on the war effort were unambiguous. In one programme, Savage suggested war protesters were 'committing sedition, or treason'. On radio, Savage happily swept away hundreds of years of history when he offered his own subtle solution to the Middle East conflict: 'We are the good ones and they, the Arabs, are the evil ones. They must be snuffed out from the planet and not in a court of law'. Savage apparently went too far and was fired in July of that year after making homophobic remarks on air.

Commentators were now talking about a so-called Fox Effect, whereby CNN and MSNBC were trying to recapture lost market share by singing from the same patriotic song book as Fox (Rutenberg 2003b; Willis 2003). The near-monopolisation of the meaning of patriotism by Republican and pro-war advocates was difficult to break through for anti-war protestors. In San Francisco, a hub of antiwar activity, counter-branding campaigns were launched to 'reclaim' the flag using 'Peace is Patriotic' bumper stickers (Salladay 2003). While media corporations were openly sponsoring pro-war rallies, one *San Francisco Chronicle* reporter was fired after it was learned he had participated in an anti-war rally on his own time. MSNBC correspondent Ashleigh Banfield, who had been feted by the network during its coverage of the conflict in Afghanistan, was reprimanded by her employer after telling students at Kansas State University that media coverage had not shown the full horrors of battle.

In bed with militainment

News organisations' desire to brand themselves as patriotic meshed nicely
with the Pentagon's and the White House's desire to choreograph the invasion. 'After September 11 the country wants more optimism and benefit of
the doubt', said MSNBC President Erik Sorenson. 'It's about being positive
as opposed to being negative' (Rutenberg 2003b). CBS News President
Andrew Heyward said he wanted audiences to know that he was 'rooting
for the US to win the war' (Bednarski and Higgins 2003). Branding synergy
between broadcasting media and the military was at the core of the
media/military relationship. Careful attention was given by the Pentagon to
make sure that their public-relation needs were integrated with the hour-by-
hour organizational requirements of broadcasters. The goal was to produce
dramatic and sympathetic stories about the troops. Their solution was to
attach, or 'embed', more than 600 reporters with specific military units.
These reporters travelled 24 hours a day under the protection of the same
soldiers they were supposed to write stories about. The decision met with
condemnation and praise. Liberal critics worried that reporters would lose
their prized 'objectivity' while living, eating and sleeping under the protection of their military keepers (Tumber and Palmer 2004: 48–63). Proponents
such as Heyward argued professional distance was maintained. 'We had
total freedom to cover virtually everything we wanted to cover', claimed
Chip Reid, an embedded reporter with NBC (Bauder 2003). Supporters also
praised the ability of embedded reporters to bear direct witness to events,
and recalled how journalists had been kept far from the battlefield in previous conflicts. 'It broadened the lens on the battlefield', said Terence Smith,
media correspondent for PBS (Kelley 2003). Others were more defensive.
'Let them try not showering for a week, sleeping out in the desert, living
through sandstorms, being under fire – I don't see these people out there',
said embedded CBS correspondent John Roberts, speaking of critics of the
programme. 'All they do is criticize' (Kurtz 2003a).

Reporters who chose to go it alone, the so-called unilaterals, were seen as
a problem. Some unilaterals were harassed and detained by soldiers as they
tried to move around the country (Houston 2003b; York 2003). During the
advance into Baghdad, the main hotel housing journalists was shelled by US
tanks, killing two cameramen. 'It is in fact a brilliant, persuasive conspiracy
to control the images and the messages coming out of the battlefield and
they've succeeded colossally', un-embedded Canadian TV reporter Paul
Workman concluded, when speaking of efforts to restrict the movement of
journalists (Ward 2003). Stories by embedded reporters were also subject to
censorship if they revealed information deemed sensitive by military over-
seers. Many commentators added that 'embeds' could only see what military
handlers allowed them to see.

American and British military media minders did try to restrict story frames to the governments' daily 'message track'. The lack of valuable information coming out of the daily briefings at the central-command media centre in Doha, Qatar, was particularly frustrating. *New York Magazine* writer Michael Wolff captured a sentiment held by many journalists who were annoyed by the successful efforts to organise and control coverage. 'It takes about 48 hours to understand that information is probably more freely available at any other place in the world than it is here. At the end of the 48 hours you realize that you know significantly less than when you arrived, and that you're losing more sense of the larger picture by the hour. Eventually you'll know nothing' (Wolff 2003). Reporters had complained during the conflict in Afghanistan about restrictions placed on their movement. Moreover, government communication teams were overwhelmed by the challenge of managing a 24-hour global news cycle. The difficulties faced by NATO media handlers in controlling information during the Kosovo conflict convinced the Pentagon that improvements were required (Tumber and Palmer 2004: 64–65). American and British media specialists responded during the Afghan invasion by creating Coalition Information Centres (CICs). With offices in Washington, London and Islamabad, the centres coordinated the release of information and rebutted opposition allegations across time zones. The CICs were modelled on the so-called war rooms used in domestic political campaigns (DeYoung 2001; Stanley 2001b; Brown 2003). The approach has since been institutionalized. The daily briefing in Doha were timed for 2:00 p.m. so as to coordinate with morning-news programmes in the United States.

After the Hussein regime collapsed, US General Tommy Franks gave the embedding programme a thumbs up. 'Embedding will happen again', he said, 'and I remain a fan' (Moses 2003). The British government had struggled to persuade a sceptical public to support its decision to participate in the invasion. But during the conflict, UK Defence Secretary Geoff Hoon gave credit to embedding for a swing in public opinion in favour of the war. 'The imagery they broadcast is at least partially responsible for the public's change in mood', he said (Cozens 2003). Hoon had identified the core issue. Fear that reporters would lose their 'objectivity' missed the point. What really mattered were the lasting images of the fight against terror. Despite tensions between British and American PR staff over this strategy, the US approach carried the day, according to John Kampfner, who helped produce a BBC documentary that was highly critical of military propaganda during the conflict.

> The American strategy was to concentrate on the visuals and to get a broad message out. Details – where helpful – followed behind. The key was to ensure the right television footage. The embedded reporters could do some of that. On other missions, the military used their own cameras, editing the film themselves and presenting it to broadcasters as ready-to-go packages. The Pentagon had been influenced by Hollywood producers of reality TV and action movies, notably Black Hawk Down. (Kampfner 2003)

One could remain true to the 'regime of objectivity' (Hackett and Zhao 1998) and still provide the Pentagon spin machine with what it wanted – dramatic stories, sometimes mythic tales, about the heroic efforts of men and women in uniform. In fact, while the embedding programme was backed by coercive force, its success ultimately depended on reporters doing their jobs as they saw fit. It was important that stories produced by Western media have an air of verisimilitude. Iraq's hapless information minister, Mohammed Saee al-Sahhaf, was nicknamed 'Comical Ali' by wags in the Western media for his obvious disinformation. But while he provided suitable fodder for late-night comics, his presence had an ideological dimension. If Disneyland exists, as Baudrillard suggests, to make the rest of the United States appear real, then 'Comical Ali's' outbursts – 'We defeated them yesterday. God willing, I will provide you with more information' – marked the sophisticated American and British propaganda as truth.

There is no reason to believe that military personnel twisted the arm of embedded *New York Times* bio-terrorism reporter Judith Miller to write the numerous stories she filed, both before and during the invasion, on the search for Iraq's WMD programme. Her stories were cited by the White House to justify swift military action. And the imprimatur of the *New York Times* brand gave them enormous credibility. The unnamed source used in the stories turned out to be Ahmed Chalabi, leader of the Iraqi National Congress (Kurtz 2003b). Chalabi was the Pentagon's favoured replacement as a possible new Iraqi leader and, therefore, had a substantial interest in the war's outcome.[3] Reports that Chalabi was the principal source for the stories raised obvious questions as to whether the *New York Times* was manipulated to make it appear *as if* the White House was citing an independent intelligence source, instead of one of its own Iraqi proxies.

The Pentagon did not force the embedding programme on an unwilling news media. Their relationship was symbiotic. Moreover, 'military and entertainment types have been meeting and greeting over the last ten years or so' at conferences geared towards merging entertainment and military-training simulation technologies (Burston 2003: 166). Hollywood executives, including top people from Warner Brothers television, CBS and Fox were meeting with White House officials about participating in counter-terrorism initiatives as early as one month after the September 11 attacks. 'We have not done a good job communicating to people about who we are', said Bryce Zabel, chairman of the Academy of Television Arts and Sciences. 'It's possible the entertainment industry could help the government formulate its message to the rest of the world' (Rutenberg 2001). Indeed, the idea to embed reporters came out of a programme produced for ABC by action-movie king Jerry Bruckheimer (*Black Hawk Down*), and co producer Bertram van Munster (reality-TV show *Cops*), with the cooperation of the Pentagon. The premise behind *Profiles From the Front Line* was to get 'up close and personal' with soldiers fighting in Afghanistan in order to tell dramatic human-interest stories from their perspective (Seelye 2002; Holson 2003; Kakutani 2003; Kampfner 2003). It was a basic story formula first made popular in the 1970s by ABC Sports maven Roone Aldridge. The Pentagon liked the show so much that the embedding programme was born.

Some stories were produced that did not show soldiers in a particularly fond light, but the overwhelming flow of live-broadcast pictures tended to produce decontexutalised tales of heroism, or simply gripping live video. Armed with portable, satellite video phones, reporters were able to keep pace with advancing military forces while filing dramatic footage of troops on the move, or fearless paratroopers leaping out of aircraft into the pitch-black night. These live shots were often given the added patina of authenticity by their fuzzy green quality. Perhaps the most famous embedded reporter was NBC correspondent David Bloom, who transmitted live pictures while strapped atop his specially outfitted vehicle, nicknamed the 'Bloom Mobile'. A content analysis of embedded coverage found that most reports were anecdotal, combat focused, mostly live and unedited. That is to say, most reports involved a live stand-up (49.1 per cent; audio-only 12.1 per cent), with the reporter describing military action (27.8 per cent), combat results (13 per cent), or precombat activity, such as troop movements (31.5 per cent). Stories about troop morale, the work soldiers did and details about weaponry accounted for another 16 per cent. 'In general', read the report by the Project for Excellence in Journalism, 'the embedded reports tended toward immediacy over reflection' (Project for Excellence in Journalism 2003). As Peter Bart writes: 'The dead and dying were always kept at PG-13 distances' (Bart 2003). Even the Pentagon and White House officials admitted, in their more grumpy moments, that media coverage tended to view the conflict 'through a soda straw'.

The myth of the saving of Private Lynch

Perhaps the most memorable story of the war was the rescue of Private First Class Jessica Lynch from an Iraqi hospital. In this story, the potential for the spectacular integration of military propaganda, the commercial interests of converged-media conglomerates, mythic storytelling, and the organizational requirements of their 24-hour broadcasters were fully realised. A documentary produced for the BBC's *Correspondent* programme went as far as to call the story 'one of the most stunning pieces of news management ever conceived'.

Lynch was travelling with the Army's 507th Maintenance Company on 23 March, when the convoy was ambushed after taking a wrong turn. The 19-year-old soldier was taken prisoner after she sustained serious injuries to her legs and spine. Five others were captured and held separately from Lynch. Eleven soldiers were killed. That much of the story remains undisputed.

Almost two weeks into the conflict, there was mounting pressure on the White House and Pentagon. Some media coverage had gone negative. Reports from mainstream American news outlets were not challenging the validity of the invasion. That would have damaged 'Brand America'. Instead, retired generals and other elite sources were starting to question whether the United States and Britain had underestimated the strength and determination of Iraqi soldiers who, at that moment, were putting up much stiffer resistance than anticipated. Many journalists had been swept up by the promise of 'shock and awe' and expectations were high that there would be a swift and painless victory march into Baghdad. That would change. Negative images of frightened US POWs released by Iraq as propaganda had become front-page news. Word that Iraqi civilians, including women and children, had been shot after the vehicle they were in failed to stop at a US checkpoint, was also making headlines. Some reports dared to raise the possibility that the military operation might slip into a Vietnam-like quagmire.

It was in this media context that reporters embedded with Centcom, in Doha, were raised from their beds on 1 April. Some reporters thought the military might have captured Saddam Hussein. The story was better. They were briefed on the dramatic tale of Lynch's rescue. Edited video of the operation was distributed by the military to eager broadcasters, who quickly beamed the images around the world. The video showed Lynch, draped in a US flag, being carried on a stretcher into a helicopter that would fly her to a US military hospital in Germany. Soon family photos of the photogenic private would be released. The image of a pretty blond American teenager, with humble roots, from Palestine, West Virginia, grabbed media attention. 'She Was Fighting to the Death', shouted a 3 April headline in the *Washington Post*. That story went on to quote unnamed Pentagon sources who said Lynch, despite having sustained multiple gunshot wounds at the hands of Iraqi soldiers, had 'fought fiercely', discharging her weapon until she ran out of ammunition. 'She did not want to be taken alive', said one official. 'Talk about spunk!' said US Senator Pat Roberts, who was also quoted in the *Post* story. 'She just persevered. It takes that and a tremendous faith that your country is going to come and get you' (Schmidt and Loeb 2003). Other broadcast and print outlets quickly followed the *Post*'s lead and wrote similar stories that would mark Private Lynch as a national hero – an icon of American grit, determination and patriotism (Chinni 2003). Seemingly over-night, Private Lynch had entered the pantheon of American heroes. And, just as suddenly, media coverage changed. 'Boy, one little POW rescue can sure change the tone of the press coverage', wrote *Post* media critic, Howard Kurtz. 'By the time Ari Fleisher [White House press secretary] faced reporters yesterday, many of the questions were about who would be running Iraq once Saddam is permanently sidelined. Goodby, quagmire' (Kurtz 2003c).

The 'good news' was soon complicated. Within days reports began to appear that contradicted the storyline as portrayed in the *Post*. Named sources at the hospital in Germany denied that Lynch had been shot and stabbed. The extent and cause of her injuries were being questioned. 'Interestingly though', writes Dante Chinni, in a detailed chronology of media coverage of the story, 'given the choice between the two stories, many news organizations chose the more theatric set of circumstances, even though the other version of events had better sourcing' (Chinni 2003). It appears the story of a pretty blond soldier displaying courage and patriotism under fire was simply too good to pass up, particularly for broadcasters predisposed to wrapping coverage in the flag. It was later confirmed that, while Lynch suffered serious leg and spinal injuries due to a motor-vehicle accident, she was never shot or stabbed. Neither did she participate in a gun battle, because her gun jammed. Further information indicates that Iraqi troops that had been guarding the hospital had left before the rescue. This means that the special forces team did not meet any significant resistance during the rescue mission, as first reported – a fact that seriously dampens the dramatic tension required for successful melodrama. On 17 June, a chastened *Washington Post* published a lengthy reassessment of the Lynch saga on its front page, in which it corrected many of the errors contained in its heavily quoted story of 3 April (Priest et al. 2003). The patriotic mythology of 'Saving Private Lynch' was a made-for-Hollywood script. Unlike Specialist Shoshana Johnson, a fellow POW whose frightened image was also widely broadcast, Lynch was, as one columnist put it, the 'archetypal blonde-in-peril' (Zerbisias 2003). Shoshana had humble origins, but she was a black single mother. The Lynch mythology was so compelling that a bidding war erupted among news media thirsting for the first interview with the 'plucky' private – what is known in the industry as 'the get'. It is the most-prized interview among celebrity journalists. Katie Couric, NBC's popular host of the *Today Show*, reportedly sent Lynch 'a bundle of patriotic books, including Rudolph W. Giuliani's memoir, *Leadership*. Diane Sawyer, of ABC News, sent a locket with a photograph of Private Lynch's family home'. At CBS News the interview pitch was on a much larger scale. A letter written by CBS News senior vice president Betsy West, offered to bundle a two-hour TV movie along with other possible media projects with CBS Entertainment, MTV and book publisher Simon & Schuster – all of which are owned by parent company Viacom. 'From the distinguished reporting of CBS News to the youthful reach of MTV, we believe this is a unique combination of projects that will do justice to Jessica's inspiring story' (Rutenberg 2003c). The proponents of media convergence at Viacom recognised a platinum promotional opportunity when they saw one. Unfortunately, after the conglomerate's plans were revealed in a page-one story in the *New York Times*, CBS News was accused of 'checkbook journalism'. The news organisation fought back by accusing the *Times* of selectively quoting from its offer, and it insisted that the editorial independence of CBS News was never in question. A month later, CBS chairman Leslie Moonves would finally concede that linking the interview pitch to an integrated multimedia entertainment package may have gone too far. In a moment of astounding honesty, Moonves blamed the new competitive environment created by large media conglomerates. 'As these companies become more and more vertically integrated, you know, sometimes you do go over the line', Moonves said (BBC News Online 2003b).

Lynch returned home to a choreographed hero's welcome on 22 July that was broadcast live. She was greeted by thousands of flag-waving well-wishers who lined the streets of the tiny Appalachian town for a glimpse of their home-grown celebrity. Some displayed entrepreneurial spirit. Souvenir hunters could purchase a 'Welcome Home Jessica' t-shirt or a CD including a song about her ordeal made by an employee of a local market. It was titled: 'She Was Just Nineteen, Became America's Queen' (Dao 2003; Whoriskey 2003). For $24.95, online shoppers could visit jessicavideo.com and purchase 'Faith and a Community'; promotional copy for the video/DVD promised to 'tell the untold story of not just one individual but a whole community that pulled together during a time of war . . . This dynamic video tells the story of Jessica's rescue and those who believed for [sic] a miracle'.

Media were forbidden from taking pictures of Lynch struggling to get off a Black Hawk helicopter, nor were they permitted to film her at the family home. Reporters were directed to the parade route and a media tent constructed for the occasion. Sitting in front of the stars and stripes, Lynch nervously read from a prepared statement in which she thanked all those people who helped 'save' her, including special forces soldiers and a handful of Iraqi civilians, one of whom was Mohammed Odeh Rehaief. The 32-year-old lawyer is said to have tipped the military as to Lynch's whereabouts. He and his wife were swiftly granted political asylum in the United States. Rehaief helped NBC with its unauthorized TV movie about the rescue, and wrote a book for Harper Collins (Priest et al. 2003). Lynch declined overtures made by NBC to cooperate with the film, but later signed a deal with publisher Alfred A. Knopf that would see her share a reported $1-million advance with former *New York Times* writer Rick Bragg.

All the reports about Lynch's homecoming produced by major US news broadcasters failed to mention the controversy over her story. However, during her statement, Lynch did make a cryptic comment connected to the media controversy. 'I've read thousands of stories that said when I was captured I said, "I'm an American soldier, too." Those stories were right. Those were my words. I am an American soldier, too'. With these comments, Lynch's carefully crafted statement provided a testimonial as to the veracity of her story, without making specific claims that could be proven factually incorrect. It testified to the truth of her story at the level of myth. Significantly, controversy over whether the Pentagon manipulated the news media in order to construct a convenient wartime hero was not considered to be a problem by locals gathered to view the parade. 'Every war needs a hero', 77-year-old James Roberts told the *Washington Post*. 'Rickenbacker

... Kennedy ... she's the hero in this war. The facts don't particularly matter' (Whoriskey 2003). The view was shared by others. 'No matter what happened, she deserves every good thing she can get', said a local restauranteur. 'We just love her' (Dao 2003). These neighbours were concerned with phatic communication, not factually accurate reporting. The power of the 'Saving Private Lynch' drama is connected to how it is used by people to reinterpret everyday social reality and strengthen social relationships. The myth of 'Saving Private Lynch' had 'existential utility', that was historically situated, and structured in domination.

To Lynch's credit, she eventually cast doubt on her status as a mythic hero during an interview on the ABC News programme *Primetime*. The Pentagon 'used me as a way to symbolize all this stuff', Lynch told host Diane Sawyer. 'I mean, yeah, it's wrong ... I don't know what they had ... or why they filmed it' (ABC News 2003). The interview was broadcast November 11, Veterans' Day, to coincide with the launch of her co-authored book – *I am a Soldier, Too: The Jessica Lynch Story*.

Final comments

The invasion of Iraq was sold to America, and the rest of the world, 'as a public good' (Rutherford 2004: 99) with the aid of a willing media. Reporters and editors were not in collusion with the White House and Pentagon to dupe the public. Such a conspiracy was unnecessary and undesirable. The successful US and British propaganda made deft use of dramatic storytelling techniques that were tailor made for the 24-hour news environment. News media organisations worked to promote the Bush administration's plans to invade Iraq not because they were pressured by the White House (unilateral reporters notwithstanding), but because the media and military shared converged interests. The legitimate fear felt by members of the American public following the terror attacks of September 11 was leveraged by the administration in order to win public approval for a unilateral invasion of Iraq. 'What is worrisome', argue Steven Kull, Clay Ramsay and Evan Lewis, 'is that it appears that the President has the capacity to lead members of the public to assume false beliefs in support of his position' (Kull et al. 2004: 596). Instead of acting as watchdogs of power, it appears the media became symbiotic collaborators.

Notes

1 The report is available online at www.newamericancentury.org.
2 David Armstrong (2002) argues that Dick Cheney had been developing plans for US domination of the Persian Gulf region as far back as 1992 when he authored

the Defence Planning Guidance, a draft paper in which the Bush administration's unilateral foreign policy was first fleshed out.

3 Chalabi eventually fell out of favour with the White House. In May 2004 his home was raided by Iraqi police and American troops looking for evidence of criminal activity by members of his Iraqi National Congress. He also faced allegations that he disclosed secret information to Iran's intelligence service.

Digital divisions: online reporting and the network society

The use of information by the powerful and privileged as a means to reinforce, even exacerbate, the structures of the digital divide has attracted considerable attention amongst critical researchers concerned with the uneven development of the internet. The term 'digital divide' itself assumes varied meanings in different contexts, but is typically used as a sort of analytical shorthand to refer to the inequalities in people's relative access to internet resources. These inequalities, which in a given society recurrently revolve around social factors such as age, class, gender, ethnicity, education, employment and so forth, are particularly pronounced when internet access is examined in global terms. 'The differentiation between Internet-haves and have-nots', as Manuel Castells (2001) observes, 'adds a fundamental cleavage to existing sources of inequality and social exclusion in a complex interaction that appears to increase the gap between the promise of the Information Age and its bleak reality for many people around the world' (2001: 247).

Understanding the digital divide necessarily involves more than measuring the number of internet connections available in any one location. Of profound importance is the need to attend to the consequences of being connected or not in the first place. The internet, Castells contends, 'is the technological tool and organizational form that distributes information power, knowledge generation and networking capacity in all realms of activity' (2001: 269). As a result, he adds, to be 'disconnected, or superficially connected, to the Internet is tantamount to marginalization in the global, networked system. Development without the Internet would be the equivalent of industrialization without electricity in the industrial era' (2001: 269). Precisely how the dynamics of differential access unfold in different social contexts around the world is very much a question of possessing the capacity – or not – to adapt to the speed of change. Technologies of global communication are being decisively recast by a myriad of competing interests, posing acute difficulties for the very legitimacy of governing institutions from one country to the next. Until the digital divide is overcome, Castells maintains, it will threaten to engulf these institutions in a series of political crises. Here again, he makes a key point for our purposes, namely that as the internet 'becomes the pervasive infrastructure of our lives, who owns and controls access to this infrastructure becomes an essential battle for freedom' (2001: 269).

In taking Castells's (1996, 1997, 2000, 2001) theorisation of the network society as its point of departure, this chapter seeks to situate online journalism within the informational politics of capitalism. I shall argue that to grasp what is at stake in this 'battle for freedom' across the digital divide, we must necessarily account for the ways in which the news media are shaping democratic deliberation and debate across what are ever more globalised public spheres. Accordingly, this chapter will proceed to examine some of the ways in which ordinary citizens are opening up alternative spaces for new types of reporting to emerge. In providing an evaluative assessment, it is the extent to which online journalism is able to challenge certain forms of social exclusion underpinning the digital divide that is of primary importance.

Informational politics

A new world is beginning to take shape before our eyes. In making this observation, Castells (2000) argues that we are witnessing the emergence of a distinctive form of capitalism – characterised as much by its globalising reach as by its flexible adaptability to change – that is actively re-writing the imperatives of time, space and distance around the globe. The organising principles of this form of capitalism may be traced to the last three decades of the previous century. It was around the early 1970s, he maintains, that the historical coincidence of three processes became evident: the information technology revolution, the economic crisis of both capitalism and statism (and their subsequent restructuring) and the 'blooming' of cultural social movements (2000: 367). In examining the interaction between these otherwise independent processes, together with the responses they engendered, he discerns the emergence of 'the network society' as a new dominant social structure.

By introducing the phrase 'the network society', Castells is attempting to pinpoint an underlying logic that informs social action and institutions throughout what is an increasingly interdependent world. The network society is the social structure of the Information Age, in his view, being made up of networks of production, power and experience. Its prevailing logic, while constantly challenged by social conflicts, nevertheless gives shape to a system of norms, values and beliefs. More specifically, Castells maintains that at the heart of the network society is a dialectical interaction between modes of production (goods and services are created in specific social relationships) and those of development (technological innovation). This interaction is neither linear nor mechanical in the manner that it operates. Nor, crucially, is it contained within the authority of the nation-state. Rather, the network society is characterised by a new power system, where the once sovereign nation-state is submitted to an array of powers and counter-powers largely beyond its control. These competing sources of power, each bearing down on the nation-state in accordance with its own logic, find their basis in 'networks of capital, production, communication, crime, international institutions, supranational military apparatuses, non-governmental organizations, transnational religions, and public opinion movements' (1997: 304). Moreover, he adds, below the state 'there are communities, tribes, localities, cults and gangs', all of which place limits on its capacity to act. It follows, then, that nation-states are becoming effectively de-centred, that is, increasingly little more than 'nodes' of a broader network of power.

For Castells, it is knowledge generation, together with information processing, which are the primary sources of value and power in the Information Age. Evolving alongside the network society, he contends, is a new informational/global economy, as well as a new culture, which he describes as the culture of real virtuality. Turning first to the dynamics of this emergent economy, Castells believes a new international division of labour is appearing, one which is underpinned by informational-based production and competition. This increasingly global economy is characterised by its 'interdependence, its asymmetry, its regionalization, the increasing diversification within each region, its selective inclusiveness, its exclusionary segmentation, and, as a result of all these features, an extraordinarily variable geometry that tends to dissolve historical, economic geography' (1996: 106). Of critical importance here, then, is the extent to which the material foundation of this new global economy is grounded by 'informationalism' as the technological basis of economic activity and social organisation. 'Under informationalism', he writes, 'the generation of wealth, the exercise of power, and the creation of cultural codes came to depend on the technological capacity of societies and individuals, with information technology as the core of this capacity' (2000: 367). The enhanced 'flexibility' of capitalism, it follows, is directly attributable to the role played by new information technologies. This role may be broadly characterised as revolving around the provision of 'the tools for networking, distant communication, storing/processing of information, coordinated individualization of work, and simultaneous concentration and decentralization of decision-making' (2000: 368).

Taken together, these factors are broadly constitutive of a new kind of culture, which Castells terms 'the culture of real virtuality'. In his words, it is 'a system in which reality itself (that is, people's material/symbolic existence) is fully immersed in a virtual image setting, in the world of make believe, in which symbols are not just metaphors, but comprise the actual experience' (2000: 381). To clarify, this culture is real, but at the same time virtual in that it is constructed primarily through processes of communication that are electronically based. This virtuality is, in effect, our 'fundamental' reality.

That is to say, in Castells's view, it is 'the material basis on which we live our existence, construct our system of representation, practice our work, link up with other people, retrieve information, form our opinions, act in politics, and nurture our dreams' (2001: 203). Hence, in trying to elucidate the lived materiality of this culture at the level of experience, it is crucial to recognise that all domains of social life are implicated ever more deeply in the time-spaces of networked communication media. The influence of information technology in transforming the social relations of inclusion and exclusion is not to be underestimated – indeed for Castells, it is of vital importance in understanding how networking has recast social life, more often than not in unexpected ways where political interests are concerned.

Cyberspace, then, is a contested terrain, crisscrossed by countervailing logics of domination and liberation. Castells's conceptual approach is richly suggestive of new ways to investigate the changing dynamics of power. 'In an informational society', he argues, power 'becomes inscribed, at a fundamental level, in the cultural codes through which people and institutions represent life and make decisions, including political decisions' (2000: 378). Power, it follows, can be both material and immaterial. In the case of the former, the consolidation of power may provide certain individuals or organisations with the means to enforce their interests or decisions, quite possibly in the absence of consensus. At the same time, however, its immateriality is implicated in the production of a new consensus around these ruling imperatives. In this latter sense, power assumes a hegemonic quality in that it encourages the framing of life experience within the boundaries of certain preferred categories, thereby furthering ruling prerogatives as a question of legitimacy (as opposed to coercion). For instance, Castells writes:

> if a population feels threatened by unidentifiable, multidimensional fear, the framing of such fears under the codes of immigration = race = poverty = welfare = crime = job loss = taxes = threat, provides an identifiable target, defines an US versus THEM, and favours those leaders who are most credible in supporting what is perceived to be a reasonable dose of racism and xenophobia. (Castells 2000: 378–379)

It is in this context, then, that Castells elaborates upon his thesis that 'cultural battles are the power battles of the Information Age' by bringing the role of the news media to the fore. It is across the field of journalism, in his view, that these cultural battles are primarily waged. Power, it follows, does not reside within the news media in the sense that they become power-holders; rather, it 'lies in the networks of information exchange and symbol manipulation, which relate social actors, institutions, and cultural movements, through icons, spokespersons, and intellectual amplifiers' (2000: 379).

In seeking to assess the specific implications of this new geometry of power for online journalism, then, the 'informational politics' of the internet warrant particular attention. To the extent that access to government is mediated by interests outside of democratic forms of control and accountability, Castells argues, the use of information becomes the 'privileged polit-ical weapon' in the age of the internet. Precisely how, and in what ways, jour-nalism must evolve and change to counter the powerful influences of the new communication system is anything but clear from the vantage point of today. The capacity of the internet to transform the guiding ethos of journalism – even at the most rudimentary level of reconfiguring what counts as 'news' in the first place, let alone any conception of a 'public sphere' – is only now beginning to register where it matters most, that is, in the minds of the people who make up its publics. People's lived experience in the Information Age, their engagement with the im/materiality of cultural forms in the contexts of their everyday life, is of paramount concern when systems of representation are at stake. It is in making use of information or analysis available from varied sources, especially those situated well beyond the borders of any one nation-state, that people can refashion new forms of collective creativity, identity and attachment.

How best online journalism might contribute to the broadening of these distant relationships, and in so doing facilitate processes of democratisation, thus becomes a pressing political question. It is this latter consideration, that is, the ways in which the internet affords the user with the opportunity to engage with news, information, imagery and commentary from afar, that is of particular interest here. In the next section, we shall briefly examine the online reporting of the tragic events of September 11, 2001 and, secondly, the use of warblogs in covering the war in Iraq. Attention focuses through-out on the ways in which online reporting engenders new approaches to eye-witness reporting, a process that is shown to be uneven, contingent and frequently the site of intense resistance from those whose interests are called into question.

Citizen journalism

The network society, to the extent that it is being built around the commu-nication networks of the internet, promises to refashion familiar conceptions of the global (see also McGuigan 1999; Volkmer 2002; Urry 2003; Allan and Matheson 2004; Gillmor 2004; Hassan 2004; Seib 2004). In attempting to pinpoint the ways in which online journalism operates within these commu-nication networks, it soon becomes all too that this is by no means a straight-forward task. To contend that journalistic forms and practices are subject to informational politics is one thing, but to demonstrate how they are being shaped by its development is a challenge of an altogether different order. There can be little doubt, however, that what is going to count as journal-ism in the years to come is being decisively reconfigured by the rise of the network society.

Early signs that this process of reconfiguration was gaining momentum were all too apparent on September 11, 2001. Less than ten minutes after the first airplane struck the World Trade Center, eyewitness accounts began to appear on the World Wide Web (see Allan 2002). People were desperate to put into words what they had seen, to share their experiences, even when they defied comprehension. Following closely behind were the major news sites – such as CNN.com, MSNBC.com, ABCNews.com, CBSnews.com and FoxNews.com in the US – with their respective journalists scrambling to post information as quickly as they could gather it from bewildered sources. As the crisis unfolded, however, most of these sites were so besieged by user demand that they became virtually inaccessible. If the day before these sites had been counting their 'hits' in the hundreds of thousands per hour, suddenly they were experiencing millions of such hits. Online news managers, like their mainstream news counterparts, were caught completely off-guard by breaking developments of this speed and magnitude.[1]

Few online journalists would dispute the claim that television led the way in covering the attacks during the early hours. The dramatic footage of crashing jetliners was indeed such that individuals with access to television were much less likely to turn to the internet than those who were deskbound, such as office workers. Online news sites, painfully aware of their users' frustrations, struggled to make the best of a desperate situation. In the early hours of the crisis, efforts to cope with the huge upsurge in traffic were varied and met with limited success. Several news sites responded by removing from their web pages any image-intensive graphics, such as banners, photographs and advertising content, so as to facilitate access. Further strategies to improve the capacity of websites to respond included expanding the amount of bandwidth available, bringing additional computer servers online, suspending user registration processes and temporarily turning off traffic-tracking software (Outing 2001; Robins 2001; Langfield 2002). The *New York Times* site even dispensed with its famous masthead to help streamline the loading process.

Still, for those restricted to their computers for information, the response time of some major news sites – if and when they actually loaded – must have seemed painfully slow. In the light of these and related difficulties associated with accessing these news sites, many users were forced to look elsewhere on the internet for information about breaking developments. Across the webscape, hundreds of websites were being rapidly refashioned as the day wore on. Many ordinary people felt compelled to post their eyewitness accounts, personal photographs, interpretations and analyses. Such 'citizen-produced coverage', to use a term frequently heard, was being produced by people who were transforming into 'amateur newsies', or instant reporters, photojournalists and opinion columnists. Their contributions to 'personal journalism', or 'do-it-yourself reporting', appeared from diverse locations, so diverse as to make judgments about their accuracy difficult if not impossible. These types of personal news items were forwarded via e-mail many times over by people who did not actually know the original writer or photographer. In so doing, they not only challenged traditional definitions of 'news', they also opened up for reappraisal the issue of who could be counted as a 'journalist'.

In stretching these familiar boundaries, so called 'personal journalists' threw into sharp relief the reportorial conventions of mainstream reporting. The richness of their accounts was extraordinary (even when allowing for those lapses where inaccuracies – accidental in some cases, deliberate in others – crept into accounts). Still fresh in many people's minds are the haunting stories and images of these eyewitnesses, some expressed in heart-rending detail, that fell outside the codified strictures of ostensibly 'impartial' journalism. The rapid and extensive circulation of this form of reporting across the webscape has meant that the human consequences of this crisis have arguably received far more extensive expression than would have otherwise been the case. News, as Dan Gillmor (2004) observes, 'was being produced by regular people who had something to say and show, and not solely by the "official" news organizations that had traditionally decided how the first draft of history would look' (2004: x). On this occasion, he adds, 'the first draft of history was being written, in part, by the former audience', an 'inevitable' development, in his view, given the new publishing tools available across the internet. 'We were witnessing – and in many cases were part of – the future of news' (2004: x).

Of particular importance here was the crucial role played by weblogs in making these forms of 'amateur', 'guerrilla' or 'DIY' (do it yourself) journalism available. Weblogs, or blogs for short, may be characterised as diaries or journals written by individuals with net access who are in possession of the necessary software publishing tools (e.g. those provided by sites such as Blogger.com) to establish an online presence. 'Most of the amateur [news] content', Leander Kahney (2001) remarked at the time, 'would be inaccessible, or at least hard to find, if not for many of the Web's outstanding weblogs, which function as 'portals' to personal content'. Managers of these blogs spent the day rapidly linking together any and all items of 'personal journalism' from 'amateur newsies' onto their respective sites. 'The Weblog world before September 11 was mostly inward-looking – mostly tech people talking about tech things', Glenn Harlan Reynolds of the blog InstaPundit.com observed. 'After 9/11, we got a whole generation of Weblogs that were outward looking' (cited in Gallagher 2002). By acting as 'unofficial' news sources on the web, these blogs linked together information and opinion that supplemented – or, in the eyes of some advocates, supplanted – the coverage provided by 'official' news outlets. 'Eyewitness reporting comes in large part from people's desire to share their stories and publish the truth', John Hiler of WebCrimson.com has argued. 'These are key features in blog-based grass-roots reporting, and a big reason that weblogs have exploded in popularity since September 11th' (cited in Bowman and Willis 2003).

Indeed, by the time of the formal declaration of 'Operation Iraqi Freedom' on 19 March 2003, the term 'blog' was rapidly being appropriated into the everyday language of journalism. To an extent never seen before, news-oriented blogs were achieving widespread public salience, being heralded as a new interactive form of participatory reporting, commentary and analysis of breaking news. In the case of those individuals blogging from Iraq, the proliferation of new media technologies – from digital cameras and computer notebooks to satellite telephones – enabled a very different kind of reporting to emerge, namely 'warblogs'.

In general terms, four categories of warblogs could be identified. First, there were warblogs associated with major news organisations (such as broadcasters like the BBC, CNN or MSNBC, together with newspapers such as the *Guardian, Seattle Post Intelligencer* or *Christian Science Monitor*). Typically these blogs were written as eyewitness accounts from the battlefield by journalists otherwise busy preparing print or broadcast reports. Second, warblogs were produced by freelance or 'sojo' reporters, writing and editing their own copy. For these bloggers, their relative freedom of movement enabled them to pursue the stories which mattered most to them – and the readers of their warblog. Freelancer Christopher Allbritton, self-described as the web's first independent war correspondent, relied on readers' financial support to make possible his blog, titled 'Back to Iraq. 2.0'. Third, 'personal' or 'amateur' journalists warblogs appeared, posted by soldiers, officers, activists, health workers, human rights campaigners, and so forth – many of them based on events they had witnessed firsthand. Their observations, impressions and opinions, taken together, covered every facet of the pro- and anti-war continuum. And, fourth, warblogs posted by Iraqi citizens proved to be especially adept at providing fresh insights into the horrors of daily life in a war zone.

Precisely what counts as truth in a war zone, of course, is very much in the eye of the beholder. Above dispute, in the view of many commentators, was that some of the best eyewitness reporting being conducted was that attributed to the warblog of 'Salam Pax' (a playful pseudonym derived from the Arabic and Latin words for peace), a 29-year-old architect living in middle-class suburban Baghdad. Indeed, of the various English language warblogs posted by Iraqis, none attracted a greater following than Salam's Where is Raed? (dear_raed.blogspot.com), which had begun to appear in September 2002. His motivation for blogging was later explained as a desire to keep in touch with his friend Raed, who had moved to study in Jordan.

In the months leading up to the initial 'decapitation attack', to use Salam's turn of phrase, the blog contained material ranging from personal – and frequently humorous – descriptions of everyday life to angry criticisms of the events around him. It was to his astonishment, however, that he discovered that the international blogging community had attracted such intense attention to his site. As word about Where is Raed? spread via other blogs, email, online discussion groups, and mainstream news media accounts, it began to regularly top the lists of popular blogs as the conflict unfolded. For Salam, this attention brought with it the danger that he would be identified – a risk likely to lead to his arrest, possibly followed by a death sentence. At the same time, speculation over the identity of the Baghdad Blogger – and whether or not *Where is Raed?* was actually authentic – was intensifying. Some critics claimed that it was an elaborate hoax, others insisted it was the work of Iraqi officials, while still others maintained that a sinister CIA disinformation campaign was behind it. Salam responded to sceptics on 21 March, writing: 'please stop sending emails asking if I were for real, don't believe [sic] it? then don't read it'. Moreover, he added, 'I am not anybody's propaganda ploy, well except my own' (cited in BBC News Online, 25 March 2003).

Enraged by both Saddam Hussein's Baathist dictatorship and George W. Bush's motivations for the invasion, Salam documented life on the ground in Baghdad before and after the bombs began to drop. This was 'embedded' reporting of a very different order, effectively demonstrating the potential of blogging as an alternative means of war reporting. His warblog entry for 23 March, 8:30 pm, was typically vivid:

> Today's (and last night's) shock attacks didn't come from airplanes but rather from the airwaves. The images al-Jazeera are broadcasting are beyond any description. . . . This war is starting to show its ugly face to the world. . . . People (and I bet 'allied forces') were expecting things to be much easier. There are no waving masses of people welcoming the Americans, nor are they surrendering by the thousands. People are doing what all of us are doing – sitting in their homes hoping that a bomb doesn't fall on them and keeping their doors shut. (Salam Pax, dear_raed.blogspot.com)

Salam's posts offered readers a stronger sense of immediacy, an emotional feel for life on the ground, than more traditional news sites. For John Allemang (2003), writing in *The Globe and Mail*, 'what makes his diary so affecting is the way it achieves an easy intimacy that eludes the one-size-fits-all coverage of Baghdad's besieged residents'. As Salam himself would later reflect, 'I was telling everybody who was reading the web log where the bombs fell, what happened . . . what the streets looked like.' While acknowledging that the risks involved meant that he considered his actions to be somewhat 'foolish' in retrospect, nevertheless he added: 'it felt for me important. It is just somebody should be telling this because journalists weren't' (cited in Church 2003).

The demands of truth

In the aftermath of the US-led invasion of Iraq, further questions continue to be raised about journalism's obligation to inform its publics while, at the same time, holding those in positions of power accountable for their actions.

In the words of US journalist Paul Andrews (2003), 'media coverage of the war that most Americans saw was so jingoistic and administration-friendly as to proscribe any sense of impartiality or balance', hence the importance of the insights provided by the likes of Salam Pax. This 'pseudonymous blogger's reports from Iraq', Andrews believed, 'took on more credibility than established media institutions'. This point is echoed by Toby Dodge (2003), who argued that Salam managed to post far more perceptive dispatches than those written by 'the crowds of well-resourced international journalists sitting in the air-conditioned comfort of five star hotels'. Communicating to the world using a personal computer with unreliable internet access, he reported 'the traumas and more importantly the opinions of Iraqis as they faced the uncertainty of violent regime change'.

Ever greater numbers of internet users, one online survey after the next appears to show, are looking for a wider array of reportorial perspectives about the realities of the conflict than are available from mainstream media in their own country (see also Allan 2004). 'Viewers first turn to television in part because TV's strength is the delivery of a narrative story line. That's what people are looking for when an event like this first begins to unfold', argued Kinsey Wilson, Vice President and Editor-in-Chief of USAToday.com, at the time of the invasion. 'Eventually, though, television starts to loop back on itself and repeats the narrative over and over again' (cited in Outing 2003). It is at this point, as he suggests, that a key advantage of online news comes to the fore. 'The best sites can move quickly to develop a story in multiple directions, add depth and detail, and give readers their own pathways to explore'. Online writer Stephen Gilliard concurs, contending that the 'war in Iraq has made world news sources far more important'. That is to say, while it is the case that 'not all news sources are reliable, there is such a gap between the way Americans see the world and the way other people do that it is invaluable to use these resources' (cited in Kahney 2003).

It is this capacity, that is, the ways in which the internet affords the user with the opportunity to engage with news and perspectives from afar, that concerns us here. While it is sometimes difficult for users to judge whether any given source is sufficiently trustworthy, the sheer diversity of the perspectives available online enables people to supplement their understanding of alternative, even opposing views. From the vantage point of most UK and US users, for example, no site in the region attracted more intense interest during the Iraq war than that associated with the al-Jazeera (www.aljazeera.net) satellite television network. Prior to the launch of al-Jazeera's website in January 2001, Arabic speakers were typically most interested in CNN.com (www.arabic.cnn.com) when looking for news online. Since the September 11 attacks, however, the page views for the Arabic-language site operated by al-Jazeera reportedly grew from about 700,000 a day to 3 million, with more than 40 per cent of visitors logging-on from the US (Ostrom 2003). Indeed, at the outbreak of hostilities in Iraq, aljazeera.net was widely recognised as receiving the most 'hits' of any Arabic site in the world.

Of critical significance here was al-Jazeera's commitment to pushing back the boundaries of Western definitions of 'objective' journalism so as to help give voice to contrary definitions of the world. In the case of the conflict in Iraq, this meant those of the Iraqi people themselves – victims, in the eyes of the network, both of Saddam Hussein's regime and the invasion of US and UK forces to destroy it. By including in its reports what were frequently horrific images of civilian casualties, al-Jazeera re-inflected Western notions of 'balanced' reporting. It was precisely these images, in the view of Faisal Bodi (2003), a senior editor for aljazeera.net, that made al-Jazeera 'the most sought-after news resource in the world'. In his words:

> I do not mean to brag – people are turning to us simply because the western media coverage has been so poor. For although Doha is just a 15-minute drive from central command, the view of events from here could not be more different. Of all the major global networks, al-Jazeera has been alone in proceeding from the premise that this war should be viewed as an illegal enterprise. It has broadcast the horror of the bombing campaign, the blown-out brains, the blood-spattered pavements, the screaming infants and the corpses. Its team of on-the-ground, unembedded correspondents has provided a corrective to the official line that the campaign is, barring occasional resistance, going to plan (Bodi 2003; see also Iskandar and El-Nawawy 2004).

At no time was this difference in news values cast in sharper relief than on 23 March, the night al-Jazeera broadcast footage of US casualties, as well as Iraqi television's interviews with five US prisoners of war. Al-Jazeera's decision to air the interviews was promptly denounced by US Defense Secretary, Donald Rumsfeld, who alleged that it was a violation of the Geneva Convention protecting prisoners of war. In reply, the network's London bureau chief, Yosri Fouda, argued that Western news reports were being constrained to the extent that they failed to provide accurate coverage. Regarding the Geneva Convention, he insisted that a double standard was being invoked. 'We and other broadcasters were not criticised for showing pictures of Iraqi dead and captured', he stated, 'or those famous pictures from Guantanamo Bay' (cited in Kafala 2003).

The more heated the ensuing furore became, of course, the more news headlines it generated around the world. The very images deemed by Western news organisations to be too disturbing to screen were being actively sought out by vast numbers of people via online news sites. According to figures compiled by popular search engines, such as Google, Lycos and AltaVista, the term 'al-Jazeera' was quickly becoming one of the most searched-for-topics on the web. Figures for the week in question indicated that the term 'al-Jazeera' (and variant spellings) was the term that showed the greatest increase on Google, while Lycos reported that it was the top search term, with three times more searches than 'sex' (a perennial favourite with web surfers). For Karl Gregory of AltaVista, the popularity of al-Jazeera's online sites was clear evidence of 'people branching out beyond their normal sources of news' (*BBC News Online*, 1 April 2003). The decision taken at al-Jazeera to broadcast the images, as well as to display them online, was justified by its spokesperson, Jihad Ballout, as being consistent with its journalistic ethos of reporting the war as it was being fought on the ground. In his words: 'We didn't make the pictures – the pictures are there. It's a facet of the war. Our duty is to show the war from all angles' (cited in Whitaker 2003). In the opinion of others, however, the network had become a mouthpiece for Iraqi propaganda. Citing the images, some military officials began ignoring questions from al-Jazeera's reporters at briefings. At the same time, two of the network's financial reporters were evicted from the floor of the New York Stock Exchange, their press credentials having been revoked (Nasdaq would follow suit, citing 'al-Jazeera's recent conduct during the war' as the reason). It was in cyberspace, however, that the backlash registered most decisively as various pro-war individuals and groups made clear their intent to make al-Jazeera a target of retaliation.

News sites of all descriptions are always vulnerable to attack from hackers –typically involving little more than webpage defacements and graffiti – but those directed at al-Jazeera's sites were remarkably vicious. The 'electronic onslaught', as aptly characterised by one internet commentator, began on 25 March, the same day the English-language site, www.english.aljazeera.net, was launched. Two days later, hackers 'crashed' both sites, effectively forcing them offline by a 'denial of service' or DOS attack. This type of attack aims to close down a targeted site by overwhelming the associated server with so much meaningless data that it can no longer handle legitimate traffic. Few sites have sufficient resources, such as the necessary bandwidth, to withstand millions of simultaneous page impressions. Such was certainly the case with both al-Jazeera sites. The English-language site was disabled virtually from the outset, while its Arabic-language counterpart struggled – with only limited success – to hold up against the storm. Efforts to restore the sites, which reportedly included re-aligning them with servers in France, encountered fierce resistance by repeated hack attacks. 'We come up for five or ten minutes', stated Salah AlSeddiqi, IT manager at al-Jazeera, 'and then the attacks bring us down again' (cited in Roberts 2003).

Later the same day, even though security protocols had been reinforced for the sites, matters went from bad to worse. Evidently, al-Jazeera's domain was effectively 'hijacked' by a pro-war hacker, who succeeded in ensuring that users were pointed to an altogether different site instead. Specifically, traffic was redirected to a pro-war webpage featuring a US flag, together with the messages 'Let Freedom Ring' and 'God bless our troops', signed by a self-proclaimed 'Patriot'. It was quickly determined that this latter site belonged to an internet provider based in Salt Lake City, Utah, albeit without their knowledge. Hackers calling themselves the 'Freedom Cyber Force

Militia' had claimed responsibility for the attack, but in any case the registration information provided to establish the webpage proved to be fictitious. Hours later, traffic intended for the al-Jazeera site was redirected again, this time presenting users with a webpage bearing the message 'taken over by Saimoon Bhuiyan'. Further attacks continued apace, one of which apparently succeeded in diverting users to a pornography site. Meanwhile, as al-Jazeera's technicians scrambled to reinstate the correct addresses for the sites, pressures of a different sort were brought to bear. As a result of the hacker attacks, the network's hosting company, along with a company brought in to help deal with the increased traffic to the sites and to provide protection against hacking attempts (both based in the US), abruptly terminated their respective services. 'It has nothing to do with technical issues', Joanne Tucker, the managing editor of al-Jazeera's English-language site, argued. 'It's non-stop political pressure on these companies not to deal with us' (cited in St John 2003; see also Granneman 2003; Gray 2003; Roberts 2003). Commenting on the repeated hacking, she added: 'It's a narrow, pro-censorship attempt to silence a news site'.

Al-Jazeera's ongoing commitment to re-writing the tacit, taken-for-granted rules of Western notions of journalistic 'objectivity' continues to enrage its critics, yet is also winning praise from others. In accepting an award from Index on Censorship for the best circumvention of censorship, Muftah Al Suwaidan, the London bureau's executive director, accentuated the importance of maintaining professional integrity under pressure. 'Since its inception, al-Jazeera has been at the forefront of the struggle to maintain free, independent and balanced reporting', Al Suwaidan asserted. 'Different people have different views but the common denominator should always remain the right of people to know and the freedom of all to express themselves' (*Guardian*, 27 March 2003). At the same time, there is evidence to suggest that the network is becoming more self-reflexive about its use of shocking images, if not to the extent demanded by US and British officials. In April 2004, staff at the network received a memo informing them that Ahmed Sheikh, editor-in-chief, was 'upset' by what he considered to be scenes of 'excessive violence' represented in some news items. 'Violence that is true to life is regarded as desensitising viewers', the memo stated, 'although some might argue that its use may serve a moral or a social point. Therefore, consideration should be given to the suitability of scenes of violence in the news' (cited in the *Guardian*, 30 April 2004). A balance needs to be struck, the memo continued, between 'the demands of truth and the danger of desensitising people'. While for some critics the memo was symptomatic of external pressures brought to bear on the network, for others it was a price worth paying to ensure that its capacity to present news from Iraqi civilians' point of view was protected.

Counting casualties

'We don't do body counts', a statement made by General Tommy Franks (recently retired) of US Central Command, is the tagline of a unique website dedicated to providing information about civilians killed in the Iraq war and its aftermath. Operating with the help of about 20 academics and peace activists, the UK-based Iraq Body Count (www.iraqbodycount.net/) maintains a running tally of the civilians reported to have been killed in incidents associated with the military intervention.

In compiling their figures from thousands of news items, the site's project team is careful to follow a strict methodological framework. Specifically, casualty figures are calculated using a thorough survey of online news reports and eyewitness accounts (where sources report differing figures, a minimum and maximum number is provided), a procedure which is independently reviewed and cross-checked by other members of the team in every instance. This approach, as the authors readily acknowledge, provides the basis for what can only be an estimate. In their words:

> We are not a news organization ourselves and like everyone else can only base our information on what has been reported so far. What we are attempting to provide is a *credible compilation* of civilian deaths that have been reported by recognized sources. Our maximum therefore refers to *reported deaths* – which can only be a sample of true deaths unless one assumes that every civilian death has been reported. It is likely that many if not most civilian casualties will go unreported by the media. That is the sad nature of war (emphasis in the original; www.iraqbodycount.net/).

The project's figures for Iraqi civilian deaths, at the time of writing, were a minimum of 13,224 and a maximum of 15,292. 'By requiring that two independent agencies publish a report before we are willing to add it to the count', the authors add, 'we are premising our own count on the self-correcting nature of the increasingly inter-connected international media network'.[2] In the absence of alternative statistics from US military officials – where evidently no effort has been made to compile them – the project's site has become one of the most widely-cited sources of information for journalists around the globe.[3]

Nevertheless, for individuals seeking to place a human face on these sorts of statistics, it is more than likely that they will have to look beyond the narrow confines of mainstream news reporting. It is interesting to note in this context the results of a Pew Internet & American Life Project study (2004) which suggested that more than 30 million internet users in the US have seen graphic war images online, approximately 28 per cent of whom having actively sought them out.[4] Indeed, according to the report's nationwide telephone survey conducted between 14 May and 17 June, 2004, internet users are much more inclined than non-users to approve of the display of disturbing war-related images on the internet. Given that events transpiring during this period included the murder and dismemberment of US contract workers in Fallujah, images taken in the Abu Ghraib prison of Iraqi prisoners being tortured, and the capture (and subsequent beheading) of US civilian Nicholas Berg, it is perhaps not surprising that access to such imagery provoked mixed responses from users. 'Millions of Internet users want to be able to view the graphic war images and they see the Internet as an alternative source of news and information from traditional media', stated Deborah Fallows, co-author of the Pew report. 'But many who do venture outside the traditional and familiar standards of the mainstream news organizations to look at the images online end up feeling very uncomfortable.'

The report's findings underscore the extent to which it is difficult to generalise about how internet users in the US relate to online news coverage of the conflict. Evidently, the men surveyed were more likely to approve of graphic and disturbing ware-related imagery being made available online than the women surveyed. 'Of the 16 percent of women who have seen the war images online', the report states, 'only 36 percent say they felt they made a good decision in doing so; 52 percent said they wish they hadn't seen them, and 3 percent said both' (Pew Report, 2004: 3). Apparently some 68 percent of the men surveyed believed it was a good decision to search the internet for extreme images not covered in the traditional media. At the same time, younger users (those 18 to 29 years of age) were more inclined to approve of the use of this imagery than older users. Further findings assert that those users situated at the higher end of the socioeconomic scale, along with those with higher than average educational obtainment, were more favourably predisposed than others. Political partisanship, it seems, was also a factor. Supporters of the Democratic Party were more inclined to approve of the use of such imagery on the internet (52 per cent of them) than Republicans (42 per cent). Although no correlation is drawn with respondents' views on the war itself, one can speculate that it is likely that self-described Democrats are presumably more inclined to see in such imagery vindication for an anti-war position than Republican users.

Bearing in mind the usual sorts of qualifications where opinion surveys are concerned (margins of sampling error, interpretations of question wording, practical difficulties, and so forth), this type of data usefully highlights the extent to which the internet is being used to supplement traditional news sources. Across the webscape, news sites are calling into question the military's preferred definitions of the conflict, not least by challenging the 'sanitized' representations prevailing in newspapers and television newscasts. 'While so much is made of the 1,000 US military fatalities', observed online journalist Linda S. Heard (2004) on the occasion of the third anniversary of the September 11 attacks, 'an eerie silence surrounds the tally of Iraqi casualties since the invasion'. Pointing out that while the deaths of the September 11 victims had been widely commemorated in public events, 'the deaths of Afghan and Iraqi civilians went unnoticed. When this inequality is publicly remarked upon, US politicians either sidestep the question or glibly parrot prepared answers'.[5] This relative silence is in sharp contrast, as discussed above, to the determined efforts made by internet users to see such types of imagery for themselves. Clearly al-Jazeera, along with various war-blogs, go some distance in challenging the normative limits imposed by mainstream media's definitions of 'balance', 'public decency' or 'good taste'. Images of the horrific consequences of warfare, it almost goes without saying, are as upsetting as they are necessary.[6]

To close, this chapter has sought to identify a number of the ways in which journalism is being reconfigured by what Castells aptly characterises as the informational politics of the network society. Online reporting, as I have sought to show, possesses the capability to bring to bear alternative perspectives, context and ideological diversity to its coverage, providing users with the means to hear distant voices otherwise being marginalised, if not silenced altogether, across the network society's breadth. Journalists' routine, everyday choices about what to report – how best to do it, and why – necessarily implicate them in a discursive politics of mediation in what are increasingly globalised public spheres. The very multi-vocality at the heart of their narrativisation of reality renders problematic any one claim to truth, and in so doing reveals that witnessing is socially situated, perspectival and thus politicised. To the extent that online reporting fosters points of human connection at a distance, and in so doing establishes new principles of trust and responsibility, it will help to counter the forms of social exclusion endemic to the digital divide.

Notes

1   MSNBC.com, for example, reportedly registered as many as 400,000 people hitting its pages simultaneously. In the case of CNN.com, 9 million page views were made per hour that morning. Where some 14 million page views would be ordinarily made over the course of an entire day, about 162 million views were made that day (Outing, 2001). Each of the other major news sites could be reached only sporadically as efforts mounted to ward off the danger of the Internet infrastructure undergoing a complete 'congestion collapse' (see Allan 2002).

2   'For a source to be considered acceptable to this project', an explanatory statement on the website states, 'it must comply with the following standards: (1) site updated at least daily; (2) all stories separately archived on the site, with a unique url; (3) source widely cited or referenced by other sources; (4) English Language site; (5) fully public (preferably free) web-access. The project relies on the professional rigour of the approved reporting agencies. It is assumed that any agency that has attained a respected international status operates its own rigorous checks before publishing items (including, where possible, eye-witness and confidential sources).

3 'The truth about who is being killed by the US air strikes', Patrick Cockburn, correspondent for the *Guardian* newspaper, pointed out, 'is difficult to ascertain exactly because Islamic militants make it very dangerous for journalists to go to places recently attacked. Bodies are buried quickly and wounded insurgents do not generally go to public hospitals. But, where the casualties can be checked, many of those who die or are injured have proved to be innocent civilians' (*Guardian*, 18 September 2004).

4 Regarding methodological considerations, the authors write: 'The results in this report are based on data from telephone interviews conducted by Princeton Survey Research Associates from May 15 to June 17, 2004, among a sample of 2,200 adults, 18 and older. For results based on the total sample, one can say with 95% confidence that the error attributable to sampling is plus or minus 2 percentage points. For results based Internet users (n=1,399), the margin of sampling error is plus or minus 3 percentage points'.

5 One exception to this general rule was a statement made by US Brigadier General Mark Kimmitt, the senior military spokesperson in Iraq, in the aftermath of a particularly violent round of fighting in Fallujah. Asked what he would tell Iraqis about televised images 'of Americans and coalition soldiers killing innocent civilians', he replied: 'Change the channel' (cited in the *New York Times*, 12 April 2004).

6 This relative silence was briefly interrupted by a study published by the *Lancet* medical journal in October, 2004. The findings of the research team, led by Les Roberts of the Johns Hopkins Bloomberg School of Public Health in Baltimore, suggested that about 100,000 Iraqi civilians (half of them women and children) had died in Iraq since the invasion. The study's data was based on information gathered from door-to-door household surveys (33 clusters of 30 households each across the country) concerning births and deaths since January 2002. Press reports (see, for example, Boseley 2004; Stein 2004) highlighted the study's findings, but they did not receive sustained attention.

The impossibility of technical security: intellectual property and the paradox of informational capitalism

Introduction

> Marx termed the twofold movement of the tendency to a falling rate of profit, and an increase in the absolute quantity of surplus value, the law of the counteracted tendency. As a corollary of this law, there is the twofold movement of decoding or deterritorializing flows on the one hand, and their violent and artificial reterritorialization on the other. The more the capitalist machine deterritorializes, decoding and axiomatizing flows in order to extract surplus value from them, the more its ancillary apparatuses, such as government bureaucracies and the forces of law and order, do their utmost to reterritorialize, absorbing in the process a larger and larger share of surplus value. (Deleuze and Guattari 1984: 34–35)

This chapter examines the contradictions of information and communications technology in the production, distribution and regulation of 'informational goods'. Information and communication technologies have facilitated, and been driven by corporate, political and military expansion (Castells 1996), as well as by deterritorialisation in all spheres of social action (Deleuze and Guattari 1984;Virilio 1994). The need and the ability to coordinate action at a distance feed into each other in the development of an increasingly 'globalised' society, and feed off the fusion of energy and information. A global 'post-industrial' society is increasingly dependent upon primary extraction activities in highly localised and highly contested spaces. This is one dimension of ongoing conflict. A second dimension is becoming increasingly apparent at the opposite end of the spatial and technical spectrum. If energy needs generate potential for intense threats to the new world order in a range of very specific locations, the potential to reproduce 'information goods' without limit either in number or location creates the opposite threat. Corporate power is threatened by scarcity on the one hand and a potential loss of scarcity on the other. The capacity to produce a near infinite number of perfect copies (of music, film, books, scientific and medical formulas, computer programs) in millions of locations across the world takes the process of deterritorialisation beyond empire (Hardt and Negri 2000). It is this second dimension that will be the focus of attention in this chapter. This dimension highlights; (1) the crisis tendencies within a system that generates surplus but which cannot survive without scarcity, as well as (2) the impossibility of technical solutions to such insecurity.

The chapter starts by outlining the dual processes of geographical expansion and technological development by which capital seeks to secure its dominance, but which in both cases set up potential for subsequent crises. Both processes are then related to the tendency for the rate of profit to fall, and the attempts to shore up this threat. The discussion is then grounded in an account of struggles over file sharing on the internet, the supposed link between DVD piracy and international terrorism, and the distribution of mobile phone ring tones. These cases illustrate the binding of technological developments within the economic, legal and cultural contradictions of a system that promotes innovation, creativity and productivity and then seeks to rein these forces in when surplus threatens profitability.

The ironic reversal

The advent of the deterritorialised rocket state, the fusion of missiles and media was supposed to secure the power of the mobile over the relatively fixed, or at least the power of those who could control propulsion and the flow of information. In large measure, and in the above terms, the rocket state has been a success. However, the dynamics of success are also capable of creating new contradictions and crises.

Thomas Pynchon's (1973) novel *Gravity's Rainbow* explores the emergence of what he calls the 'Rocket State' in the aftermath of World War Two and in the context of the Cold War (Kellner 2001, David 2005). The fusion of military competition and corporate global expansion created the conditions for the emergence of the 'Rocket State'. Nazi Germany exemplified the development of modern methods of scientific domination towards a particular logical extension. Totalitarian control over an occupied territory, and the concentration of enemies of that regime for the purpose of extermination required the development and application of modern scientific methods of military control, administration and execution. Pynchon, drawing upon the work of Max Weber, refers to Nazi Germany as the 'Oven State'. The 'Rocket State' dispenses with the need for physical occupation of territory, instead developing the dual technologies of long-range nuclear missiles and global telecommunications. Such a state can effect extermination and propaganda on a global scale, by technical means that detach the host society of almost all manifest expressions of its totalitarian dominion. Dispensing with the need for an overtly militarised civil society, the 'Rocket State' can threaten and enact huge acts of destruction and extermination, while projecting, at home and abroad, the image of itself as a peace loving, consumerist, democracy. Paul Virilio (1994) addresses similar themes in his discussion of deterritorialisation and the fusion of war and media, and again presents an account that gives primacy to the rising power of the military post-industrial complex, rather than to growing contradictions within such processes.

Developments in ICTs (information and communication technologies) bound up with globalisation/deterritorialisation are routinely presented in academic writing and in mass media as forces of both regulation and deregulation. In one instance such developments are announced as being the death knell of national regulation as to restrict something in one jurisdiction would only encourage re-location and re-importation across increasingly porous borders. However, the relative mobility of capital is facilitated by the increasing non-materiality of goods, even while ICTs also enable the coordinated movement and production of physical objects at a global level. So, even as globalisation is said to represent a form of deregulation at one level, it also facilitates attempts at increased regulation and integration at a higher level. This regulation/deregulation process operates not only in economics, but also at political, cultural and military levels of action. The power to enact regulation and deregulation where and when it is convenient is the power to control global society. Such power is premised upon the mobilisation or resources and the fuelling of mobility. What happens when millions of people across the planet, relatively fixed as individuals, but distributed as a network across the whole planet, start reproducing without payment the 'things' that corporations seek to sell at a profit? Such unregulated production challenges the 'monopoly rent' available to those capable of securing sole rights to access or of giving access to a particular 'thing'. At this point the multitude outstrips empire (Hardt and Negri 2000), in both productivity and universality, and in a way potentially less controllable than physical migration. It is at this point that capitalist corporations, who themselves called for deregulation of local protections, call out for global regulation to protect their monopoly rent. However, it is by no means assured that the systems set in place to facilitate such corporate regulation and deregulation will not be successfully subverted for other purposes.

An old problem – the tendency for the rate of profit to fall and the rise of monopoly capitalism

The rise of the networked economy and informational goods witnesses the reinvention of an old spectre within capitalism, that of uncontrolled surplus. Unchecked, this surplus threatens to transcend the very system that brought it into existence. Marx's account of the tendency for the rate of profit to fall relies on a distinction between the 'law/tendency' itself (Marx 1995: 419–437) and an array of counteracting forces that mediate against the 'law/tendency' (438–446). While industrial capitalism contains barriers to market entry that shore up the rate of profit, these are being stripped away within a global network economy of informational goods.

Marx's account of the tendency for the rate of profit to fall and of his analytical separation of the law/tendency from the many tendencies mediating against it, rely on the labour theory of value (as developed by Smith and Ricardo). In an idealised 'textbook' market, price tends towards cost, and cost tends towards the labour embodied in a product (capital being dead labour). Increased investment in technology increases productivity thereby reducing the overall amount of labour embodied in each unit of production. While this increases the rate of surplus value extraction in the short term, competition will reduce prices in the long run as other capitalists follow suit with increased fixed capital investment. The rate of profit is thereby driven down as the value of goods falls towards the diminished amount of labour embodied in each unit of production. Alternative strategies to increase profitability (such as longer hours, lower wages, cheaper imported capital goods and the intensification of working practices other than by capital investment) increase the level of surplus value extraction without reducing the amount of labour embodied in each unit of production, but such counter-tendencies are only short lived too as such inefficient production runs up against both worker resistance and competition from more capital-intensive and thereby more efficient forms of production.

The tendency for the rate of profit to fall can be set against increased overall profitability if a lower profit margin per unit is counterbalanced by an increase in the overall number of items produced and sold. If an increase in capital intensity leads to increased worker productivity, this counterbalance between reduced profits per unit and increased overall output would, it might seem, be logically necessary. However, this assumes all the increased production can be sold. In conditions of market saturation prices will fall below their overall cost of production, to that of their variable, that is marginal, costs (that of living labour). In such conditions capital (dead labour) is not valorised and it is at that point that players leave the market. The rounds of capital intensification that precede such a moment generate levels of productivity that outstrip the capacity of wages (the value of labour power) to buy them, unless (1) prices fall to a level where the sum of commodity prices equals the sum of wages (the point noted above where capital is not valorised), or (2) where profit is transposed into consumer credit (a solution only if repayment is permanently deferred). Another option (3) is market expansion, the opening up of new realms of the world in which surplus production (commodities that cannot find an exchange value at home) can realise the value embodied in its production. This was seen as a primary motivation for colonial expansion in earlier epochs of capitalist expansion, along with the search for cheap capital goods as noted by Marx himself. Hardt and Negri (2000) discuss the work of Lenin, Hilferding and Kautsky, who all noted the curious perversity of a society where over-production represented a source of crisis. In today's global empire the 'exo-colonial' expansion of the past is supplanted by 'endo-colonial' intensification of a world already 'inside capitalism' (Virilio 1984). Such intensification of capitalism within ever deeper layers of life creates new markets, but does not eliminate the crisis tendencies that compel such intensification. The tendency for the rate of profit to fall is universal within market systems of production, while the tendency itself compels the adoption of innovative methods of expansion and/or intensification in the attempt to offset it. Such offsetting strategies may or may not succeed.

An interesting example of over-production as a source of potential crisis occurs in the networked economy of informational goods. One fundamental characteristic of informational goods is that they extend the principle of capital intensification to a new level. The capital investment required in the production of a new programme, drug, film or musical piece, is, once created, a fixed capital cost to be set against an almost non-existent variable cost, the labour involved in the production of each additional copy of that item. Market forces would, in textbook conditions, reduce the rate of profit to almost nothing in such circumstances if barriers to entry into the market are not created. One consequence of the global network economy is that barriers to market entry in the production of additional units of already existing informational goods are in fact radically reduced. Secondary entry into the market does not require the kinds of fixed capital investment required by market leaders and the natural monopoly afforded by being first is reduced to almost nothing when such goods can be transferred/replicated electronically. The conditions necessary for capital to make a profit from such goods (1) the capacity to bind fixed capital (property) and variable capital (labour) together, such that surplus value drawn from the latter can be accumulated by the former, and (2) the capacity to restrict market entry and so uphold 'monopoly rent', are potentially suspended. The tendency for the rate of profit to fall takes on an unprecedented level of intensity.

As Deleuze and Guattari (1984) suggest, for all capital's attempts to deterritorialise production within networks of ever more intense and extensive circulation, when confronted with the possibility of a form of productivity that takes surplus beyond the fixities of ownership and monopoly rent, it is corporations who call loudest for reterritorialisation. The solution being sought by corporations and their lobbyists is to limit market entry in the simultaneous process of electronic production/distribution through forms of legal, technical and cultural protectionism. The war on internet piracy can be seen as the latest frontier in the war against the falling rate of profit.

Background to specifics – Napster to New Napster

On 12 February 2001 the Ninth Circuit Court judges in Los Angeles decided that the internet music share service Napster was guilty of vicarious infringement of copyright and should cease its activities. The charge of vicarious infringement was brought against Napster because it was found guilty of aiding the illegal sharing of copyrighted music, despite not actually disseminating music itself. Napster was a piece of software developed in 1999 by Shawn Fanning that simply allowed users to freely share music in cyberspace by scanning individual computers and creating a central registry of music for downloading. Napster's ethos to aid sharing and create its own virtual community was also its weakness and eventual undoing. Napster's essential weakness were host servers that not only created this central registry of users and the music they held for sharing but that the digital transfer of music was conducted through these same servers. This centrality gave the American recording industry the target they desperately needed to hold someone legally responsible for both the breaking of intellectual property and copyright law and for a drop in music sales. It is Napster's technical fallibility that has since been superseded by new generations of file-sharing software.

The recording industry claimed that Napster was responsible for a dramatic fall in music sales in the United States and for encouraging widespread breaking of copyright law. The recording industry attempted to ban the software before its official release to the internet. However, recorded music sales were beginning to tumble as far back as 1997 (Kemeny and Rushe 2003), two years before Fanning began developing the system code for Napster, and only continued this decline during Napster's lifetime and beyond. These two central arguments over (1) copyright infringement and (2) responsibility for falling sales are still raging today. The only difference is that this debate has been widened from a local issue to a global problem.

Napster's enforced closure has been met with an array of technological solutions designed by the internet and music-sharing community who seek to avoid the legal accusation of vicarious infringement of copyright. Napster's fallibility was its central registry. A new generation of sharing software was developed to avoid the need for any central registry or server. Instead, the sharing of music takes place direct between the users. This technical evolution has created a major problem for the global recording industry because responsibility cannot be attributed to one or two software organisations, but rather, many millions of people who share music and other copyrighted data globally on a daily basis. In a repeat of history, the recording industry attempted to prevent the widespread dissemination of this new generation of music-sharing software by taking companies such as Kazaa, Grockster and Morpheus to court under the same legal charge as Napster. In April 2003, Judge Stephen Wilson adjudged in a Los Angeles district court that these music share companies could not be held responsible for the activities of their users (Glasner

2003). Judge Wilson drew the parallel with video recorders in which the manufacturer cannot be held responsible for the copyright-infringing activities of their consumers because the technology also has legal, non copyright-infringing uses. This single decision completely alters how the global recording industry will have to evolve its business for the twenty-first century (if it is not to be rendered redundant), and how it seeks to limit the unregulated practices of cyberspace music sharing.

Since April 2003 the global recording industry has embarked and sustained a continued campaign on many fronts with the sole purpose of destroying these 'New Napster' technologies and return recorded music to centralised control. This campaign has included the legal targeting of individuals who swap music on internet networks, targeting the Internet Service Providers to disclose personal and private information about individuals, seeking changes in the law to both criminalise individuals and extend the power of copyright owners, and lastly, the development of surveillance and encryption technology to make sharing difficult. Despite various degrees of success and irrespective of public consternation the recording industry is unapologetic about its actions. Recent and ongoing legal disputes have highlighted the significance of attributions and interpretations of responsibility, and show how even the biggest corporations do not always get what they want despite economic and political power. The legal failure against the 'New Napster' technologies in the US and other regions of the world have called for technical solutions to restrict music being disseminated in cyberspace and new methods of surveillance employed in government-like fashion to identify users for direct legal action. Much of the recording industry's mixed success has been due to the denizens of the internet also seeking technical solutions to the recording industry's actions and the very character of the internet. The internet developed from the late 1960s not to recognise territorial, legal or cultural differences – just to transfer data via the quickest most effective route. In many ways it transcends the limitations of the physical world as its infrastructure does not recognise social and cultural norms. Unfortunately for the recording industry, they must pursue actions within the limitations of the physical world, and in fact change their actions depending on the territory they are targeting. Different nation-states interpret copyright law differently, with varying degrees of emphasis placed on individual liberty and freedom. The recording industry is attempting to erase the problems of localised cultural, legal and political differences by pursuing global homogeneity of intellectual property, patent and copyright laws with the aid of the World Intellectual Property Organisation (WIPO), but this still requires localised 'reterritorialising' enforcement.

Contra technological determinism – the dialectic of technology

Technology that is developed for a single purpose can actually be capable of fulfilling an alternative purpose. The history and development of technology is filled with these twists. Clingfilm was a domestic offshoot of napalm used during the Vietnam conflict, and non-stick materials used for cooking were developed during the 1960/70s space race to prevent particles sticking to space craft are but a few examples. The notion that technology has a logic of application, or that technology automatically embodies the social relations of power that structured its creation is brought into question. Research by sociologists into workplace technology highlights the dialectical nature of technology, both in the complex and contradictory processes that structure the development and evolution of technological artefacts, and in the dynamics of technology's utilisation. The work of Zuboff, Grint and Woolgar, Burawoy, Collins and Pinch, Bogard and others explore this dynamic in a variety of situations (see David and Kirkhope 2004).

Technical security of informational goods in the globalised world becomes increasingly difficult to enforce, due to the schizophrenic character of technology. Any technology designed to secure and limit use can conversely also have the potential to secure anonymity and limit surveillance of those engaged in illicit use. Security and controlled dissemination of informational goods cannot be assured. Like intellectual property and copyright law, technical systems of regulation can be ignored or manipulated in such a fashion as to suit the agendas of those wishing to benefit from them. Success of the many technical methods to regulate and control the dissemination of informational goods relies on social forces (of trust and belief) not reducible to corporate (technical) control. In the network society post-industrial corporations have attempted to introduce many forms of technical restriction, but with limited success. Contemporary encryption software is not without its fallibilities, as algebraic mathematical code designed to prevent unauthorised access always has the potential to be broken and/or leaked throughout cyberspace. Likewise, technical security via government/corporate surveillance technologies are not without their weaknesses as methods can be found to play such approaches off against themselves. Corporate solutions all to easily become the next generation of means by which such corporations are threatened, even if the potential inversion by challengers is never itself totally secure.

The lock is also the key. This is the dialectic of technical security's impossibility. The capacity of the media industries to survey those who seek to share files requires the capacity to break forms of anonymity and encryption software. This capacity by its nature is also the technical capacity to break the encryption used by the media industries themselves to protect their informational property. In reverse, the technical attempts by the file sharer's to evade detection by authorities can never be absolutely secure.

All attempts at digital rights management have failed due to this technical dialectic. The cases of mini-disc, super audio compact disc, ATRAC, QuickTime, Windows Media Player and digital versatile disc all show that any technical systems designed with encryption in mind can and have been 'cracked' and keys made universally available (see David and Kirkhope 2004 for a more detailed account). Similarly, the technical strategies of file-sharing systems such as Darknet, Freenet and Zeropaid are all vulnerable as the technologies they use are all techniques that can be used against them. The technical coin always has more than one side. Outcomes at any given moment will reflect legal, economic and political processes rather than technical necessity.

Managing 'the horror'

Steve Woolgar (1988) highlights the range of methods adopted to shore up what is said to be 'truth' in the scientific arena. He refers to these attempts to fend off the underlying ambiguity and contingency of all knowledge claims as 'managing the horror' (1988: 33–35). He identifies the following: (1) Indexicality and Reflexivity – the cyclical process of using examples to clarify categories while using categories to give meaning to examples; (2) Passing off the shared assumptions of a network as independent verifications via triangulation; (3) Presenting theoretical models that have been invented as objects in the external world that have been discovered; (4) By looking at knowledge production in reverse, the linkage between current social arrangements and current legitimate knowledge appears to justify current social arrangements as the best reflection of 'truth', rather than showing knowledge to be a mirror of its conditions of production; (5) Feedbacking – the process whereby shared language reinforces the view that shared beliefs reflect reality; and (6) Appeals to Authority – where reference to a respected person is taken as equivalent to conclusive evidence. All these processes are amply displayed in the attempts made by corporations and their lobbyists to shore up their claim that the defence of monopoly rent in the area of informational goods is in the common good. In order to do this a double process is set in motion. The first step is the creation of a threat to everyone, and secondly there is the attempt to reassure 'everyone' that 'they' can be protected. Recent attempts to link 'piracy' of informational goods with international terrorism highlight such attempts to fabricate threat and security, but also the potential dangers of adopting such a strategy.

FACT or fiction: the claim that piracy funds terrorism and the idea that it is terrorism

The ability to reproduce virtual goods in millions of homes and offices across the world at virtually no additional cost per unit of production threatens to bring down the rate of profit. Even the capital goods (a networked computer, a CD burner, etc.) required to produce copies of virtual products are available to millions, either by ownership, or via work, study or other means of access. If market forces tend to encourage cost cutting and the reduction of prices towards the cost of production, as unit costs fall to next to nothing the only way to offset the tendency for prices to fall, and for the rate of profit also to fall, is for market forces to be regulated so as to protect the monopoly rent. But it is this level of monopoly rent (such as can be charged by record companies who have sole rights to market specific artists) that encourages people to 'enter the market'. In the attempt to regulate the actions of 'pirates', in conditions where many people are prepared to buy from them, corporations and their lobbyists have made increasingly extreme claims. 'Piracy funds terrorism and will destroy our society and your future enjoyment' (UK Federation Against Copyright Theft cinema commercial 2004). The rather curious linkage between the destruction of society and having one's night in with a video ruined by poor quality is in itself a rather crude jump, but no less crude is the attempt to substantiate the claim that piracy funds international terrorism. The use of the most extreme associations is designed to win over the public to corporate attempts to shore up their own profitability, even while such claims, may, if not believed, further undermine the claims of elites over their actions to 'protect us'. The multi-million pound campaigns of 2004 have recruited celebrities and politicians, policemen and so-called 'experts' to offer carefully crafted and coordinated messages to the public asserting the link between piracy and terrorism. The actress Helen Mirren claims 'It is increasingly clear that the money people spend on fake DVDs goes straight into the pockets of organized crime and international terrorism' (press release sent out across the UK in 2004 by FACT – see www.fact-uk.org.uk/home/htm). Television presenter Jonathan Ross just wanted to let everyone know that fake DVDs put money into the pockets of 'some very unsavoury individuals indeed' (Industry Trust for IP Awareness Limited 2004).

Organising a string of coordinated press releases and advertisements the array of corporate funded lobby groups sought to create the impression of overwhelming evidence for the link between copyright infringement and international terrorism. Through multiple and circular acts of self-reference, 'evidence' appeared to amass. One lobby group would cite another's claim that evidence existed. The other would in turn subsequently cite the first. Claims made by such lobby groups at local, national, regional and global forums were again cited as evidence.

To date the only evidence for a link between paramilitaries and DVD piracy comes from Northern Ireland, where the peace process has, it would appear, left some (active and/or former) paramilitaries to focus upon making money by illegal means (Burkeman 2004). Considering that Northern Irish paramilitaries have been implicated in just about every legal and illegal means of making and laundering money, the significance of this link is limited. Yet this has not prevented corporate lobbyists from extrapolating the general and seemingly universalist claim that 'piracy funds international terrorism'. In its successful defence against claims that such an extrapolation was a misrepresentation liable to mislead, the Federation Against Copyright Theft told the Advertising Complaints Commission that it could not release further 'evidence' because it was confidential and sensitive (ACC website). It did go on to cite statements and claims made by representatives of various international agencies attesting to the link, but all these again boiled down to the Northern Irish connection. Linking piracy and international terrorism in the context of the 'war on terror' seems designed to encourage people to think of al-Qaida trading pirated DVDs for flying lessons. Vague claims about 'international terrorism' allow insinuations to be generalised, even while the defence of such claims are highly localised.

Such attempts however may backfire if the insinuations come to be seen as deliberate manipulations. While a bomb threat was issued to the Northern Irish police counterfeit squad, no bomb was detonated and, in the context of the peace process, the migration from paramilitary to economic criminality makes the link with terrorism all the more ambiguous. As one researcher of terrorist finance, Rita Katz, puts it: 'I have never found, in any of my investigations, any terrorist attacks financed by the grey market [in pirated DVDs]' (cited in Burkeman 2004). Making the suggestion that the 1993 bombing of the World Trade Center may have been financed in part by the sale of counterfeit textiles as part of the case for claiming piracy of music and film funds international terrorism (FACT spokesman cited in Burkeman 2004) may only serve to undermine the credibility of such claims even further.

While the claims of those like Baudrillard (1995) and Virilio (1984) concerning the merging of media and war give powerful insights into the concentration of power, it should not be concluded that such a melding will act to abolish scope for resistance. The merging of military 'facts' and media 'fabrications' may discredit the supposed realism of the former rather than reinforce power. The increased critical consciousness that has emerged as a result of the British and US governments' attempts to construct a significant 'weapons of mass destruction' threat in Iraq may be the template here. But this may be only the explosive reaction against the fusion of media and war, representation and reality.

There is another ironic and implosive reaction that may be just as damaging for corporate interests. One amusing take on the suggested link between piracy and international terrorism can be found amongst peer to peer file sharers, where the act of downloading music and film programmes for free is being re-represented as a good way to ensure that you are not in any way inadvertently funding terrorists. Given the claims made by corporate lobbyists that a huge, but unknown, percentage of CDs and DVDs are fake then, so the implosive logic runs, it is every citizen's duty to cut out the risk and download free from the web. For those who question their own government's involvement in criminal military activities, downloading from the web also has the added advantage of ensuring no taxation goes towards funding 'state terrorism'.

Of course this is not quite how the corporate lobbyists want their message to be read. As one respondent to a chat room put things: 'Because you're not paying tax on the download, tax that would've been used in The War Against Terror. Actually if you download movies instead of going to the cinema you are a terrorist! Wink.' Whilst this is a joke, we can expect another high-profile campaign some time soon making just this kind of claim. What we should not expect is that such campaigns will be particularly successful, either in persuading people or, if persuaded, of channelling their actions in directions best suited to corporate interests.

Protecting 'music': corporate self-preservation versus 'radical' ring-tones

In very recent years there has been an unexpected rise in popularity of 'ring-tones' for mobile phones on a global basis. In 2003 $3.5 billion was spent on ring-tones globally which equated to 10 per cent of the world music market (Petridis 2004). Currently in the United Kingdom, ring-tones out sell CD singles by 3–1. This phenomenon is set to rise still further with the increase in choice and new generations of mobile phones with more sophisticated gadgetry. Put simply, ring-tones are thirty-second clips of music (or any sounds) developed specifically for today's mobile phones to play when a recipient receives a telephone call. They are usually obtained by a recipient downloading the music from a mobile network or via the internet.

Little is actually understood why people wish to purchase a ring-tone of their favourite song which can cost anything from 30 pence (or nothing if shared through sending to others as a text message attachment) to £3.99 in the UK for a 30 second clip when an average CD single costs £1.99 for two to three full songs. Whether it is the convenience of mobile technology or an individual's desire just to personalise permissive technology is still open to speculation. Regardless, the global ring-tone market is burgeoning and to such a degree that executives within the music industry believe sales should be incorporated into mainstream music sales charts.

Since before the birth of Napster technologies, the global music industry has existed in a state of cultural and economic transition where its very relevance in the networked world has been questioned. The music industry is fighting to retain its dominant position in global economics. To preserve this position the music industry is adopting strategies to gain a larger share of the ring-tone market. When a consumer purchases a ring-tone, the revenue is divided between the record labels, the artists and the mobile phone operators.

Often the record label either receives the smallest share, or in some cases, does not receive any revenue whatsoever. Ring-tones are not direct copies or fac-similes of a piece of music. Instead, the service operators who sell the ring-tones produce a version or derivative that is compatible with existing mobile phone technology. Rather like a cover version, the royalties from a ring-tone sale are owed to the composer or song writer and not the record label, which are essentially large distribution and advertising ventures. The music indus-try are worried that they are being taken out of this loop and the services they offer will no longer be relevant in the networked world, plus the fact that potentially they could be losing out on billions of US dollars annually. Historically, the music industry has enjoyed centralised control over the dis-semination of music, but the pervasiveness of informational technology net-works has threatened this centralised dominance. Networked technologies have democratised how people access and procure informational goods. The music industry is attempting to preserve or even secure its position in the ring-tone market by introducing 'Mastertones'. New generations of mobile phones have increasingly sophisticated circuitry that allows for the exact rep-lication of music. Mastertones are actual pieces of music from the recording artists themselves, rather than derivatives or poor versions of the original recordings. The music industry aims to create a new market for their sole control and exploitation. Steve Woolgar stated that all aspects of social, eco-nomic and political life stand to be affected by the continued growth of elec-tronic technologies (2002: 1–2). The music industry has been accused of not evolving or changing to reflect societal and cultural changes of how people procure entertainment. This diversity into a new breed of ring-tones is a des-perate attempt to preserve the dominant position as key controllers of global entertainment.

New Napster/New world order – the search for legitimacy in new business models

The ever-popular and pervasive spread of information and communication technologies into often new areas of social life has called for the global media content industries to evolve their practices. The rise and fall of Napster has left an indelible mark on many global corporations. The freedom of access to informational goods has directly challenged the dominant position of tradi-tional industries whose monopoly was once assured. Perhaps the greatest success in the fall of the Napster software was not the victory for the record-ing industry to protect its copyright but conversely, the production of new generations of increasingly decentralised sharing information software. The internet has given people the relative freedom to choose what they watch, read and listen to. The old business models in which dominant industries decide what people should choose are slowly waning. The technical evolution of 'New Napster' file-sharing technologies has prompted corporations to seek new business models – often simply to exist.

At the time of the Napster trial, voices within Sony (Mann 2003) did note the possibility of increasing profitability in the context of free music downloading by means of selling more of the hardware necessary to download with. However, this strategy was not adopted. Sony is now promoting a payment-based download service for access to the work of mainly Sony signed artists. ATRAC downloads are encrypted so as only to play on the individual machine they are downloaded to. This is designed to prohibit sharing. As such, Sony now seeks to profit from both hardware sales and the sale of musical content. This parallels the development of similar but incompatible systems such as i-tunes and a string of Microsoft Windows-based platforms. However, this proliferation of these incompatible and encrypted payment-based platforms only encourages the use of free peer-to-peer systems that offer compatibility at no cost. It also encourages the ongoing cracking of the various forms of encryption being used.

So far the recording industry has taken legal action against individuals in the United States, Canada, Germany, Spain and the Netherlands with a mixed success. They have sought changes and extension to copyright laws and a general call to have the practice of using internet-based file-share services a criminal offence, despite these technical networks also having legitimate uses. The recording industry are aware that they are always one step behind technological developments in the virtual world, therefore there has been a massive growth in the last twelve months in legal, sanctioned music download websites. Steve Redmond of the British Phonographic Industry (BPI) has declared that litigation against people in the UK will commence before the end of 2004 (Johnson 2004: 19). On 7 October 2004 the BPI announced its intention to prosecute twenty-eight specific individuals they claim are 'serial uploaders', i.e., those placing numerous music files on the internet for others to download. However, currently the BPI only know the IP (internet protocol) addresses of these target individuals. On 14 October 2004 the High Court in London granted an order requiring internet service providers to reveal the names and addresses of those accused (*New Musical Express* 2004). There is the risk that such actions will create negative reactions both in the British court system but also among the public. The BPI is openly unrepentant, explaining that court action and creating a culture where such activities will not go unpunished are more important than public relations. Whether individual actions are successful is not the point. Such policies will be widely reported in the media creating an arena of suspicion and doubt in the minds of individuals who download music and other content from the internet. The recording industry hopes such a culture of fear may lead to a fall in the use of internet file-share services and if this can be sustained then the development of new business models will continue.

The global recording industry aims to secure its once dominant position and acquire legitimacy with new business models. Global capitalism works from the principle that it must forever grow and expand into new territories until every facet of social life is dominated. Industry sanctioned and supported legal music download sites have grown in popularity immensely to the point that the UK now has its own 'Top 10' reflecting current tastes, and many other industrialised societies will shortly follow. Back in 1999 the recording industry also targeted the manufacturers of personal digital music players stating that they encouraged the illegal sharing of copyrighted music. Today these products are condoned with the support of large multi-national corporations such as Microsoft and Apple Computers because following the unexpected success of Apple's iTunes music download site, people who buy digital players are more likely to purchase legal digital content from the internet. Daniel Bell explains that what is radically new today is the codification of theoretical knowledge and its centrality for innovation, both of new knowledge and for economic goods and services (1988: 8). In other words, the global content industries are using technical and business innovation in their attempts to sell existing or 'old' information goods and services by new methods to the consumer. Whether this drive to sell in new ways will succeed in driving out sharing in virtual space, or vice versa, remains open to contestation.

Conclusions

Capitalist expansion into the networked economy of informational goods has extended the principle of capital intensification to a new level and a new dimension of crisis. The network economy, in reducing the cost of production for informational goods, also has the potential to eliminate barriers to market entry, and collapse the rate of profit. It is only through the security and regulation of such informational goods that profit can be made. Technical security systems are used to protect informational goods by controlling their dissemination. The security of such goods, despite expensive and elaborate methods of encryption and surveillance, cannot be assured because the same systems can be reworked to provide anonymity, counter-surveillance, de-encryption and the dissemination of such de-encryption keys. File-sharers have the ability (through technologies which are in part subversions of those produced by corporations themselves) and the motivation (in large part a reaction to levels of profitability sustained by the longstanding monopoly position of the content industries) to resist attempts at technical security. Corporations are attempting to legally package informational goods as though they were physical goods, while enjoying the minimal costs of production/distribution that is the consequence of their non-physical aspect. Unfortunately for them, this play of deterritorialisation/ reterritorialisation can be instantly reversed by those who resist them. Technical security alone is not enough to secure profitability. In the absence of pure technical security, those that seek to defend informational property rights have combined means of legal enforcement with media driven propaganda, but as this chapter demonstrates, even in these arenas the capacity of the powerful is never assured, and is significantly threatened.

Global financial markets and the ICT revolution: perfect market or (im-)perfect domination?

The reorganisation of global capitalism over the past two decades involves changes in production and finance. In production, commodity chains have been increasingly stretched worldwide (Gereffi and Korzeniewicz 1994); and, in addition, finance has been liberalised heavily. Both processes have been mediated by significant advances in information and communication technologies (ICTs). This chapter concentrates on their impact on global financial markets rather than global production. Particularly important here is the role of ICTs in enabling global finance to compress time and space at the same time as it promotes time-space distantiation (Harvey 1989, 2003; Giddens 1990). According to neoliberals, these changes have given rise to the most 'perfect market' yet realised. However, adopting a neo-Gramscian cultural international political economy approach (Jessop and Sum 2001: 89–101; Sum and Jessop 2004), this chapter questions the perfectibility of markets. It highlights instead the inherently discursive and material nature of economic relations and their embedding in a complex and entangled web of different scales of action from global to local. Thus no market can be perfect and none operates without significant selectivity's that affect different market agents and those outside the market in different ways and to different degrees. On the discursive level, this chapter argues that the discourses of 'perfect market' and 'neoliberal finance' are one of the key mechanisms in and through which the US has been rebuilding its financial hegemony. And, on the material level, it argues that the 'Dollar-Wall Street' regime (Gowan 1999), which is a leading advocate of the mystifying neoliberal discourse, is a key factor in generating and spreading structural contradictions, major crisis-tendencies, and strategic dilemmas on a global scale. These crises have serious economic, social and political disruptions for the working and non-working population in developing countries and the dilemmas that policy-makers confront in dealing with them make it hard for any piecemeal and partial reforms to overcome them. The resulting disruptions have not only encouraged passive revolution but are also prompting counter-hegemonic resistance on national, regional and global scales.

Emergence of the global cyber-financial order and the hegemony of finance

The global cyber-financial order (see below) has emerged under specific technological and economic conditions that have become significant since the 1970s. The key technological influence was the development of global communication and information infrastructures that were enabled by: (a) increased computer power and enhanced communications capacity, such as high-capacity microwave and fibre optic systems; and (b) the commercialisation of strategic military capabilities developed by the US – most notably communication satellites in the 1970s and the internet in the 1990s. Satellite technology provides a global space for telephone, telex, TV and fax. With its capacity for rapid digitisation and transmission of data, the internet has become a key tool for the convergence of computer (PCs, laptops, software), communication (satellites, mobile network, e-mail applications), and information (databases, data exchange, images). This convergence of communication and information technologies has played a supportive role in the globalisation of financial markets. The heart of the ICT revolution was the transformation of money into electronic signals and the creation of new forms of money. Apart from the expansion of automated credit card transactions, new electronic monies include fund transfers, automated clearinghouses in wholesale banking, and computer-based home banking. These changes enabled banks and other financial institutions to expand their operations in time and space to tap new sources of capital and invest them around the globe. They moved onto 24-hour banking, trading, fund transfer and on-line services. Instant transmission of 'electronic money' and 'virtual banking' operations across borders were no longer a dream after the establishment of automatic clearing houses, wire-transfer systems (such as Fedwire and Bankwire in the US), international interbank clearing networks (such as the New York-based CHIPS, and SWIFT), and the adoption of International Accounting Standards. In this regard, banks and non-banks (e.g. stock exchanges, hedge funds and pension funds) were increasingly tied into global finance markets focused on the key markets located in New York, London, Tokyo, Hong Kong, Singapore and Frankfurt (McMahon 2002: 144–145).

Such technological and infrastructural changes cannot bring about an effective global cyber-financial order without parallel or complementary developments in policies, economic common sense and institutions. Until the 1960s and early 1970s, the dominant thinking in the Bretton Woods system was that the strength of a country's currency was closely tied to trade balance and that the central banks' role was to maintain currency stability through foreign exchange reserves and credit/interest rate controls. This system experienced some key changes initiated unilaterally by the Nixon administration. First, it took the control of financial relations out of the hands of state central banks and increasingly centred them upon private financial operators.

Second, it ended the role of gold as a global monetary anchor and allowed the dollar itself to become unambiguously the dominant international money. Third, it substituted the fixed exchange rate system by the dollar exchange rate.

These changes enabled the US to reassert its hegemony, this time, through finance rather than overwhelming technological superiority. The liberation of capital from state control enables it to flow freely. In this regard, Eurodollars, which were held outside the US, can now flow anywhere and even be redirected back to the US (or, more specifically, Wall Street in New York). In this way they reinforced the positions of the US dollar as a hegemonic, dominant and master international currency. This enabled the US to dominate by: (a) running continual balance of payments deficits by issuing US Treasury securities that central banks of surplus nations are more or less obliged to buy with their surplus dollars; (b) allowing or forcing the price of the dollar to vary against other currencies so that other economies bear the costs of adjustment rather than the US – enabling the latter to maintain higher levels of capacity utilisation and employment, to maintain higher levels of growth, and to protect domestic markets; and (c) controlling interest rates on the basis of domestic considerations without too much regard to external repercussions because of the large size of the domestic market compared with its major trading partners. In contrast, any changes in the US exchange and interest rates would have worldwide repercussions through the dominance of dollar-denominated loans, bonds, and contracts (Gowan 1999: 16; and Patomäki 2001: 74–76). In short, this system allowed (and still allows) the US to supply its consumers and companies with foreign goods while spending abroad militarily and keeping interest rates relatively low – especially by international standards. This worked both to inflate its bubble economy and to protect it from the worst consequences of the subsequent collapse (Hudson 2003: 78).

This drive to transform the Bretton Woods system into one based on private finance and a dollar standard was mediated by free market and, especially, neoliberal discourses in academic, policy and financial circles. For example, the best-known advocates of neoliberal/'prefect market' discourse in finance were McKinnon (1973) and Shaw (1973). They portrayed interest rate controls by the state as market 'distortions' and advocated financial liberalisation.[1] This would, they argued, enable the allocation of global and national resources to be determined by private market forces rather than the state. They coined the term 'financial repression' to describe state financial controls in developing countries. They recommended full financial liberalisation as vital for economic development because the removal of all barriers and distortions in the financial market would permit a 'perfect market' to function. In general, neoliberal discourse sees the free movement of capital resulting in efficient allocation of saving for the most productive investment.

This neoliberal way of thinking about finance was also promoted by US officials from the Federal Reserve, international organisations and institutions such as the IMF, the World Bank, think tanks, central banks and transnational banks, as well as local(ised) actors, such as bank managers, market analysts and lay investors. Given that these actors often occupy privileged positions as financial experts and/or policy-makers at the global, regional, national or local level, they are able to promote a free-market understanding of finance and investment in and through their speeches, research reports (and executive summaries), table and charts, business press, investors' chronicles, indices, popular economic/management literature, media, and so on. For illustrative purpose, this chapter chooses a typical speech given by the US Federal Reserve Chairman, Alan Greenspan, to the Fifteenth Annual Monetary Conference of the Cato Institute in Washington in 1997. In this speech, the chairman promoted the following neoliberal view on global finance:

> As a result of very rapid increases in telecommunication and computer-based technologies and products, a dramatic expansion in cross-border flows and within countries has emerged. The pace has become truly remarkable. These technology-based developments have so expanded the breadth and depth of markets that government, even reluctant ones, increasingly have felt they have had little alternative but to regulate and free up internal credit and financial markets.
>
> In recent years global economic integration has accelerated on a multitude of fronts. While trade liberalisation, which has been ongoing for a longer period, has continued, more dramatic changes have occurred in the financial sphere.
>
> World financial markets undoubtedly are far more efficient today than ever before. Changes in communications and information technology, and the new instruments and risk-management techniques they have made possible, enable an ever wider range of financial and nonfinancial firms today to manage their financial risks more effectively . . .
>
> The solid profitability of new financial products in the face of their huge proliferation attests to the increasingly effectiveness of financial markets in facilitating the flow of trade and direct investment, which are so patently contributing to ever higher standards of living around the world. Complex financial instruments – derivative instruments, in one form or another – are being developed to take advantage of the gains in communications and information technology. Such instruments would not have flourished as they have without the technological advances of the past several decades. They could not be priced properly, the markets they involve could not be arbitraged properly, and the risks they give rise to could not be managed at all, to say nothing of properly, without high-powered data processing and communication capabilities. ('Globalization of Finance', Remarks by Chairman Alan Greenspan at the Fifteenth Annual Monetary Conference of the Cato Institute, Washington, D.C., 14 October 1997, www.federalreserve.gov/boarddocs/speeches.1997/19971014.htm)

This kind of market-friendly discourse shared some discursive understandings of the orthodox economics and, in general, tenets associated with the Washington Consensus. Hegemonic codes such as 'market', 'efficiency', 'integration', 'higher living standards' were deployed and resonated with other actors. They normalised and translated these ideologically sophisticated theories into commonsensical codes for wider public dissemination and consumption through national policies, popular economic literature, investors' chronicles and specialised columns/programmes on the media. Nationally, this neoliberal 'common sense' obliges the state to reduce its controls on interest rates and credit allocation to allow 'greater freedom to market forces' in the private financial sector. Internationally, it demands removal of controls and regulations on inflows and outflows of capital. Insofar as this occurs, it furthers the rise of the global cyber-financial order.

Under pressure from international agencies, the US, and other dominant forces, developed countries in the OECD were the first to embark on the liberalisation of capital account by removing controls, lowering subsidies, and reducing taxes that affect capital account transactions. The UK, under Thatcher, ended such controls in 1979. Holland followed in 1981 and West Germany in 1982. Denmark liberalised in 1988, Italy started a phased liberalisation in the same year, and France began phasing out capital controls in 1989 (Gowan 1999: 36). This liberalisation wave gradually allows for the unrestricted purchase and sale of financial and real assets across borders. Action on the capital account was followed by liberalisation of bond markets in the 1980s and of equity markets in the 1990s. In addition, the growing institutional intermediation of savings has given increased prominence to pension funds, hedge funds, and other intermediaries in global financial markets.

From the late 1980s, financial markets in developing countries have also undergone rapid changes (see table 5.1). Encouraged by the US, the IMF and the World Bank, developing countries launched policies to open their capital markets. A contributing factor alongside diplomatic and material pressures was their construction by the World Bank, the Clinton administration, and other circles as 'emerging markets' that offered 'fresh investment opportunities' and a market-led route to development. The idea of 'emerging market' was further circulated and naturalised as a common-sensical (and, of course, profitable) investment category by investment analysts, fund managers, and other members of the financial profession (Sidaway and Bryson 2002: 405). Following 1987, one after another of these countries liberalised their capital markets by allowing foreign investors to invest in their firms. For example, Brazil rewrote its foreign investment law in May 1991. Resolution 1832 Annex IV stipulated that foreign institutions could own up to 49 per cent of voting stock and 100 per cent of non-voting stock. Similarly, January 1992 signified a partial opening of South Korean stock market to overseas investors, after which they could own up to 10 per cent of domestically listed firms. Table 5.1 provides a more detailed outline of the particular changes that occurred since late late-1980s in some major emerging markets. By 1995, thirty-five so-called 'emerging markets' had fully opened capital accounts.

Table 5.1 Stock market opening in some 'emerging markets'

Country	Official liberalisation date	Details
Argentina	November 1989	Free repatriation of capital, remittance of dividends and capital gains.
Brazil	May 1991	Change in foreign investment law which stipulates that foreign institutions can own up to 49 per cent of voting stock and 100 per cent of nonvoting stock. Economic ministers approve rules allowing foreign direct investment; 15 per cent tax on distributed earnings and dividends but no tax on capital gains.
Indonesia	September 1989	Minister of Finance allows foreigners to purchase up to 49 per cent, of all companies listing shares on the domestic exchange, excluding financial firms.
Korea (South)	January 1992	Partial opening of the stock markets to foreigners. Foreigners can own up to 10 per cent of domestically listed firms; 565 foreign investors registered with the Securities Supervisory Board.
Malaysia	December 1988	Budget calls for liberalisation of foreign ownership policies to attract more foreign investors.
Mexico	May 1989	Restrictions on foreign capital participation in new direct foreign investments liberalised substantially.
South Africa	1996	Restrictions on foreign membership in the Johannesburg Stock Exchange lifted.
Taiwan	January 1991	Implementation date of phase two of liberalisation plan. Eligible institutional investors may now invest directly in Taiwan securities, subject to approval.
Thailand	September 1987	Inauguration of the Alien Board on Thailand's Stock Exchange. The Board allows foreigners to trade stocks of those companies that have reached their foreign investment limits.
Turkey	August 1989	Foreign investors permitted to trade in listed securities with no restrictions at all and pay no withholding or capital gains tax provided they are registered with the Capital Markets Board and the Treasury.

Source: Adapted from Bekaert et al. 2003: 56–57.

Table 5.2 Countries and territories with offshore financial centres

Region	Offshore financial centres
Africa	Djibouti, Liberia, Mauritius, Seychelles, Tangier,
Asia and Pacific	Australia, Cook Islands, Guam, Hong Kong, Japan, Macau, Malaysia, Marianas, Marshall Islands, Micronesia, Nauru, Niue, Philippines, Singapore, Thailand, Vanuatu, Western Samoa.
Europe	Austria, Andorra, Campione, Cyprus, Gibraltar, Guernsey, Hungary, Ireland, Sark, Isle of Man, Jersey, Liechtenstein, Luxembourg, Malta, Madeira, Monaco, Netherlands, Russia, Switzerland, UK.
Middle East	Bahrain, Dubai, Israel, Kuwait, Lebanon, Oman.
Western Hemisphere	Antigua, Anguilla, Aruba, Bahamas, Barbados, Belize, Bermuda, British Virgin Islands, Cayman Islands, Costa Rica, Dominica, Grenada, Montserrat, Netherlands Antilles, St. Kitts and Nevis, St. Lucia, Panama, Puerto Rico, St. Vincent and the Grenadines, Turks and Caicos Islands, United States, Uruguay.

Source: Singh 2000: 106.

As part of its promotion of the Washington Consensus, the IMF encouraged financial liberalisation and the holding of US dollars as a reserve currency through its Article VIII and structural adjustment programmes. The former requires member countries to avoid imposing restrictions on current account transactions; the latter requires debtor countries to liberalise their capital account and hold US dollars as part of the conditions for loans. For example, when American advisers were given a free hand in Russia in the mid-1990s, they insisted that the Russian central bank hold US dollars as counterparts to the creation of roubles (Hudson 2003: 80). Apart from the IMF, the World Bank, under the 1997 Financial Services Agreement (FSA), secured the commitments by 102 members to open up their financial services in banking, insurance, securities and financial information (Singh 2000: 9). This international push has created a new transnational financial space. This involves the role of some 69 offshore financial centres throughout the world to the current and capital accounts of national states with liberalised financial markets and a reserve system mainly based on the dollar. Transactions in these centres are exempted from tax and free from interest and exchange regulations (see table 5.2). Global financial actors can thus bypass traditional sovereignty demands for disclosure, regulation and taxation when conducting their transactions.

This transnational financial space is particularly supportive of financial innovation, which is initiated above all by financial engineers in the US and further promoted by market analysts, bank managers and business columnists. Together they create a culture of investment or even speculator identities that are prepared to experiment the financial innovation to 'make money from money' (e.g. derivatives, securities, hedge funds) or to 'make money without money' (e.g. insider trading) (see table 5.3). For example, derivatives, which involve the short-term trading of stock-index futures and interest-rate futures, are highly speculative, involve high risks for investing firms, and spread shocks throughout the system at high speed before states have a chance to react effectively.

These developments on the macro and micro levels have shifted social relations and the mode of wealth creation away from production to finance. Compared with the 1960s, this mode is more associated with the search of

Table 5.3 Type and purpose of financial instruments

Types	Purposes	Instruments
Instruments to provide capital for new products and services	For radical innovations and large investment in production and infrastructure	Bank loans, venture capital and other
	To facilitate investment or trade in goods and services	
Instruments to help growth and expansion	For incremental production expansion	Bonds
	To facilitate government funding	
Modernisation of financial services	Incorporation of new technologiesfor better services	Automatic tellers E-banking Virtual transfer
Profit-making and spreading investment and risk	Instruments to attract small investors	Mutual funds, certificates of deposits
	Instruments to encourage and facilitate big risk taking	Derivatives, hedge funds
Instruments to refinance obligations or mobilise assets	To reschedule debts or restructure existing obligations	Brady bonds, swaps Real estate, futures
	To acquire and mobilise 'rent'-type assets	
Instruments that 'make money from money' and 'make money without money'	To take advantage of legal loopholes	Deposits in tax havens
	To take advantage of incomplete information ('to make moneywith money')	Foreign exchange arbitrage, leads andlags
	To take advantage of illegal information ('to make money without money')	Insider trading, financial fraud

Source: Adapted from Perez 2002: 139.

capital for quick profits through the buying and selling of short-term secondary financial instruments. Heikki Patomäki called it 'high finance' in the post-Bretton Woods era (2001). According to the Bank of International Settlements, the value of trade in global foreign exchange was estimated to be seventy times the value of world trade in goods and services in 1995. In terms of foreign exchange alone, it has grown explosively. In 1986, daily global foreign exchange turnover was only $ 18.3 billion, whereas by 2002 the volume of foreign exchange markets had reached the level of $ 3,700 billion a day. Only about 5 per cent of this foreign exchange turn over was used to finance trade in goods and services. Most of the rest were purely financial transactions. Apart from foreign exchange, other growing areas were interest rate, currency, and commodity derivatives. The first two comprise over 97 per cent of the total value of derivatives traded. The total estimated notional amount of outstanding derivative contracts stood at $ 111 trillion at the end of 2001 (see figure 5.1). This data aims to show that the size and short-term nature of international financial flows. The size of these flows can overwhelm the official reserves that central banks stockpile in order to contain fluctuations. Global official reserves in 1977 totalled nearly 17 days of global foreign exchange turnover. Yet despite a quadrupling of this reserve in the interim, they totalled less than one day of global turnover by 1995. This severely limits the ability of Central Banks to moderate and control fluctuations of their exchange rates, as was seen in the Asian currency crisis in 1997.

Figure 5.1 The growth of derivatives
Global derivatives markets (USDbn, amounts outstanding)

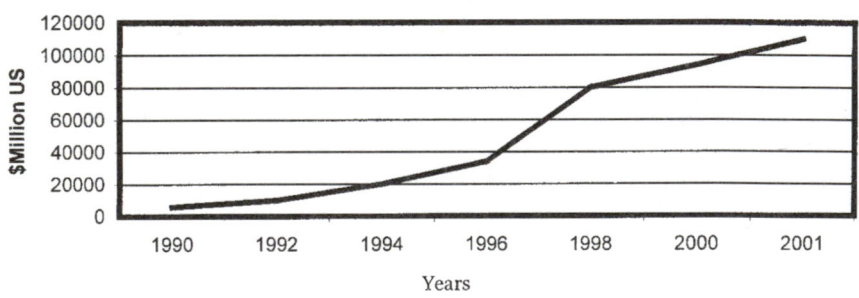

Source: BIS, Annual Reports (various).

'Perfect market' or domination by market-oriented financial actors?

The emergence of these neoliberal discourses, financial sites and financial instruments provided a potential transnational space for capital to roam. Apart from its discourse, this space is far from being a 'prefect market' in which actors participate with equal information and access for the most efficient allocation of financial resources. This chapter argues that this space is dominated by market-oriented actors whose financial activities can be analysed on three levels. They are: (a) the disciplinary nature of financial market; (b) the increasing conglomeration of the financial sector; and (c) the disproportionate gain of rentier income by financial actors.

First, the disciplinary nature of the financial market is discernible in part in the activities of the IMF and credit-rating agencies. IMF conditionalities micro-manage events in developing countries through structural adjustment programmes. Developing countries are disciplined according to the Washington Consensus and are required to structurally adjust their economies in line with its neoliberal criteria, especially during financial crises. The mechanism deployed here was imposition of economic requirements such as cutting budget deficits by tightening fiscal policies, restricting central bank credits to government, etc. (Peet 2003). Apart from the IMF, credit-rating agencies, such as Moodys or Standard and Poors, construct panoptic knowledge that passes judgments on the creditworthiness of security issuers such as transnational corporations, municipalities and states (Sinclair 1994: 133–159). These agencies use both qualitative and quantitative information for assessment. Far from providing equal and neutral information, the credit-rating agencies construct knowledge that naturalises neoliberalism and to discipline security issuers in accordance with these market standards. It rewards high rates to those who abide by its ideals and punishes deviants (Patomäki 2001: 94).

Second, the organisation of financial capital is far from a perfect market. Mergers and acquisitions of financial institutions have led to the increasing centralisation and concentration of the sector. This trend was confirmed in the Group of Ten findings (2001: 2), which noted that there was a high level of merger and acquisition activity in the 1990s among financial firms in the thirteen countries studied. M&As in the financial sector mainly involved banking firms; but others combined banks, insurance and other financial entities to become financial conglomerates. In Europe, for example, conglomeration has gathered pace since the 1990s. Between 1985 and 1999, the value of merger and acquisition deals involving a commercial bank and an insurance company was $ 89.6 billion, or 11.6 per cent of all acquisitions by European financial institutions. Well-known examples include Allians in Germany and Credit Suisse in Switzerland. In the US, despite sanctions imposed by the Banking Act 1933 on mergers between banking and insurance corporations, Citicorp and Traveler Group combined to form Citigroup in 1998 in anticipation of the repeal of this law. This occurred in November 1999, when Congress passed the new Gramm-Leach-Bliley Act, which allows firms to combine banking, insurance and security services. For example, Chase Manhattan Bank merged with JP Morgan to form JP Morgan Chase in 2000. The same increase in conglomeration of financial operations can be found in Asia. For example, Fuji Bank, Dai-Ichi Kangyo Bank and Industrial Bank of Japan merged to form the Mizuho Financial Group that became the world's largest bank in 2000. This trend to conglomerate has concentrated financial capital in some mega banks (see table 5.4).

Table 5.4 The top 15 mega banks, 2000

Rank	Bank	Home country	Assets ($m.)
1	Mizuho Financial Group	Japan	1,259,498
2	Citigroup	United States	902,210
3	Deutsche Bank	Germany	874,706
4	JP Morgan Chase & Co	United States	715,348
5	Bank of Tokyo-Mitsubishi	Japan	675,640
6	HSBC	United Kingdom	673,614
7	Hypovereinsbank	Germany	666,706
8	UBS	Switzerland	664,560
9	BNP Paribas	France	645,793
10	Bank of America Group	United States	642,191
11	Credit Suisse	Switzerland	603,381
12	Sumitomo Bank	Japan	540,875
13	ABN Amro Bank	Netherlands	506,687
14	Credit Agricole Groupe	France	498,426
	Industrial & Commercial Bank of China	China	482,983

Source: Based on *The Banker*, July 2001: 132.

Third, through their domination of the market, financial actors can lay claims on a disproportionate share of income. An examination of the share of rentier income, which is defined as income that accrues from financial market activity and the ownership of financial assets, showed that there has been a marked increase during the neoliberal period since the early 1980s. According to Epstein and Power (2003: 5–6), the decades of 1960s and 1970s and the 1980s and 1990s, the rentier income in OECD countries has gone up more than non-financial ones. For example, the UK went up by 143 per cent and the US by 92 per cent (see table 5.5). These authors also show that the non-financial profits share of eight out of twelve countries have grown; but these increases were generally smaller than those in rentier income (see table 5.5). In short, these data indicate that rentier income rose dramatically during the neoliberal period in most of the OECD countries. In most cases, these increases have also gone hand-in-hand with increases in non-financial industrial income – though the latter grew more slowly. This growth in financial and industrial income is achieved at the expense of labour, especially the non-skilled. The latter is especially vulnerable to the flexibilisation of labour market as well as to

Table 5.5 Rentier income share (not including capital gains) on financial assets in some OECD countries 1970–2000

Country	Average decade share 1970s (% of GDP)		Average decade share 1990s (% of GDP)		Percentage change over the period and 1960s/1970s 1980s/1990s	
	Rentier Income Share	Non-financial profit share	Rentier Income Share	Non-financial profit share	Rentier Income Share	Non-financial profit share
Australia	7.92	12.66	12.97	7.91	88.4	−26.76
Belgium	11.69	11.66	21.81	12.92	84.4	18.30
Finland	6.04	7.37	8.75	10.56	31.5	−19.33
France	6.24	6.39	21.19	11.07	155.0	23.25
Germany	5.02	12.09	7.43	11.16	90.9	−26.02
Japan	12.30	9.02	11.22	8.25	19.7	−12.54
South Korea	4.69	7.32	11.28	8.23	112.1	9.90
Luxembourg	6.14	6.14	12.41	12.41	53.3	53.31
Netherlands	13.47	9.86	20.97	15.33	47.2	43.90
Norway	6.03	10.74	9.56	15.20	65.9	29.31
UK	6.33	13.45	14.16	15.95	143.0	16.19
USA	22.47	10.65	33.49	9.97	92.4	0.89

Source: Selected and adapted from Epstein and Power 2003: 11, Table 1.

episodes of corporate downsizing under the domination of the neoliberal globalisation.

In addition to noting the general unevenness in power and profits associated with transnational financial space, we should also consider the central role of the US and the dollar therein (cf. Gowan 1999; Hudson 2003). Gowan calls this the 'Dollar-Wall Street' regime. It comprises the IMF, the US Treasury, Anglo-American financial markets, offshore centres, and non-state private financial actors (e.g. commercial banks, stock exchanges, credit-rating agencies). Together they promote the neoliberal financial project that helps to rebuild US hegemony that is based on the power of global finance and the US dollar. While this regime is centred on Wall Street and the US Treasury, it also has many multilateral aspects rooted in the activities of leading private actors registered in New York and the City of London and their regional counterparts in Tokyo, Frankfurt, Zürich, Hong Kong, Singapore, São Paulo, and so on (on leading global and regional financial centres, see Beaverstock et al. 1999). Together, they form a hierarchically ordered set of financial centres coordinated by a transnational elite of central/commercial bankers, stockbrokers and financiers located in the major world cities (see table 5.6).

Table 5.6 Hierarchy of financial centres located in world cities

First-tier world cities
London, New York, Paris, Tokyo, Chicago, Frankfurt, Hong Kong,
Los Angeles, Milan, Singapore

Second-tier world cities
San Francisco, Sydney, Toronto, Zurich, Brussels, Madrid, Mexico City,
Sao Paulo

Third-tier world cities
Amsterdam, Boston, Geneva, Jakarta, Johannesburg, Bangkok, Beijing,
Rome, Stockholm, Warsaw

Source: Adapted from Beaverstock et al. 1999, Tables 6 & 7.

The global cyber-financial disorder and counter-hegemonic challenges

This neoliberal financial order is not free from contradictions and instability – some of which are played out in developing countries. This financial order renders developing countries depending on short-term capital flows for their main source of credit. Given the short-term and footloose nature of such flows, developing countries are prone to capital flight, currency and financial instability, and crises. The Mexican financial implosion of 1994–95 marked the beginning of a series of financial crises throughout the 'emerging markets'. Its crisis was followed by the Asian crises of 1997–8, their diffusion to Russian and Brazil shortly after, thence to Turkey in early 2001, and to Argentina in 2002 (Wade and Veneroso 1998: 2–23; Sum 2002: 70–71). This spiral of financial crises gave rise to economic stagnation and disparities in power and wealth that are inherent in capitalism. There are three main problems here as seen from developing countries' viewpoint (Sum 2001: 151–157; Grabel 2002: 37–41).

First, neoliberal finance renders developing countries vulnerable to capital flight and currency instability. This is especially evident regarding portfolio investment. In Asia in 1997, for example, sudden outflows of portfolio investment triggered vicious cycles of additional capital flights. Such flights destabilised the domestic currencies and increased the cost of imports as well as inflationary pressures. Second, neoliberal finance induces a speculation-rather than production-led economy. Compared with production-oriented economies, it is cheaper and easier for investors to obtain project finance. In almost all cases, neoliberal finance induced a speculative bubble in real estate and stocks and shares. Such speculative activities involve high risks and investors and borrowers are vulnerable to reversals of capital inflows and depreciations of domestic currency. The bursting of speculative bubbles often ends in financial crisis. Susan Strange dubbed this phenomenon 'casino capitalism' (1986). In addition, neoliberal finance diverts investment away from production that is central to long-term employment and income for developing countries. Third, neoliberal finance also limits governments in developing countries to implement social policies. Fear of capital flight prevents these countries from undertaking economic and social policies that may signal an anti-corporate orientation (e.g. environmental and labour policies that may increase costs of production). With the onset of the crisis, these countries, under the structural adjustment programme of the IMF, have to institute deflationary policies that drove viable concerns into bankruptcy and intensify unemployment and inequality.

During the Asian Crisis, Thailand, Indonesia and South Korea were the three countries most subject to IMF conditionalities through the economic requirement associated with the structural adjustment programme (e.g. cutting the budget deficit by tightening fiscal policies, restricting central bank credits to government). In the case of South Korea, this package had devastating economic and social impact, including bankruptcies, unemployment, pay cuts. These in turn prompted de-globalisation sentiments. Writing more specifically with reference to a local site, Kim reported the following changes in Seoul (2002: 181–186). A total of 9,894 local companies were put out of business in the fourteen months to the end of 1998. From November 1997 to January 1998, there were more than 1,200 bankruptcies each month. Seoul's unemployment rate increased to almost 10 per cent by July 1998. For those fortunate enough to keep their jobs, salaries were cut by around 30 per cent on average. In general, the unskilled working class has been the main victim. There have been many strikes, street protests and bitter jokes, for example, IMF as the acronym for 'I'M Fired' – demonstrating the local resistance to such shake-ups. With fewer than half of females being economically active (in a formal sense), most households depend on their male earners, if any; they have been severely affected by bankruptcies, unemployment and pay cuts. In addition, de-globalisation sentiments were extremely strong between late 1997 and 1998. Economic and social stresses were attributed to the IMF's structural adjustment programme and the government. The IMF was seen as the representative of global investors opening up Korea rather than as a 'rescuer'. The financial crisis was also called the 'IMF crisis' and the buying rush of foreign companies for bankrupted firms was seen as a threat on economic sovereignty.

Similar economic and social disruptions can be found in other post-crisis developing countries with Indonesia experiencing political turmoil as well (Sharma 2003: 123–179). With rising unemployment and skyrocketing prices of basic commodities (in large a result of reductions in government subsidies), thousands of Indonesian took to the street demanding the resignation of Suharto. Under immense domestic and international pressure, Suharto finally resigned on 21 May 1998. Observing these disruptions, Malaysia took the lead to resist the neoliberal and IMF hegemony by imposing capital controls in September 1998 (see box 5.1).

Box 5.1 Some ways of controlling capital flows in Malaysia 1998

Residents are freely allowed to make payments to non-residents only up to RM 10 000 or its equivalent in foreign currency (except for payments for imports of goods and services)

Investments in any form abroad by residents and payments under a guarantee for non-trade purposes require approval

Domestic credit facilities to non-resident correspondent banks and non-resident stockbroking companies are no longer allowed

Residents require prior approval to make payments to non-residents for purposes of investing abroad for amount exceeding RM 10 000 equivalent in foreign exchange

Residents are not allowed to obtain ringgit credit facilities from non-residents

Resident travellers are allowed to import ringgit notes up to RM 1 000 only and any amount of foreign currencies, and to export only up to RM 1 000 and foreign currencies only up to RM 10 000 equivalent

Source: Adapted from Third World Network, www.twnside.org.sg/title/radical-cn.htm, accessed on 28 November 2003)

There were also regional proposals, such as Japan's idea of an Asian Monetary Fund (AMF), to counteract the domination of the IMF (Sum 2002: 69–70). With a possible capitalisation of US $ 100 billion, the AMF symbolised a regional source of finance that could provide quick and flexible disbursements to alleviate regional currencies in crisis, as well as to provide emergency balance-of-payments support to crisis-hit economies. In other words, the AMF idea proposed a new form of regionality that could by-pass the IMF and could deepen the regional cooperation under the leadership of Japan. This idea attracted much interest from Malaysia, Taiwan, Thailand and South Korea. Unsurprisingly, however, the US and the IMF opposed the AMF. By constructing a new sphere of regional lending activity, the latter was seen to threaten the IMF's hegemony and its debt conditionalities.

Coexisting with these kinds of institutional resistance were the changing discourses that originated from within the heartland of financial capitalism. Actors from the neoliberal tradition began to question its prevailing regime of truth. Such Damascene critics include prominent economists such as Bhagwati, Krugman, Sachs and they deployed the pages of the *New York Times*, the *Wall Street Journal*, and the *Washington Post* to question this neoliberal cyber-financial order. Bhagwati argued that capital markets are by their nature unstable and require controls. Krugman outlined the case for exchange controls as a response to crisis. Bhagwati went further by noting that free capital mobility is promoted by the 'Wall Street-Treasury Complex' that equates its interests with the 'good of the world' (1998: 12). Sachs, a prominent Harvard 'marketeer', focused more on the folly of the IMF's policies during the crisis. Specifically, he criticised the austerity measures of tightening money, high interest rates and tight fiscal policies under the structural adjustment programmes and argued that they have transformed a liquidity crisis into a financial panic in the Asian context. He proposed that the IMF should revise its standard formula for economic reform, make its decision-making more transparent, and become more accountable for the impact of its policies (Sum 2002: 72).

In the midst of this elite 'dissent' and paradoxes related to the Asian Crisis, the US and the corporate sector, acting through the G7, pushed through a passive revolution (cf. Gramsci 1971)[2] and to neoliberalism. The discourse on 'new international financial architecture' was deployed in 1999 to reformulate neoliberal financial capitalism via the formation of the *Financial Stability Forum* (FSF) and Group of 20 (G20). The Forum drew its forty members from national representatives from the G7 countries and well as experts coming from the IMF, World Bank, Bank for International Settlements (BIS), the OECD, the International Organization of Securities Commissions, the International Association of Insurance Supervisors, etc. Together they adopt a policy discourse that promotes international financial stability by managing risks/problems that stem from 'emerging markets' and not the US-led international financial order. The symbolisms of 'corruption', 'transparency' and 'corporate governance' are deployed to map the objects of financial governance.

In terms of 'transparency', for example, countries are encouraged to publish economic data especially those on short-term indebtedness and the state of their foreign exchange reserves. As for 'corporate governance', these countries are encouraged to comply with international financial standards and codes of conduct as defined by the FSF. Instead of being critical of the 'IMF-Treasury-Wall Street' complex, this norm-mediated construction is biased towards the neoliberal agenda by providing better domestic information for foreign capital to make decisions on lending and investment in the 'emerging markets'. It thus favours the interests of the G7 and the financial constituencies in the global order. Apart from its neoliberal bias, subsequent development on best-practice core standards in twelve policy areas further subjects 'emerging markets' to the neoliberal surveillance of the IMF, World Bank, and standard-setting bodies (see table 5.7) (Soederberg 2002: 615). These webs of surveillance not only enhance the policing of the 'emerging markets'; they also turn sensitive political issues concerning global finance (e.g. the domination of Dollar-Wall Street regime) into technical issues concerning standards and benchmarking. This deflects attention from the main sites of authority and their exercise of power.

Table 5.7 Best-practice core standards in 12 policy areas under the Financial Stability Forum

Policy areas	Key standards	Standard-setting bodies
Monetary and financial policy transparency	Code of Good Practice on Transparency in Monetary and Financial Policies	IMF
Fiscal policy transparency	Code of Good Practices in Fiscal Transparency	IMF
Data dissemination	Special Data Dissemination Standard	IMF
Insolvency	World Bank Insolvency Initiative	World Bank
Corporate governance	Principles of Corporate Governance	OECD
Accounting	International Accounting Standards	International Accounting Standards Board
Auditing	International Standards on Auditing	International Federation of Accountants
Payment and settlement	Core Principles for Systemically Important Payment Systems	Committee on Payment and Settlement Systems
Market integrity	The Forty Recommendations of the Financial Action Task Force	Financial Action Task Force
Banking supervision	Core Principles for Effective Banking Supervision	Basel Committee on Banking Supervision
Securities	Objectives and Principles of Securities Regulation	International Organization of Securities Commission
Insurance supervision	Insurance Supervisory Principles	Internationa lAssociation of Insurance Supervisors

In contrast to the highly selective FSF, membership of the G20 is drawn from broader constituencies. They included the G7, European Union, the IMF, the Fund's new International Monetary and Financial Committee, the World Bank, as well as the Bank's Development Committee, and ten 'emerging market' countries (Argentina, Australia, Brazil, China, India, Indonesia, Mexico, Saudi Arabia, South Africa, South Korea, Turkey). Despite its broad membership base, its areas of concern were mainly limited to: (a) stock-taking of progress made by members in reducing vulnerabilities to crises; and (b) monitoring these countries for compliance with FSF codes and standards. Such concern with domestic vulnerability to financial crises leaves the neoliberal financial order and the domination of US dollar unquestioned. Even if its broadly based membership seems more inclusive than the G7, it can be argued that it is no more than a case of 'inclusive neoliberalism' that lends legitimacy to the work of FSF and, more generally, financial liberalisation.

Compared with investment provisions related to the Multilateral Agreement on Investment or the World Bank's policy on debt, there is a marked absence of high-profile counter-hegemonic campaigns concerning global financial regulation and the process of the FSF and G20. However, anti-globalisation demonstrations against the annual IMF(-WTO) meetings became more prominent since 1999. These struggles mostly coalesced around IMF-imposed structural adjustment and the predatory activities of finance capital. In October 2000 on the occasion of the G20 meeting in Montreal, the *Halifax Initiative* hosted an international conference in which major transnational NGOs explored alternative ways to build a more equitable global financial system, e.g. Tobin Tax, tax havens, debt cancellation, finance for development, etc. (see Table 5.8).

Table 5.8 A sample of NGO projects on global financial issues

Major financial issues	*Research/policy studies*
Financial regulation	
Tobin Tax	AFROAD 4-country study on Tobin Tax; ATTAC Tobin Tax study
Tax havens	OXFAM tax havens study
Derivatives	Derivatives Study Centre on derivatives regulation
Debt	
Debt cancellation	Jubilee 2000 campaign; OXFAM research on debt, trade and other financial issues
Ecological debt	ECEJ study of 'ecological debt'
Role of the international financial institutions	
Regional mechanisms	Focus on Global South on Asian Monetary Fund
World Bank's Poverty Reduction Strategy Plans (PRSPs)	African critique of PRSPs
Structural Adjustment Programme	Structural Adjustment Participatory Review Initiative
Finance for Development	
Performance requirement for FDI	Critique of US African Growth Opportunities Act
Mobilization of domestic resources/ debt cancellation	Critique of EU-ACP negotiations and pressures for 'liberalization

Source: Adapted from Halifax Initiative, A Canadian Coalition for Global Economic Democracy, www.halifaxinitiative.org/updir/GFS_doucment.pdf.

In response to rising concerns of the NGOs and grassroots organisations in developing countries after the Asian Crisis, the UN, in conjunction with the IMF, the World Bank and the WTO, organised the International Conference on Financing Development in Monterrey in March 2002. The final 'Monterrey Consensus' examines five mechanisms for development. These included domestic resource mobilisation, foreign direct investment, trade, official development assistance (ODA), and debt reduction. During the negotiation process, developing countries emphasised the need for more international source of finance (e.g. ODA). This was sharply contested by the developed countries which emphasised the focus should be 90 per cent on domestic resources and 10 per cent on international sources. In terms of international sources, the Monterrey Consensus contains few new commitments – it reiterates Doha on trade, encourages private investment and a positive domestic enabling environment; it reaffirms HIPC on debt reduction and continues to call for compliance with the existing 0.7 per cent target on ODA without any specific timetable (Foerde 2002: 7). In this regard, it can be argued that the Monterrey Consensus makes no real attempt in redesigning the international financial architecture. Some NGOs even see it as reinforcing the neoliberal model of development; but, this time, involving the United Nations in 'bluewashing'[3] the neoliberal agenda of the 'Washington Consensus'.

Conclusion

This chapter uses cultural international political economy to critique the global cyber-financial order and the hegemonic and counter-hegemonic challenges thereto. The cyber-financial order emerged under the development of global communication and information infrastructures since 1970s. These technological and infrastructural changes cannot bring about a global cyber-financial order without parallel development in policies, economic common sense/identity, and institutions. The transition from the Bretton Woods system to one that was based on transnational private finance and the domination of the dollar was mediated by new discourses on 'perfect competition', 'efficiency', 'emerging markets', 'offshore centres', 'financial innovation', etc. These discourses helped to shape the everyday life of a culture rooted in the investment and speculation that are essential for the building of the global cyber-financial order. Discursive claims apart, this transnational financial space was far from a 'perfect market'. This chapter argues that it was actually dominated by market-oriented actors who disciplined and normalised the market and earned a disproportionately high rentier income. This US-dominated financial order was not free from contradictions and instability. The spread of Mexican financial crisis of 1994–95 to Argentina in 2002 demonstrated the vulnerabilities of the 'emerging markets' and the fragility of this order. The imposition of the IMF conditionality upon the crisis economies has given rise to bankruptcy, unemployment and pay cuts. Co-existing with grassroots resistance was the change in discourses among the prominent economists in questioning the legitimacy of the IMF and its structural adjustment programme. Mediated by this 'elite dissent', the projects on 'international financial architecture' and, later on, the 'Monterrey Consensus' were introduced to deepen the hegemony of neoliberalism. These projects not only re-iterated the FSF standards that technicalise the surveillance of the 'emerging markets'; they also deflected public attention from the hard core of financial capitalism and that is the global domination of the dollar and the Dollar-Wall Street regime.

Notes

1 The key components of financial liberalisation include: (a) deregulation of interest rates; (b) removal of credit control; (c) privatisation of government owned banks and financial institutions; (d) liberalisation of restrictions on the entry of private sector and/or foreign banks and financial institutions into domestic financial markets; (e) introduction of market-based instruments of monetary control; and (f) liberalisation of capital account (Singh 2000: 36-8).
2 The passive revolution process involves dominant group seeking to maintain hegemony via discourses and material measures to incorporate other forces that could threaten its dominance.
3 'Bluewashing' means using the reputation of the United Nations to present a more humanitarian image for neoliberalism.

6 Sharon Beder

Corporate propaganda and global capitalism – selling free enterprise?

This chapter examines the way in which capitalism has been underpinned by a self-conscious propaganda campaign on the part of the world's major corporate powers.

Corporations have used a variety of propaganda techniques not only to dominate markets but also to attempt to monopolise the realm of ideas where dissent and alternate voices might be heard (Ewen 1996; Beder 2002). The rise of corporate propaganda since the 1970s has been particularly aimed at selling the idea of free, unregulated business enterprise and an accompanying policy agenda that facilitates the expansion and spread of global capitalism. Ideas associated with the maintenance and expansion of capitalism as a social and economic system have progressively taken on the status of accepted wisdom in policy circles.

Public relations responses to counter-culture challenges

Capitalism came under attack during the late 1960s and early 1970s when the counter-culture movement brought with it a proliferation of public interest groups that challenged the authority of business and sought government controls over business activities. Confidence in free enterprise and the consonance between profits and public welfare declined sharply. Anthony Sampson, in his book *Company Man*, argued that this 'revolt marked a watershed – the end of the consensus between corporations and society' (Sampson 1996: 122)

In many industrialised nations protests focused on the social and environmental impacts of business activities and the first-wave of modern environmentalism was born. These environmentalists blamed development and the growth of industrial activities for environmental degradation. Their warnings captured the popular attention, resonating with the experiences of communities facing obvious pollution in their neighbourhoods. Many governments responded with new environmental legislation to cope with the grossest sources of pollution, introducing clean air and water acts and new regulatory bodies to implement and enforce these acts (Beder 1996: xii).

Throughout the 1970s, in various business meetings, corporate executives lamented their decline in influence: 'The truth is that we've been clobbered', the chief executive officer of General Motors told chiefs from other corporations. (quoted in Vogel 1989: 194) As a result US corporations became increasingly politically active, getting together to support a conservative anti-regulatory agenda and financing a vast public relations effort aimed at regaining public trust in corporate responsibility and freedom from government regulation. Corporations began to adopt the strategies that public-interest activists had used so effectively against them – grassroots organising and coalition building, telephone and letter-writing campaigns, using the media, research reports and testifying at hearings (Beder 2002). To these strategies corporations added huge financial resources and professional advice. 'A new breed of public affairs professionals began emerging' who could service corporations in their new activism (Grefe and Linsky 1995: 3).

Corporations established 'public affairs' departments, increased the funding and staffing of those departments, and allocated responsibility for public affairs to a senior company executive, such as a Vice-President. Chief Executive Officers (CEOs) also devoted increasing amounts of their time to government relations (Saloma 1984: 67). A survey of 400 American public affairs units in large and medium-sized firms in 1981 found that most received more than half a million dollars each year in funding and more than half were set up after 1970 (Vogel 1989: 195–197).

Businesses cooperated in a way that was unprecedented, building coalitions and alliances and putting aside competitive rivalries. Broad coalitions of business people sought to effect 'a reorientation of American politics.' In the US the Chamber of Commerce and the National Association of Manufacturers (NAM) were resurrected and rejuvenated and new organisations such as the Business Roundtable (for large corporations) and the Small Business Legislative Council (for small businesses) were formed to lobby government (Himmelstein 1990: 132; Ricci 1993: 156).

This trend towards corporate activism could be observed in other countries too. In Australia corporations 'substantially increased their level of resources and commitment to monitoring and influencing the political environment'; ensured their senior executives were effective political operatives in their dealings with politicians and bureaucrats; hired consulting firms to help with government submissions; and established government relations units within their companies with direct access to the chief executive officer (Bell and Warhurst 1992: 58–59; Wanna 1992: 73).

Corporate money was invested in political campaigns but more importantly it was invested in other forms of political influence, particularly those aimed at influencing the political agenda through the dissemination and selling of ideas: 'Right-wing business men like Richard Mellon Scaife and

Joseph Coors, and conservative treasuries like the Mobil and Olin foundations, poured money into ad campaigns, lawsuits, elections, and books and articles protesting "Big Government" and "strangulation by regulation", blaming environmentalists for all the nation's ills from the energy crisis to the sexual revolution' (Sale 1993: 49). In the US, corporations put large amounts of money into advertising and sponsorships aimed at improving the corporate image, countering ideas from opposing groups, and putting forward corporate views. The full range of public relations and mass communications techniques was utilised including front groups; Astroturf (or PR-generated grassroots campaigns) utilising computer-generated demographic data and increasingly sophisticated telecommunications techniques; and infiltration of the school curriculum with corporate sponsored and designed 'educational' materials (Beder 2002).

During the 1980s, under Reagan's administration, the numbers of trade and professional associations, corporations and interest groups with offices in Washington continued to grow. By 1985, an estimated 80,000 employees of these associations were being serviced by accountants, lobbyists, lawyers, trade paper journalists, public relations advisors, direct mail consultants, economists and think tanks (Sale 1993: 43). It was a huge information industry and all this information was shaped and presented to promote the interests of the associations and corporations generating it.

Selling free enterprise

In response to the significant decline in confidence in free enterprise in the 1960s and 1970s, the US Advertising Council launched a major campaign in 1976 to promote free enterprise, or as the Council termed it: 'create greater understanding of the American economic system' (Ad Council 1976e: 1). This campaign has been described as 'the most elaborate and costly public-relations project in American history' (Rippa 1984: 306).

The idea for this campaign came from the chairman of the board of Procter and Gamble, the largest advertiser in the US, who called for American people to be better educated about the free enterprise system, so that business people need not be defensive about their work (Parenti 1986: 73; Sethi 1977: 61). The campaign was supported by so many major corporations that the Ad Council boasted the list of supporters read like a 'who's who in American business' (Ad Council 1976b: 1). It was also supported by the US Department of Commerce (Ad Council 1976d: 3).

The campaign attempted to educate the public about the benefits of free enterprise, distributing millions of booklets to schools, workplaces and communities. The stated premise of the campaign was that people were economically illiterate and therefore needed economic education. The unstated premise was that if people were educated to view the free enterprise system as business people saw it they would appreciate and defend it rather than criticise it.

The multimillion dollar campaign included media advertisements, dedicated newsletters, films, teaching materials and training kits, and booklets, point of sale displays, messages on envelopes, and flyers included with bank statements, utility bills and insurance premium notices (Ad Council 1976b: 1,5). The Ad Council told the media that 'every communications technique that is appropriate for such a campaign will be used in this effort, which we anticipate will carry over for a three to five year period' (Ad Council 1976e: 6).

Teacher education was targeted because of the influence of teachers on millions of children. Various university chairs of free enterprise or private enterprise were funded by corporations. Classroom materials were also produced for the purpose of selling the free enterprise system to school children. Four million packages of *Industry and the American Economy* (an eleven-booklet package), were distributed to students and teachers throughout the nation (Rippa 1984: 308).

Various oil companies got involved. Phillips Petroleum Company supported the production of a series of five films entitled 'American enterprise' with an accompanying teachers' guide. Amoco Oil Company produced a twenty-six-minute film and teachers' guide to explain how the free enterprise system works. The Exxon Company got together with Walt Disney Educational Media Company to produce a twenty-two-minute film for high school students about two children that go into business (Ad Council 1976c: 3). The US Chamber of Commerce also produced films, teaching materials and booklets on the economic system and a package entitled 'Economics for Young Americans' that included film strips, audio cassettes, lesson plans and text on productivity, profits and the environment (Ad Council 1976a: 7).

In the late 1970s US business was spending a billion dollars each year on propaganda of various sorts 'aimed at persuading the American public that their interests were the same as business's interests'. The result of all this expenditure showed in the polls when the percentage of people who thought that there was too much regulation soared to 60% in 1980 (up from 22 per cent in 1975) (Carey 1995: 89; Parenti 1986: 74).

Similar but lesser efforts occurred in other countries. In 1978 AIMS of Industry, which had been formed in Britain 'by leaders of free enterprise industry . . . to promote a free market economy and to defend freedom and enterprise', held an International Conference in London on 'The Revival of Freedom and Enterprise' and organised a Free Enterprise Day (Ivens 1978: back cover, v).

Facts about Business launched a schools programme in the UK in 1975 – 'Business and Profit' – which included a free booklet and purchasable wall charts and study folders. By 1978 the programme was being used in a quarter of all secondary schools in Britain and they launched another called

'Discover British Industry' which was taken up by over 400 schools in the first four months (Broadway 1978: 63).

In Australia, after the election of a 'progressive' Labour government in 1972, the Australian Chamber of Commerce reacted with a nationwide 'economic education campaign' to promote free enterprise and in 1975 Enterprise Australia was established by the Free Enterprise Association (funded by multinational companies such as Esso, Kodak, IBM and Ford Motors) to take part in the 'propaganda warfare for capitalism' (Carey 1995: 87–88, 105, 112–114).

The Australian Chamber of Commerce and Enterprise Australia used surveys of school leavers to find the 'deficiencies' in their attitudes to the free enterprise system and then circulated corrective material through schools. Additionally business groups such as chambers of commerce, the Australian Bankers Association and the Australian Mining Industry Council ran conferences and made presentations to teachers, business people and school students (Carey 1995: 112–117)

Neoconservative think tanks

Think tanks also took a leading part in the war of ideas in various countries. In the US in particular, conservative foundations and large corporations established and/or funded a new set of think tanks which were ideologically compatible with right-wing causes and corporate interests, promoting the free market and attacking government regulation.

> Funded by eccentric billionaires, conservative foundations, and politically motivated multinational corporations, right-wing policy entrepreneurs founded think tanks, university centres, and political journals, and developed the social and political networks necessary to tie this nascent empire together. The end product was a tidal wave of money, ideas, and self-promotion that carried the Reaganites to power. (Alterman 1994: 59)

This influx of money meant not only that conservative think tanks proliferated but that other think tanks moved towards the right. As Jerome Himmelstein points out in his book *To the Right*: 'The political mobilization of big business in the mid 1970s gave conservatives greater access to money and channels of political influence. These helped turn conservative personnel into political leaders and advisers, and conservative ideas, especially economic ones, into public policy.' (Himmelstein 1990: 129, 146)

As an example, the Heritage Foundation, one of the largest and most important of the Washington-based think tanks was formed in 1973. Early support came from beer magnate Joseph Coors and petroleum tycoon Edward Noble. It promotes deregulation of industry, an unrestrained free market and privatisation. The *Economist*'s *Good Think-Tank Guide* of 1992 described the foundation's ideology as 'red-blooded, celebratory capitalism'. *The Economist* noted: 'First, they help to set the agenda of the political debate. They inject arguments (neatly packaged for a copy-hungry media) into the public arena before they are raised by politicians. This both softens up public opinion and pushes the consensus farther to the right' (*The Economist* 1989: 54).

Edwin Feulner, president of the Heritage Foundation, described to an Australian audience in 1985 the role of think tanks. He said that whilst people like Milton Friedman were 'the *first-hand* dealers of ideas' who explained and expanded upon ideas, think tanks introduced these ideas into the policy arena, marketed them and sought to change government policy:

> It takes an institution to help popularise and propagandise an idea – to market an idea. Think-tanks are *second-hand* dealers of ideas. Organisations . . . host conferences, lectures and seminars and publish policy reports, books and monographs to popularise an idea. Through 'outreach' programmes an institution can promote an idea on a continuing bases and cause change. But this takes time.
>
> Procter and Gamble does not sell Crest toothpaste by taking out one newspaper ad or running one television commercial. They sell it and resell in every day by keeping the product fresh in the consumer's mind. The institutes I have mentioned sell ideas in much the same manner. (Feulner 1985: 22)

The Heritage foundation spends only 40 per cent on actual research. More than half its budget goes on marketing and fund raising, including 35–40 per cent of its budget on public relations. All this marketing enables the Foundation to successfully attract mass media coverage for its publications and policy proposals. The Foundation claims that it usually gets 200 or more stories nationwide from each of the position papers it publishes (Weaver 1989: 572; Gellner 1995: 502; Smith 1991: 171, 201, 287).

Other conservative think tanks also focused on the marketing of ideas. The American Enterprise Institute (AEI) was said, in the 1980s, to operate 'as the most sophisticated public-relations system in the nation for dissemination of political ideas' (Moore and Carpenter 1987: 146).

Similarly, the rise of Thatcherism in Britain can be attributed in large part to the endeavours of two think tanks. The first was the Institute of Economic Affairs, IEA. It set out to gain wide acceptance for the 'philosophy of the market economy' through education directed at the opinion leaders such as intellectuals, politicians, business people and journalists.

During the 1970s the IEA managed to enrol several academics and influential journalists to promote economic liberalism, as well as some prominent MPs, most notably Margaret Thatcher. In its early years the IEA also had some influence in the universities and produced undergraduate and secondary school texts. It had trained young economists at the IEA early in their careers and these economists provided the personnel for free-market think tanks established in the 1970s and 1980s (Cockett 1994; Desai 1994: 29).

The Centre for Policy Studies, CPS, was to some extent an outgrowth of the IEA. It was founded in 1974 by an active member of the IEA, Keith Joseph, together with Margaret Thatcher, who had also been associated with the IEA. Joseph, a former Tory Minister, is credited with Thatcher's conversion to economic liberalism (Ashford 1997: 23). The CPS was set up to convert the Tory party to economic liberalism and formulate policies for the Party that were in line with this philosophy (James 2001: 495).

These two think tanks 'provided the ideas which gave intellectual shape to the instincts and energy of Thatcherism' in Britain. They helped to convert the Tory leaders to economic liberalism whilst they were in opposition and gave the Thatcher government 'a style of politics whose cutting edge was its ideological crusade' (Desai 1994: 31; James 2001: 497). Once in power Thatcher set about implementing the economic ideology she had been imbued with, including monetarism, privatisation and government spending cuts.

Even after Margaret Thatcher's departure, the ideas of the conservative think tanks continued to influence Prime Minister John Major. Richard Cockett, who has charted the rise of conservative think tanks in Britain in his book *Thinking the Unthinkable* notes that a new consensus, which included keeping government control of industry to a minimum, has been achieved by those think tanks. The free market ideas of think tanks such as the IEA have become the new conventional wisdom.

Neoliberalism and globalism

The new economic liberal or neoliberal agenda promoted by neoconservative think tanks in English-speaking countries consists of a basic policy formula involving government spending cuts, privatisation of government services and assets, removal of tariffs (particularly in other countries) and deregulation of business activities; all in the name of free markets, competitiveness, efficiency and economic growth. It involves the replacement of government functions and services with those provided by private profit-seeking firms in the name of the public interest. In reality such policies are promoted by those who are likely to gain most from them.

This new agenda not only assisted the expansion of capitalism into areas previously controlled by government and removed many of the controls on business, but it facilitated the expansion of global capitalism. In particular the adoption of policies such as reduced government spending, privatisation, trade and financial liberalisation, and the deregulation of foreign direct investment opened up investment opportunities for multinational corporations around the world.

These policies were taken up by policy networks supported by large corporations and international financial interests and incorporated into an economic reform agenda for both developed and developing nations, referred to as the 'Washington Consensus'. This policy prescription was actively promoted by the World Bank and the International Monetary Fund (IMF) and was the driving force behind the structural adjustment packages being imposed on all developing nations with debt by the IMF. The policies were also adopted voluntarily in affluent countries by governments of many different political persuasions during the 1980s, including the conservative governments of Margaret Thatcher in Britain, Ronald Reagan in the US and labour governments in Australia and New Zealand.

The Washington consensus was a policy prescription that benefited multinational corporations and international financial institutions, often at the expense of local business, and always at the expense of the poor. The United Nations Development Programme (UNDP) admits that privatisation benefits multinational corporations by allowing them to get access to industries in developing nations that had previously been closed to them and to buy up established enterprises sometimes at cut rate prices: 'In many countries the privatization process has been more of a "garage sale" to favored individuals and groups than a part of a coherent strategy to encourage private investment' (quoted in Avery 1993).

Michel Chossudovsky, Professor of Economics at the University of Ottawa, outlines how these policies have transformed low-income countries into open economic territories and 'reserves' of cheap labour and natural resources available to multinational companies and consumers in high-income nations. In the process, governments in low-income countries have handed over economic control of their countries to the World Bank and the IMF, which act on behalf of powerful financial and political interests in the USA, Japan and Europe. Having handed over this control, they are unable to generate the sort of local development that would improve the welfare of their own people (Chossudovsky 1992: 13).

The theories behind the new policy prescriptions which were promoted by neoconservative think tanks provide a means for covering and legitimising the vested interests that stand to gain from the policies. The policy prescriptions that suited multinational corporations, including reductions in taxes, minimal regulations and freedom to trade and invest anywhere in the world, were justified by a body of economic theory that promoted these policies as being in the public interest: 'An elegant body of microeconomic theory shows that under certain circumstances the general good . . . will be promoted by a set of competitive markets and integration into the world economy.' (Williamson 1994: 16)

The theories emanated from particular economics schools such as the Chicago School in the US. Even in the mid-1980s the Chicago School represented a minority economic opinion (Easton 1988: 75). Nonetheless economics departments in universities throughout the English speaking world, outside of the US, began teaching neo-classical theory as orthodoxy (Carroll 1992: 9).

An interview conducted by scholar Jane Kelsey in 1998 with Michael Porter, the founder of The Centre of Policy Studies at Monash University in

Melbourne and later of another Australian think tank, The Tasman Institute, revealed the influence that individual economists and the corporate-funded think tanks wield in the field of agenda setting and policy formation:

> As Porter tells it, high flying graduates from elite US universities such as Stanford, Harvard, and Chicago . . . moved into government and quickly became senior advisers in countries such as the UK, the US and Chile. Porter himself went to the IMF, then to the Reserve Bank of Australia and later . . . became Professor at Monash University. 'Government was very exciting at the time' (Porter said). Because the political parties were basically doing nothing very well so the think tanks were able to fill the breach'. Well resourced special units were attached to the offices of political leaders in many of these coun- tries, feeding new ideas into government. (Kelsey 1999: 63–64)

By the 1980s most Western countries were moving towards smaller govern- ment and market liberalisation.

The work ethic and inequality

The propaganda disseminated to directly sell free enterprise was supported by that aimed at indirectly providing legitimacy to the inequalities it created and ensuring the compliance of workers in the capitalist system. As hundreds of corporations downsized and moved their production to devel- oping nations as a result of globalisation, and government services were made more 'efficient' in preparation for privatisation by shedding thou- sands of workers (Beder 2003: 197, 232), the need to reinforce the work ethic in developed countries grew. This was not only to motivate the remaining workers, particularly those who now had insecure, temporary or part-time work, but to ensure that welfare did not become an attractive alternative, and to legitimise a system that had thrown so many out of work (Beder 2000).

An ideology of work has been promoted in Western societies since the early days of modern capitalism 'as a means of masking the drudgery and necessity of work' (Gini and Sullivan 1989: 9) and ensure a willing work- force for employers. But more than this the work ethic provides legitimacy for the wealth being accrued by a minority of the population in terms of reward for hard work, initiative and the ability to take advantage of oppor- tunities that supposedly abound in a capitalist society. The work ethic turned wealth into a measure of worthiness and success while poverty and unem- ployment became indicators of laziness and lack of character (Beder 2000).

In response to the decline in faith in the American Dream that followed the wave of downsizing in the US, business people and the politicians they supported frantically promoted the American Dream. Bill Clinton gave speeches on it. The House Republicans put out a book in 1995 entitled *Restoring the American Dream* which claimed that anyone in America could succeed whatever their skin colour or current income level (*The Mall of Dreams* of 1996 at page 23).

In the mid-1990s a whole spate of books were published on how to promote and rejuvenate the American dream, including *Reviving the American Dream* by Alice Rivlin, *The Success Ethic, Education and the American Dream* by De Vitis and Rich, *Facing up to the American Dream* by Jennifer L. Hochschild, *The American Dream* by Edmond Morris, *Recovering the American Dream Through the Moral Dimension of Work, Business and Money* by Robert Wuthnow, *The Good Life and Its Discontents* by Robert J. Samuelson and *Chasing After the American Dream* by Thomas Kerr.

Bill Gates's devotion to hard work was mythologised by business magazines. The mainstream media also promoted the idea of work leading to success and this was not limited to the US. Programmes such as *60 Minutes* in Australia (Woolley 1999) propagated the idea. Such media portrayals of self-made business people as heroes were complemented by the media's negative portrayals of the unemployed as bludgers and undeserving wretches who were trying to avoid work (Beder 2000: 161–169).

Work-for-benefit schemes became prevalent throughout the English speaking world as politicians translated the theme of undeserving welfare recipients into policy. Such schemes ensured that welfare recipients were deterred from choosing an 'easy' life on welfare; that the unemployed would acquire work habits; and that there was a ready and somewhat desperate reserve labour force to ensure that those in work feared for their jobs and maintained a downward pressure on wages (Beder 2000: 174–187).

The new welfare reforms, including compulsory work-for-benefit schemes, also reinforced the idea that unemployment had been caused or at least exacerbated by the welfare system rather than factors such as the massive corporate and government downsizing that occurred during the 1980s and 1990s (Beder 2000: 187).

Business coalitions and free trade

Whilst the Ad Council and individual corporations sold the message of free enterprise to the general public and the neoconservative think tanks sold a neoliberal policy prescription to governments and policy makers facilitating the global spread of capital in the name of free enterprise, corporations from the major industrialised nations joined forces to form formidable coalitions with huge influence to lobby in international fora for free trade in goods and services and free investment worldwide.

Early efforts were focused on the Uruguay Round of the General Agreement on Tariffs and Trade (GATT) and transferred to the World Trade Organisation (WTO) when it was formed in 1995. For example, the

European Round Table of Industrialists (ERT) is a leading lobbying force for free trade and claims credit for achieving a final agreement in the Uruguay Round. Its Trade & Investment working group worked closely with the US Business Roundtable 'in backing the launch of the Uruguay Round' and supporting the ongoing negotiations (ERT 2003a; ERT 2003b: 40).

The ERT describes itself as a 'forum of around 45 European industrial leaders aiming at promoting the competitiveness and growth of Europe's economy' (ERT 2003c). ERT was modelled on the US Business Roundtable and uses the rhetoric of competitiveness to promote deregulation, privatisation and free trade (Balanyá, et al. 2000: 20–21). Membership is by invitation only and includes Chairs and CEOs of major multinational companies headquartered in Europe. Current members are from companies including Bayer, Fiat, BP, Royal Dutch/Shell, Unilever, Hoffmann-La Roche, Total, Volvo, Renault and Siemens.

ERT was credited with being the driving force behind a single European market by former Commission President, Jacques Delors (Doherty and Hoedeman 1994). It applied itself with similar vigour to the GATT negotiations. ERT Assistant Secretary General, Caroline Walcot said in 1993: 'We have spoken to everybody. We have made press statements. We have written to Prime Ministers. We have done *everything* we can *think* of to try and press for the end of the Uruguay Round' (quoted in Balanyá, et al. 2000: 24–25).

The ERT is just one of the many corporate coalitions campaigning for the expansion of free trade. The World Economic Forum (WEF) is another. The WEF is a private group of top-level business people who meet annually at the Swiss ski resort of Davos, and at numerous other more specialised meetings during the year, to network, have private discussions, share information and ideas, form alliances, and influence policy-makers. A 'club atmosphere' is deliberately cultivated and a 'privileged, informal, framework for intensive business networking' is maintained (World Economic Forum 2000).

But business people also come to WEF meetings to set the economic and political as well as the business agenda worldwide. The WEF is not a decision-making body but one that has influence through the financial power of its members. It wields influence through bringing the world's top business people and top policy makers together at its meetings. Government leaders are invited to WEF meetings enabling business leaders to have high-level access to government ministers, prime ministers and presidents. The WEF's web pages describes its deliberate role in shaping the global political agenda and claim: 'Over the past 27 years, the World Economic Forum has evolved into a major force for economic integration at the corporate as well as the national economic levels' (World Economic Forum 2000).

According to researcher James Goodman, 'WEF strategising drove the neo-liberal agenda in the 1980s . . . It offered a proactive forum, removed from the public gaze, and played a central role in diffusing neo-liberalism and was highly effective in extending the reign of the market.' Similarly, Kees van der Pijl, in his book *Transnational Classes and International Relations*, states that '[u]ntil well into the 1990s, the WEF was a pivot of neoliberal hegemony' (quoted in Murphy 1999). During the 1980s and 1990s the ERT and WEF and other business coalitions managed to conduct their lobbying behind the scenes and advance the cause of the expansion of global capital without much public attention. This all changed at the end of the 1990s. With the completion of the Uruguay Round of GATT negotiations and the creation of the WTO, a logical progression for multinational corporations was a more concerted push to deregulate investment.

In order to bypass developing nation opposition it was decided to secretly negotiate a far-reaching treaty amongst OECD nations, and then to invite (or coerce) accession from developing countries. Formal negotiations on a Multilateral Agreement on Investment (MAI) began in 1995 aimed at removing national regulations restricting foreign investment and improving protections for foreign investors. However the text of the draft agreement was leaked to the public and the protest campaign that followed helped to bring the negotiations to a halt, forcing the agreement's corporate backers to move their efforts to the WTO.

Business coalitions feared that the collapse of the MAI talks and the controversy surrounding the MAI might stall or reverse precariously-balanced moves to progress investment deregulation in the WTO (USCIB 1998). These fears were realised at the WTO Ministerial meeting in Seattle in 1999. Developing nation opposition to a new round of negotiations was supported by over a thousand NGOs – environmental, labour, consumer and development – prior to the Seattle meeting (Madeley 2000: 12). More than 50,000 people from all over the world protested at the meeting itself. These were the 'largest demonstrations witnessed in the US since the Vietnam War' (Hoedeman and Doherty 2002: 65).

The MAI controversy had instilled greater public scepticism about the claimed benefits of trade and investment deregulation, and the failure of the negotiations instilled a belief in opponents that it was possible to slow – perhaps even reverse – the corporate agenda. De Jonquieres noted in the *Financial Times* that 'the unexpected success of the MAI's detractors in winning the public relations battle . . . has set alarm bells ringing.' From now on it would be 'harder for negotiators to do deals behind closed doors and submit them for rubber-stamping by parliaments. Instead, they face pressure to gain wider popular legitimacy for their actions by explaining and defending them in public' (de Jonquieres 1998).

In response to the growing public opposition to free trade negotiations, particularly with regard to services and investment, business launched a new public relations campaign. Opposition to the expansion of free trade rules was labelled 'globophobia', and business groups sought to portray free trade in a more favourable light. Hoedeman and Doherty from Corporate Europe Observatory (CEO) describe how: 'Since Seattle, US business has engaged in a multi-faceted, multimillion-dollar counter-campaign involving individual corporations, lobby groups like the Business Roundtable (BRT) and the US Chamber of Commerce, corporate-sponsored think tanks, and of course the ever-faithful PR industry' (Hoedeman and Doherty 2002: 67, 71). Similarly Phillip Babish from the National Radio Project noted how 'corporations are showering the US Congress with well-funded lobbying campaigns and pro-free trade think-tanks are engaging in an information war for public opinion' (Babich 2000).

It was generally recognised that the internet had played a major role in mobilising opposition to MAI and the WTO at Seattle so PR firms advised that business interests also utilise the internet to promote the pro-free trade message and attack anti-WTO NGOs (Hoedeman and Doherty 2002: 70–71). A host of new websites emerged including the BRT's goTrade site, which was in place whilst business was lobbying Congress for presidential authority to fast track free trade agreements.

In business coalition meetings around the world there has been much discussion on how to present globalisation as more than just a market or economic force. It is now presented as being beneficial to developing countries. For example Bill Gates, at the WEF's Asia-Pacific Summit in September 2000, dismissed the thousands of protestors outside the meeting by arguing that globalisation was good for the poor.

Fred Bergsten, Director of the Institute for International Economics (IIE), told the 2000 meeting of the Trilateral Commission – another international body supporting capitalist expansion – that the backlash against globalisation was threatening 'the prosperity and stability of the world economy'. 'All this occurs after two decades when a market-oriented philosophy, the so-called "Washington consensus", seemed to gain near-universal approval and provided a guiding ideology and underlying intellectual consensus for the world economy, which was quite new in history' (Bergsten 2000). He argued that a response required public education 'first and foremost' to show how globalisation was beneficial to all countries and most groups, although clearly there would be costs and losers and this also needed to be admitted (Bergsten 2000).

WEF members similarly recognise that free trade leads to winners and losers and often results in greater inequalities but their problem is not how to prevent or ameliorate those inequalities but how to strengthen 'public faith in a market economy' and show ordinary people that they too can benefit from it. In an article entitled 'The Case for Capitalism' Walter Mead pointed out that for the first time there is a 'broad degree of consensus among economists and policy makers about what ought to be done . . . The trick, as always, is winning public support for good policies' (Mead 2000).

Conclusion

The 1970s were marked by a crisis of confidence in business and a challenge to the legitimacy of unfettered capitalism. Corporations responded to this challenge with a barrage of propaganda and sophisticated public relations techniques. These campaigns were not only aimed at countering specific government regulatory moves and popular movements calling for more regulation, but also at restoring faith in the benevolence of business and the sanctity of free enterprise. Nowhere were the efforts to sell the merits of free enterprise so well-financed, widespread and coordinated as they were in the US.

The liberalisation, deregulation and privatisation of the 1980s that made the possibility of global markets a reality was facilitated by a shifting ideological consensus achieved by corporate-funded think tanks – many of which were set up as part of the response to the 1970s legitimacy crisis. These think tanks not only promoted free enterprise and small government but they disseminated and marketed the ideas and theories of a minority of neoconservative economists. Such theories gave a public-interest rationale to liberalisation, deregulation and privatisation that provided cover for the self-interested motivations of corporations.

However, the dislocation and increasing inequalities that have resulted from these policies created a further crisis of legitimacy for global capitalism, leaving corporations with no choice but to continue to sell themselves as well as their commodities on a global scale. Within affluent countries the resulting unemployment and declining work conditions required propaganda aimed at renewal of beliefs such as the work ethic and the American Dream which provided some sort of justification for the inequalities and hope for the dispossessed. In poorer countries the resulting unemployment and declining affordability of food and basic services required propaganda aimed at renewal of faith in the benevolence of free trade and investment, and neoliberal structural adjustments, for the economic growth of developing countries.

The communications industry has developed to accommodate the growing communication needs of global capital. 'For the past two decades the disparate international tribes of ad men and PR consultants have been quietly consolidating their power by forging giant conglomerates.' Two of the three biggest of these, WPP and Omnicom, were founded within a year of each other in the middle 1980s. 'Together they now manage the hearts and minds of global populations for their transnational corporate clients' (Beder and Gosden 2001).

The UK-based WPP Group alone consists of over 160 companies including some of the world's largest firms in the areas of advertising – J. Walter Thompson, Ogilvy and Mather, Young & Rubicam – and public relations – Burson Marsteller, Hill and Knowlton. WPP employs 62,000 people in

1400 offices in 103 countries and its revenue for 2002 was just under £4 billion (www.wpp.com/). WPP founder and CEO, Martin Sorrell told *Forbes Magazine* in 1999: 'It is politically incorrect to say so, but our big clients are becoming more coordinated.' That is why providers of communication services must also be coordinated and centralised (quoted in Beder and Gosden 2001).

The necessity of this proliferation of corporate propaganda in recent decades supported by a massive communications industry shows that ideology still plays a vital role in supporting and legitimising global capitalism and its goals.

'The revolution will now be televised' – strategies of communication and class conflict in Brazil

Introduction

This chapter examines Brazil's developing democratic political culture and the tensions within it. These tensions are most clearly explained by the persisting class conflict of a society split between the majority of impoverished and landless peoples and a wealthy capitalist class that governs through a shifting, historic alliance that cuts across political, economic, cultural and military institutions (Arcenanux 2001; Branford and Kucinski 2003; de Staal 2003; Inter American Commission on Human Rights 2004). In particular, this chapter examines the role that the means of mass communication play in the struggle between the Workers' Party (PT) and its incumbent President Lula da Silva, and the dominant media institution, the Globo network. It is difficult to overstate the importance of Globo in the evolution of Brazilian political culture since its rise to prominence under the military dictatorship that seized power in 1964. Globo's success has been based significantly around its willingness and tendency to represent the interests and ideals of Brazil's traditional ruling class (Henry 2003; Hinchberger 2004). How have the PT and President Lula sought to deal with a means of communication that is at best antagonistic towards them, and more often overtly hostile? What the ongoing experiences of Lula's Presidency illustrate is the centrality of communication to political struggle in a democratic polity, even when the struggle has historically been one of a brutal class conflict. Pessimistic readings of the Lula administration have tended to emphasise the structural constraints placed upon it by forces within Brazil and without, such as the landowning classes, the IMF or the interests expressed in US foreign policy. In this view it is almost inevitable that the Lula Presidency will undergo the same pressures and be forced into similar concessions as those faced by progressive political movements in South America such as the Chavez administration in Venezuela or that of Aristide in Haiti. The implicit threat here is that Brazil must conform to financial orthodoxy or face a variety of economic, political and potentially military pressures.

Such views are not without foundation. However, this view fails to acknowledge the potential for resisting such pressures that the PT can bring to bear. As a coalition and network it has been built up over decades through a succession of often-conflicting coalitions that have helped to create an organic and far-reaching social force pushing for an agenda of social justice, the basis of which would be land reform. Thus *the PT is in itself a means of mass communication* that has been central to the expression of the interests of Brazil's poorest and most disempowered sectors (Keck 1991; Branford and Kucinski 2003). It has acted as the means of communication for the political and economic interests of those not represented or reflected in the agenda of Globo and the Brazilian ruling classes. This has been a carefully developed and self-conscious Gramscian strategy on the part of the PT to build a counter-hegemonic movement to challenge the entrenched hege-monic social forces that have dominated Brazil's modern history (Branford and Kucinski 2003). What has transpired during the two years of the Lula Presidency is an increasingly complex domestic struggle between three groups: Globo, Lula and the PT, and the state, most recently over the parlous financial position that Globo finds itself in. Rather than being simply the hegemonic voice that shapes Brazilian political culture, President Lula has been able to use neoliberal principles to deny Globo access to state funds to support its ailing network on the grounds that this is bad econom-ics. This has seen him push the ultimate decision onto Brazil's congress (Liderdigital 2002; Castilho 2004). Indeed, such has been the success of Lula's commitment to neoliberal orthodoxy that he has gained the endorse-ment of the world's business press. For example, *Business Week* has gone so far as to note that it is President Lula, not President Bush, who is the current favourite of the IMF (Adams 2003). Nonetheless, there are grave dangers for the PT's progressive goals in these strategies as there is an inherent class tension and conflict in the structure of Brazilian society. Simply, at some point Lula will not be able to pursue both his progressive agenda that centres around an expanded public programme in areas such as housing, health care, welfare, education and land reform, and at the same time run his administration in accord with the demands of the IMF and the world's major financial institutions that require, amongst other things, reductions in public spending. It is our contention that this structural contradiction means a conflict of some kind is inevitable for the Lula administration. The choice it has to make is over which social group it is willing to have this conflict with. Broadly there are two alternatives open to President Lula and his administration. These options can be seen as two ends of a continuum between which the Lula administration can manoeuvre: First, if they con-tinue to renege on their commitment to social justice as their critics charge, then President Lula and his administration will be in conflict with their sup-porters if they wish to force through neoliberal policies; two, they can choose to mobilise their popular support base in order to challenge neoliberal pressure brought to bear both nationally, regionally and globally through a variety of formal and informal institutions. Either strategy involves significant risk and danger. The choice that Lula and his administration make will depend upon a range of contingent factors, but its meaning will be stark for those elected governments outside of the core capitalist states that attempt to pursue a programme of social justice. The symbolic importance of the Lula Presidency cannot be overstated for this very reason: *Can progressive governments in the Periphery and the Semi-Periphery achieve social justice for the majority of their populations in a capitalist world system?* The point here is that there is nothing inevitable about the failure of the Lula Presidency to deliver on its policies. These are political choices that agents make and utilising the means of communication is central to either outcome. If Lula pursues the option of resisting neoliberal policies, then he will be reliant upon the PT to act as a means of communication to mobilise and organise popular support for his plans. If, by contrast, his administration is increasingly compromised and co-opted by political and economic institutions at the local, national, regional and global level, then it will depend upon the mainstream corporate media for support in the face of popular protest.

This chapter will proceed as follows. It will begin by providing a brief overview of the background in which the PT emerged in a Brazil restored to democracy in 1985. It will then go on to examine the relationship between Globo and the PT and Lula both before and after the latter's successful presidential campaign in 2002. It needs to be stressed that Globo is the most powerful national broadcaster in South America and that it dominates Brazilian broadcasting to a degree unknown elsewhere in the hemisphere. For this reason it is the focus of our concern as it represents the most extreme example of a powerful national media organisation in the World System. There are other significant broadcasters in Brazil but given Globo's historical importance and role during the period of the dictatorship it is the institution to be reckoned with in terms of media power and Brazilian political culture. The relationship between Globo and the PT is a crucial one in that the means of communication are central to the logistics of politics in a democratic polity. In different ways socialists and liberals alike have stressed the role of the struggle for ideas (hegemony or consensus) in democratic politics and this is part of the ongoing class conflict in Brazil. The stakes, of course, are dramatically higher than those found in a core capitalist state such as the UK. Brazilian political culture has a modern history of widespread terror and violence by the state and its military forces against those committed to social justice (Skidmore 1997; O'Shaughnessy 2002). Thus the challenge facing the Lula administration is to push its progressive agenda as far as it can without provoking such a response from those forces opposed to it that it calls into question democracy itself (Power 2000).

Our approach is broadly sympathetic with that of World System Analysis

(WSA) but is one that seeks to utilise insights from Realist social theory that both complements and develops WSA. The organising issues of this chapter can be stated simply:

- What does the relationship between the PT and Globo tell us about the role of the means of communication in the construction of contemporary Brazilian political culture?
- What does the history of the PT in opposition and government tell us about the possibility of successful progressive political movements securing reform through representative democracy in the Periphery and the Semi-Periphery?

Part one: the re-emergence of democracy in Brazil

The position of the Lula administration and the state of contemporary class conflict in Brazil has to be placed in its broader historical context. In this section we will provide a brief analysis of the context within which the Lula administration now finds itself and in so doing will set out the major structural and institutional forces that have influenced the development of Brazilian political culture. There are two major structural factors in Brazilian history that have helped to shape its current condition, and these are concerned with land ownership patterns and the politics of the Cold War period. In WSA terms, Brazil occupies a crucial place in the Semi-Periphery of the World System, similar to that played by South Africa in the African continent. As the important regional power it has a crucial role to play in stabilising social order in the region and supporting the extraction of wealth from the region by the core capitalist states. Its bloody and violent modern history can be rooted in its relationship to the Capitalist World System and the need for the core to extract wealth from the Periphery and Semi-Periphery (Wallerstein 2003).

As has been common to many South American societies, Brazil is a country where ownership of land has rested in the hands of a small minority of the population who have derived immense wealth and power from this (de Staal 2003). There have been periods of intense class struggle and state violence in Brazil around this issue and it is of fundamental importance for the Lula administration that if the agenda for social justice is to be a serious one then it requires a dramatic change in patterns of land ownership in Brazil. The Landless Workers' Movement (MST) has been a major factor in the PT history and they are already aggrieved at what they see as the failings of the Lula administration (Branford and Rocha 2002; Branford 2003; Wallerstein 2003).

The second major structural factor in Brazilian history is more recent, and is rooted in the impact of the Cold War. Falling firmly in the purview of the US-led Western bloc, Brazil was subject to a variety of mechanisms of control, intervention and influence from US companies and foreign policy through to US state support for the Brazilian military (Sader and Silverstein 1991; Skidmore 1967,1997; Henry 2003). As the Cold War intensified, the establishment of so-called National Security States throughout South America with US backing swept through the continent from the early 1960s and this tendency hit Brazil in 1964 with the overthrow of the Goulart Presidency. Goulart was a nationalist politician who sought to direct state support for modest investment in health, education and welfare for Brazil's impoverished majority population. In the binary geo-political context of the Cold War this modest agenda was presented as a move towards communism, and used to justify the ensuing military coup and US support for what followed: twenty years of military dictatorship with a fascist- style government. This period saw the intimidation and often destruction of key sections of Brazilian civil society and massive human rights violations that even now are still being revealed (Skidmore 1988; Dassin 1998; Levine and Crocitti 1999, section V; Henry 2003). What, then, of Globo's role in this period?

The classic and ideal liberal view of the media in a democratic society is that it acts as the 'Fourth Estate' (Keane 1991; Curran and Seaton 2003; see McNair elsewhere in this volume) a critical voice exposing those with power to public scrutiny. Globo, led by Roberto Marinho and his family, chose to pursue a different path (Bellos 2003). Rather than attempting to defend the deposed democratic government they very quickly moved into a position of support for the dictatorship. In return this allowed Globo to expand and take over much of Brazil's print and broadcast media. For twenty years Globo benefited from this capacity to support a regime that terrorised large sections of Brazilian society (Henry 2003). Nonetheless, this relationship needs to be seen as a contingent one. Globo and the Marinho family were not, in principle, committed to military-style fascism; they were instead committed to their own power and influence. This was illustrated in 1984–1985 when they switched their position on the return to democracy plebiscite from an initial one of continuing support for the dictatorship to one of support for democracy when it became clear that the pro-democracy movement, in which Lula and the PT played an important part, was going to win (Stepan 1989; Sader and Silverstein 1991; O'Shaughnessy 2002). The task for Globo was one of preserving the power and wealth they had accrued under the dictatorship in the new political order of party democracy. The role for Globo was one of watchdog, patrolling the boundaries of Brazil's newly re-emerging democratic political culture by attacking those that went beyond the limits of what Brazil's ruling classes saw as legitimate policies. Thus as has been well documented, Globo ruthlessly sought to attack Lula's candidacy at successive presidential elections deploying all manner of propaganda to argue that he was unfit to govern (O'Shaughnessy 2002). Nonetheless, it needs to be stressed here that even with the vast array of propaganda weapons at its disposal, Globo could not stop the progress of the PT and its allies. Indeed, over the following fifteen years the PT achieved a variety of political victories, both nationally and at the state level, enabling it to begin to pursue progressive polices such as its experiments with participatory budgets at a local level (Branford 2003). These involved local people in the decision-making process around what budgets should be spent on. Despite successive propaganda campaigns against Lula during the presidential elections of 1989, 1994 and 1998, his share of the vote remained solid.[1] Globo, unsurprisingly, sided with the parties that supported the interests of big business, usually the Liberal Party, and supported their presidential candidates. However, so corrupt and inept was the perception of these administrations that by the 2002 presidential elections the opposition to Lula and the PT had become so bereft of credibility at home and abroad that the PT were in a much stronger potion to challenge the dominant political and economic interests in Brazil (Kingstone 1999; BBC News Online 2002). Even Globo saw Lula as a credible candidate worthy of support by the 2002 presidential election. The end of the Cold War in the early 1990s meant that Globo could not simply present the PT and Lula as covert Soviet agents who were not to be trusted. Instead this period of 'New World Order' helped to open up a political space for those committed to social justice around the world to focus and organise against neoliberal capitalism without being easily marginalised by the kind of propaganda campaigns and 'red scares' that were so familiar throughout the Cold War.

This period was crucial for the PT and for Lula as it sought to build its coalition of support and establish an alternative network of communication and political culture through grass roots activism and the development of a wide coalition of groups. This represented a very different form of political communication from that offered in the soap-opera-dominated programming of Globo's TV network. What unfolded in this period was an attempt to establish a grassroots political coalition of the disempowered in Brazil, and in doing so reinvigorate and stretch the boundaries of Brazil's emerging democratic political culture. It is important to focus on this as the goals and legitimacy of the Lula administration are rooted in its aspiration to help give voice to the needs of the majority of Brazilian citizens who lived, and continue to live, in dire poverty. The Gini index table of measurement of equality gives Brazil in 2004 a mark of 60.7, with zero meaning perfect equality. This leaves Brazil ranked the fourth most unequal country in the world (Rubin 2002; ECLAC 2004; Infoplease 2004). In terms of poverty the World Bank has recently published its 2004 report on Brazil that highlights anti poverty measures and the link between high inequality and deep poverty in Brazil. The report notes the following

> Despite Brazil's impressive advances, the poorest one-fifth of Brazil's 173 million people account for only a 2.2 percent share of the national income. Brazil is second only to South Africa in a world ranking of income inequality.

More than one-quarter of the population live on less than $2 a day and 13 percent live on less than $1 a day. Brazil's Northeast contains the single largest concentration of rural poverty in Latin America. Past development programs have failed to make a major dent in a region in which 49% of the population is classified as poor. (*World Bank Report* 2004)

Around 70 per cent of Brazilians live in poverty and around 58 million live on less than $1 per day. This is even more shocking when you consider that Brazil is the eleventh richest country in the world (Hernandez 2004).

Brazil in the World System

Having set out the domestic aspects of contemporary Brazilian political culture we also need to recognise its place in the emerging World System. The political economy of contemporary Brazil is situated in a world system that provides a framework that serves to enable and constrain the range of choices open to actors and institutions alike. Brazil stands at the forefront of countries in the Semi-Periphery by virtue of its economic, cultural and military power. We want to develop the Core-Periphery dynamic of WSA and argue that a more complex model is needed that account not only the chain of capitalist exchange but which also allows for a layered social order that can be seen as having local, national, regional and global connections. WSA is often criticised for over-simplifying the structure of the World System and there is something important to this criticism. In developing our model in this way we do not seek to reject the fundamental principles of WSA, that the World System is organised through a hierarchy of power and exchange. Rather we are merely developing it in a way that allows for the greater complexity of the political, economic and cultural relations that shape it. It is useful to think about this complex structural relationship in terms of interconnected layers at the local, national, regional and global level. Through this, the nature of the obstacles and the possibilities open to the Lula administration and the PT become more apparent:

Local
At the local level the PT have been successful over the past two decades in securing political representation at a variety of levels and ultimately the Presidency. This has enabled them to implement a variety of policies aimed to empower their grassroots constituency. For example, the introduction of participatory budgets has been a mechanism enabling ordinary Brazilian citizens to have a meaningful say in where resources are to be allocated at the local level. Unsurprisingly the impact of these policies has been mixed but they would have been unthinkable under the past military dictatorship (Keck 1991; Branford and Kucinski, 2003, chapter 4; Ortellado 2002; Baiocchi 2003).

National

At the national level the PT face the continued opposition of the dominant institutions and social groups in Brazil. The land-owning classes are fiercely opposed to the agenda of the Landless Workers' Movement and since gaining power President Lula has backtracked on aspects of the PT policy commitments to the Landless Movement (Gentile 2004). It must be stressed that the Lula administration faces a broad-ranging class alliance that has historically controlled Brazil's military, its economy, its political institutions and its cultural institutions. Globo is an important part of this class alliance and has played a prominent propaganda role, attempting to monitor the boundaries of legitimate political culture.

Regional

At the regional level there have been interesting developments in recent years that could, potentially, prove to be very important to the aspirations of the Lula administration. A number of populist nationalist governments with nominally left-wing or progressive agendas have taken office in Venezuela, Argentina, Bolivia and Peru and they represent a potential regional alliance resistant to neoliberal orthodoxy and in favour of the masses that they aspire to represent (Painter 2004). It is clear that Washington views this possibility with grave concern and has sought to separate these states in its diplomatic relations to undermine the possibility of such an alliance emerging (Agence French Press 2004; Burbach 2004). Nonetheless, if the PT and the Lula administration is serious about its agenda for social justice then working with these administrations at the regional level seems to be a prerequisite.

Global

Finally, developments in Brazilian political economy have to be situated within the global context of capitalism and the global state system. As was made clear before the electoral success of Lula, if his administration failed to adhere to the structures of neoliberal orthodoxy, Brazil could expect to be hit with a variety of disciplinary economic measures. Indeed, during the first two years of the Lula Presidency Brazil's economy went into a slump from which it is only now making a tentative and unstable recovery (Bellos 2004). The Brazilian economy remains vulnerable to the pressures exerted by capitalist investors who have the ability to move their investments instantaneously as a process of continual monitoring, surveillance and discipline of the administration's economic policy (Dudley 2002; Udry 2002; ECLAC 2004; Cardoso 2004). The recent fate of the Argentine economy and society was a sobering lesson for the Lula administration before it had barely taken office. The liberalisation of the Brazilian economy, which has its roots in the brutal policies of the military dictatorship, makes it particularly vulnerable to a variety of economic pressures through international financial institutions and capitalist investors alike. Facing down this kind of economic reality is a major test for the administration. Similarly the global state system exerts pressure on Brazil as a part of the regional security structure that has emerged post-Cold War under US tutelage. The US has established military bases in a number of South American countries, including Brazil, for the first time in its history (Petras 2002). The sovereignty of Brazil is as contingent, permeable and fragile as that of any other country in the Periphery and the Semi-Periphery and the existence of foreign military bases on its soil and the soil of its neighbours is an illustration of the geo-political power relations of the region. The US remains hegemonic regionally and globally, it is the only superpower with a global military reach, and it has shown that it is increasingly prepared to use this military capacity to promote and protect its interests. If the PT and its potential allies in the region were to make serious challenges to the Washington-dominated economic orthodoxy then this would undoubtedly lead to confrontation on a variety of levels. The experience of the Chavez administration in Venezuela is salutary here. Although there is no direct evidence to show US involvement in the attempted coup d'etat, the US has voiced repeated objections to the Chavez government and offered rhetorical support for the coup, just as it had done for those opposing President Aristide in Haiti (Petras 2002; Burbach 2004).

Out of this complex array of actors, institutions and forces emerges a clearer picture of the position of the PT and the Lula administration. Any polices that it chooses to pursue need to be understood in the context of this framework of power relations. A great deal hinges upon the ability of the Lula administration to deliver on long-standing promises made to their constituents. The contradictions that a co-opted or conformist Lula Presidency finds itself in can be traced back to its long-standing campaigning for and promotion of the rights of ordinary Brazilians. The relationship with Globo remains a key factor in this process and we will turn now to the role that both Globo and the PT play in Brazilian political culture.

Part two: Globo against the PT – understanding power and ideology in Brazilian political culture

The rise of Globo

The Globo network began in 1925 set up by its founder Roberto Marinho. However, it was the emergence of the dictatorship in 1964 that saw Globo rise to pre-eminence in Brazil, then regionally until it reached the point where it held the greatest control over any domestic media network in the capitalist world, at its peak controlling around 75 per cent of advertising revenue (worth $6.4bn in 1998) in Brazil, 54 per cent of the audience figures and reaches 99.98 per cent of the population. It now stands as arguably the fourth largest media network in the world (Bellos 2004; Ketupanet 2004; MIT 2004)

Any analysis of the Globo network has to recognise its place in the political-economy structure of power in Post-Second World War Brazil. Like any capitalist media institution, it cannot be understood simply as the Fourth Estate, independent of outside interests. Rather, in Globo's case it has been heavily integrated into the political, economic and cultural structure of Brazilian political culture and increasingly into wider networks of global communication with the more powerful of News Corporation (News Corporation 2004).

As we have already suggested, Globo is not simply subordinated to the interests of the military or any particular political party. Its strategy is to support and work with those in power wherever possible. The ideology of Globo is not simply that of conservatism or neoliberalism or even fascism after its support for the military dictatorship. Instead its strategy is one of opportunism and pragmatism, directed by the permanent need to retain its power and influence. In short, Globo will work with anyone prepared to do business with it and who does not threaten its business empire, even the current administration, once its bête noire. The ideology of the company is that of capitalism, to make profits, to pursue private wealth and power and to dominate markets in order to destroy competition, by turns working with and using the state to promote and protect its power (Henry 2003). By and large this strategy has been highly successful for Globo and there is an interesting parallel between Globo and the PT and the relationship of New Labour to News Corporation in the UK. In any country the media have a crucial role to play in its political culture as they are the institutions that frame, present, organise and structure the news, entertainment and information that informs public opinion and debate. In the UK, News Corporation has long been condemned by politicians and academics alike for the coarsening of British political culture and the 'dumbing down' of detailed political analysis. In short, the company has been accused of promoting a political ideology that furthers the interests of the (non-UK) company at the expense of the needs of a democratic political culture. Thus, the *Sun* newspaper claimed to have won the 1992 election for the Conservative Party and this was a view shared by many politicians at the time (Nineham 1995; Cohen 2000; BBC News Online 2004a).

In the 1980s and early 1990s the company was seen as being highly influential on British political culture, promoting a ruthless brand of consumer capitalism that was propagandistic in its support for the Conservative Party. Indeed, the logical conclusion was that News Corporation and the British Conservative Party shared the same ideology. However, by the mid-1990s and the emergence of Tony Blair as leader of the Labour Party this began to change, as the Labour Party made overtures to News Corporation that Labour had fundamentally changed its political beliefs, subordinating them to the needs of the market and of consumer sovereignty. This conversion was symbolically and practically sealed by the famous visit paid by Blair in 1995 to News Corporation headquarters (Cohen 2000). Subsequently, News Corporation began to shift its allegiance to supporting New Labour at the 1997 election, something that would have been inconceivable in 1992. Just as Globo was able to shift from being a supporter of the pro-dictatorship movement to supporting the pro-democracy movement, and ultimately supporting Lula, News Corporation simply works with those it can do business with and who have power. Its party political loyalties are no deeper than this. Similarly in Brazil the Globo network has had to work with the administration of President Lula in order to continue to promote its interests in such things as developing the new communication infrastructure for the country.

What conclusions should we reach about the power and role of Globo in Brazilian political culture? Orthodox models of media power are usually based on positivist assumptions about the universal law-like nature of social orders.[2] In practice this reduces political activity to models that assume meaningful generalisations are based upon invariant cause-effect relations that hold over time and space and that can ultimately be transformed into some form of statistical analysis (Sayer 1992). We reject such models as they rest on a series of flawed assumptions about the nature of social orders and the social relations that obtain within them. This is a complex issue and there is neither the time nor space to go into a detailed account of it here but when considering the power and influence of Globo in Brazilian political culture we argue that any analysis has to work from the following assumptions:

Understanding societies – closed and open systems

Classic political science when formulating models for analysis views social and political systems as closed units of analysis in which variables and relations persist over time in potentially unchanging patterns of behaviour. The task of the political analyst is therefore to study these patterns and where possible test for significance (Hay 2002). However, this only works as an approach if it is plausible to view social and political systems in this way. How realistic, if you like, is such an assumption? In international relations James Rosenau made a claim that illustrates the importance of this point for how we approach the study of society when he said:

> As a focus of study, the nation-state is no different from the atom or the single cell organism. Its pattern of behaviour, idiosyncratic traits, and internal structure are as amenable to the process of formulating and testing hypotheses as are the characteristics of the electron or molecule . . . in terms of science-as-method (physics and foreign policy analysis) are essentially the same. (Rosenau 1980: 32)

In our view such assumptions are simply unwarranted. Societies are not closed systems that can be understood by reducing them to their constituent parts. Rather they are open systems, in which agents and institutions have a history and identity that are rooted in a complex array of emergent relations across time and space. For example, can you understand the rise of Globo in Brazil without locating it in its local, national, regional and global context? Our argument is that you cannot and therefore the idea that Brazilian political culture can be understood as simply the outcome of a discrete system is flawed.

Causality and tendencies

The question of causality is usually central to considerations of media power over political culture, the assumption being that a cause is a law-like relation that is invariant and holds over time and space, producing the same outcomes time after time. Such a claim works on the assumption that the behaviour of people can be controlled and directed by a media utilising an array of symbols, messages and signs to stimulate certain responses from its audiences. Whilst there is little doubt that the use of such things as fear, nostalgia, scapegoats and constructions of officially sanctioned enemies are powerful weapons in the hands of the mainstream media and states alike, the idea that invariant causal relationships hold in social and political systems makes no sense. People are agents who interpret, read and challenge information as well as simply accepting it. Any analysis of the power and relationship between a particular media and its audience has to take into account the specific social and historical context. Whilst propaganda might have proven to be a powerful tool in mobilising popular support at certain times and places in the US or the UK, it is not invariant. Contra Rosenau's claim, states are not atoms and people are not rocks. They are meaningful actors who develop ideas about the social and political world that in themselves act as causal mechanisms shaping their potential choices. Does this mean we reject the idea that causal relations obtain in social and political systems? No. Rather, we argue that what the example of Globo in Brazil shows us is that causality is a complex relationship in social and political systems, rooted in specific mechanism that have an array of causal powers. Causal powers are rooted in individuals, the meanings, ideas and beliefs they hold, in institutions, in social relations, in group identity. What we see emerging then is a complex picture of causal mechanisms that renders the kind of model building advocated by Rosenau and other political scientists completely inappropriate for the study of social and political systems. However, and this point is crucial, those powers are often challenged in open systems by other causal mechanisms, so we would not expect to see invariant patterns of behaviour in our analysis. The relationship between Globo and the PT is a classic illustration of these assumptions. If the power of propaganda was capable of causing linear, predictable, effects on its audience, the rise of the PT in Brazil would make no sense at all. In the aftermath of the return to democracy the PT in general and Lula in particular were subject to terrible forms of 'Black' propaganda by Globo, which was determined to help crush what it saw as an incipient threat to its interests (O'Shaughnessy 2002). Indeed, this is a striking example in that it destroys the explanatory power of positivist approaches working with a Humean cause–effect models that would predict regular and invariant outcomes. The PT has enjoyed little or no significant mainstream media, quite the opposite. And yet despite all of the political, economic and cultural opposition to it, it continued to gain support throughout Brazil, winning elections at a variety of levels and ultimately securing the Presidency. If the mainstream capitalist media really had the power to continually control political culture in an instrumental manner then this would make little or no sense. Where, then, does this leave us in terms of understanding the role of Globo in Brazilian political culture, its power and its relationship to the PT?

First, it must be stressed that we do not reject the importance of understanding causality in social and political analysis. What we argue for is a rejection of the idea that causal mechanisms produce invariant patterns of events in social and political systems in the same way that they do in (very) limited parts of the natural world (Bhaskar 1998). Globo has causal power as an institution to influence Brazilian political culture. It can utilise a variety of propaganda tactics to attempt to influence, intimidate and scare the population. However, this is not in itself sufficient as a form of power to produce anything like uniform outcomes. There are many causal mechanisms at play in an open social and political system that challenges Globo and its power. The PT gained success and popularity by creating alternative forms of communication, based around an organic and grassroots form of political and social mobilisation. In such a framework different ideas and experiences can be expressed, discussed and analysed. On this understanding the ideas that agents possess about the social and political world become causal mechanisms in themselves in that they help to direct the choices that agents make. None of this is to deny that in terms of reach and agenda-setting ability, the Globo network is a hugely powerful institution in patrolling the boundaries of debate in Brazilian political culture. But it is necessary to point out that it is not all-powerful and conventional political science models that work on the kind of assumptions that we have set out above are fundamentally flawed and should be rejected as appropriate methods of inquiry for the social sciences. A concern with questions of causality and power in social and political analysis is an attempt to understand what must exist in order for particular outcomes to have occurred, it is not an attempt to predict what will happen in the future on the assumption that social relations produce invariant outcomes. So the question that concerns us here is, given the immense power of Globo, the array of opposition forces facing the PT at a variety of levels (local, national, regional and global), how has it secured the popularity and success it has? Our answer to this is that it has, in significant part, been based around its ability to form an alternate means of communication in Brazilian political culture that operates outside the mainstream capitalist media. The power of ideas and of the meanings that people attach to events and relations is crucial to understanding political change but it is far more complex and protean than the Humean cause-effect models testing for statistical significance utilised by political science can allow for (Sayer 1992). Rather than pursuing neat, parsimonious and mathematically based models that ultimately predict what will happen in such relationships, we need to develop rich, detailed, historical and structural analyses of the events that concern us, locating the causal mechanisms, relations, agents, institutions and ideas that brought them into being. In addition, it is crucial to understand the meanings that actors have, whether as individuals or as members of social groups, for the events and relations that concern us. This latter point takes us to the need to understand the social production of ideas and meanings, an issue far removed from the parsimonious theorising of political science.

Having considered some important technical questions about the role of power, ideology and causality we want to turn now to the relationship between Globo and the Lula administration. Has this led to a shift in the balance of power between the institutions? Has the Lula administration been able to use its democratic legitimacy to assert its own agenda both against and through the Globo network?

Part three: 'The revolution will now be televised' – Lula in office

By the time of the 2002 presidential elections in Brazil the political system had become seriously compromised by the succession of corruption and impeachments scandals that had undermined the previous administrations (Kingstone 1999). Even with the support of the political and economic elites in Brazil and of the major cultural institutions such as Globo, it became impossible to defend the practices of these administrations in such a way that made Lula and the PT a less attractive alternative. Indeed, sections of the business press nationally and globally, and Globo itself, saw the prospect of a Lula administration in reasonably positive light, as an opportunity both to show the genuine democratic openness of the Brazilian system and perhaps for a Lula administration to organise a less corrupt and inefficient but ultimately neoliberal government (Henry 2003). The latter depended, of course, for the business community, on the degree to which Lula was prepared to either jettison or play down traditional policies of redistribution and work with the economic orthodoxy overseeing Brazil's economy through the auspices of the IMF. During the campaign Lula repeatedly made the point that he wanted to work with the business community at home and abroad in order to modernise and improve the Brazilian economy (Dudley 2002; Elliott 2002). Globo had to reckon with what was being presented as a moderate President who had learnt the lesson of previous electoral defeats to temper his rhetoric on social justice in favour of policies that the business community were comfortable with. There is a darker side to this support of course, in creating an opening for the Lula administration a Faustian bargain can be discerned. On the one hand, if Lula works with the demands of the business community and international financial institutions, he will be limited in the extent to which he will be able to pursue the policies that the PT have campaigned for over the previous two decades. The likelihood is that he would lose support and his party would be charged with co-optation by its natural constituency. The failure of the Lula administration would also be useful to the dominant institutions and classes in Brazil in that it would enable Globo, for example, to point out how radicals committed to social justice fail when in office. A salutary lesson for the rest of the Periphery and Semi-Periphery too. In effect, they aren't up to the job, can't deliver on their promises and aren't to be trusted. This latter scenario is a distinct possibility given the disastrous performance of the Brazilian economy since Lula's electoral success. High praise from the IMF for adherence to their policy prescriptions will not necessarily secure lasting votes in the favelas for the PT or for Lula at future elections. And yet this is precisely what the Lula administration has received, illustrated by a speech from IMF President Rodrigo De Rato after a recent visit to Brazil. He said: 'The advances made by the Brazilian government are very impressive. President Lula's administration has adhered to disciplined macroeconomic policies and developed an ambitious structural reform agenda' (de Rato 2004).

Is it possible for Lula to work within the system and deliver on his party's promises without incurring sanctions nationally and globally from capitalist investors, international financial organisations and governments in core capitalist states? This is the crux of the dilemma the Lula administration finds itself in. So how has Lula sought to implement his policies and secure his position with the electorate during the two years of his administration? How has his position been viewed by Globo and how, in turn, have Globo sought to promote their interests under President Lula?

Governance, strategy and communication – Lula in power

The significance of the Lula Presidency for progressive political parties in the Periphery and Semi-Periphery is enormous. Brazil is potentially a regional superpower and can lead the way in challenging neoliberal policies and their disastrous impact on the poorest sectors of society. In office the Lula administration has sought to utilise a strategy that sees it asserting its international role and challenging where possible, the actions of the core capitalist states. For example Brazil has played a significant role in peacekeeping activities in Haiti and has helped to develop the Mercosur trading bloc in South America (Burbach 2002a; Deibert 2004). In addition the Lula administration successfully challenged the US at the WTO for illegal subsidies for its cotton farmers (ABC News 2003; de Staal 2003; Deibert 2004; Hernandez 2004). This has garnered substantial praise for Lula's administration from a range of business and financial bodies, keen as they are to monitor his commitment to neoliberal norms. At this regional and global level the symbolic power of the Lula administration is impressive, it communicates the idea of a responsible, prudent and modest government seeking to work within established economic boundaries. But this is where the conflict emerges that the Lula administration inevitably faces, the first two years in office have also seen Brazil's economy slump dramatically as he has adhered to IMF policy prescriptions (*Socialist World* 2003; BBC News Online 2004b; Chossudovsky 2003; *The Economist* 2003).

Despite relative success over the past twelve months Lula has caused immense frustration amongst sections of his grassroots support (Branford 2003). Just as other charismatic figures committed to social justice in the Periphery and Semi-Periphery, such as the Mandela administration in South Africa, failed to deliver on their promises for supporters, so the same charge has justifiably been levied against Lula. The nature of the PT success and of Lula's popularity has been a unique example of both grassroots activism to create an alternative framework for political culture to develop, and one of manipulating the image of Lula as the Trade Unionist and humble defender of the people. In office Lula has sought to distance himself from the more radical sections of the PT and its allies, criticising the Landless Peasant movement for being too radical in its actions and ambitions. The danger for Lula is that in so doing he loses the goodwill and support of those he depends upon for electoral success and is increasingly reliant on those who are his traditional political enemies, the business community and Globo. Such a position leaves him exposed and vulnerable in a way familiar for progressive political figures in other South American countries. The Lula administration has so far been effectively regulated and disciplined by the power of the financial markets. Rather than taking on these powerful forces Lula has been trying to work with them to introduce piecemeal changes where possible.

There is something of an irony here in that in the period of Lula's administration the Globo Corporation has run into a major financial crisis that has seen them turn to the state for support. Globo's investment in the internet in Brazil has seen it incur massive debts and the only options it has are to default, open up to foreign investment (thus losing control for the Marinho family over the company) or to persuade the state to help. The all-powerful Globo Corporation has ended up in a situation where it must turn to its former enemy for support. No doubt the irony of this has not been lost on Lula and so far he has been careful not to succumb to Globo's demands. It required a major change in Brazilian law for foreign investors to take a significant stake in the Globo Corporation. Thus far both Globo and other Brazilian media institutions have proven to be largely unattractive to foreign investors (*Financial Times* 2003; Aragão 2004). Again, what this illustrates is that the power of Globo is in no way an absolute and that in fact the company has been made vulnerable by the very neoliberal principles it has sought to promote and which led to its seeming omnipotence (Kepp 2002; Chossudovsky 2003).

Thus far it has been difficult for Globo to offer substantive and damaging criticisms of the Lula Presidency, even with a looming corruption scandal involving the head of Brazil's Central Bank (Deibert 2004). This is unsurprising as Lula has been pursuing policies that largely reflect the interests of Globo and its allies in Brazil's ruling classes. The problem for Lula is that in failing to deliver sufficiently for his support base he is potentially undermining the decades long strategy of communication and dialogue that underpins his natural political community. The first two years of the Lula administration have been punctuated by disappointment for his supporters and conditional support from his traditional political enemies. No doubt recent improvement in economic performance will help the PT and Lula's Presidency at mid-term elections but the real conflict lies ahead as Lula has to work out his strategy for pursuing social justice and how he intends to communicate it to his supporters and those powerful institutions and classes who would oppose it. It is far from clear that his administration has resolved this dilemma and any analysis has always to bear in mind the tremendous national and global pressure that progressive governments face, be they in the Periphery or Semi-Periphery. For example a comparable state in the Semi-Periphery to Brazil has been South Africa (Seidman 1990). As with Lula's Brazil, to note the failure of the Mandela administration to deliver on its promises of housing, health, welfare and education is not to condemn the ANC as simple political opportunists but to acknowledge that all Southern governments operate in a World System that is not of their design and is not structured to promote the interests of their general populations. It is geared towards promoting the imperialist interests of the core capitalist states and their corporations. As the example of South Africa makes abundantly clear, profit for the corporations of core capitalist states is more important than the needs of the impoverished millions of ordinary Black South Africans (Seidman 1990). That is the simple, but universal truth, facing any government in Lula's position: The accumulation of capital, profit, comes before human need. To ignore this is to make the mistake of assuming that they act simply in bad faith. So what conclusions can be drawn as to the options open to the Lula administration in its relations with Globo, Brazil's economic and political elites and with its natural support base?

Conclusions: into the great unknown – the possibilities of progressive politics in the South

The main question facing the Lula administration is one that connects with the ambitions of progressive social and political movements across the

World System: is it possible for a progressive social and political movement to achieve its aims within the constraints of a capitalist world system (Burbach 2002a; Baiocchi 2003; Wallerstein 2003)? What strategy is best for achieving these ends? What this chapter has examined is the way in which social and political struggle in Brazil has taken place against the backdrop of a mainstream capitalist media that has been openly hostile to the policies and ambitions of the PT and its allies. However, what has also been illustrated is that even with effective control of the means of communication, dominant classes do not simply govern as they wish and do not always dominate the political agenda as they would want to. The example of the PT and its allies shows how political culture is formed by a complex array of factors. It is not simply the outcome of voting patterns and public opinion surveys. Politics is inflected into all areas of popular culture and everyday life and the PT alliance has utilised a network of communication to help develop a political culture that is organic and embedded in the myriad practices of Brazil's most impoverished communities. If it had not been able to develop this communicative strategy, it would not have been possible for it to obtain the political and social successes it has, without political power it was never going to gain the support of the Globo Corporation. What conclusions can we reach about the importance of the means of communication in Brazilian political culture? What options are open to the Lula administration in pursuit of its potential goals?

The first conclusion to be drawn from the example of the PT is that it is possible to counter an overtly hostile mainstream media if you have a strategy that is grassroots based, able to work with disparate communities and is embedded in the communities that it aspires to serve. For Gramscians this is a counter-hegemonic strategy, a war of position in which the subordinate social forces utilise their comparative strengths to build an alternate ethical and political community to the mainstream political culture. This is a useful way of conceptualising the strategy of the PT. Ownership and control of the means of communication is a necessary part of political power but clearly it is not sufficient or static and challenges to it can succeed.

Second, having secured office Lula has sought to direct the mechanisms of state towards certain aspects of his political programme but has sacrificed much of the PT's traditional policy goals in order to gain credibility with the national, regional and global financial and political institutions. In its relationship to Globo and other sectors of Brazil's mainstream media Lula's administration has recently introduced legislation to establish a government run journalism council which would have the power to accredit and regulate journalists (Deibert 2004). This is a worrying development in that whatever the answer is to the problems of a capitalist media in Brazil, authoritarian solutions have a tendency to produce authoritarian outcomes. In effect, this move is one towards a type of state censorship. It is difficult to see how such a policy is in the broader interests of the PT if it wishes to remain an organisation that works with rather than controls those it aspires to represent. It is easy to write off the prospects for Lula's Presidency and many left-wing critics have done just that. There are a number of directions that the administration could take and they each reflect the fault-lines along which class conflict in Brazil has long been directed:

Compromise

Having taken office the administration can continue to move in a piecemeal manner, taking as many of its supporters with it as possible and hoping to keep in favour with the national and global institutions and actors that oppose it. The approach of Lula so far has been something like this, hoping to build a broader constituency to strengthen the legitimacy of the PT and his administration at home and abroad. The problem with this is that in the medium term it threatens to undermine his natural supporters as he fails to deliver on the wide-ranging reforms that are needed in order for Brazil to deal with its major problems of poverty and landlessness. The rhetoric from Lula towards the Landless Workers' movement since he has taken office is not especially encouraging here for those hoping for a more through commitment to policies of social justice. It will also mean that the administration has to rely more on the support of its traditional enemies in the mainstream media, a dangerous strategy as such support is contingent upon the administration not straying far from neoliberal norms. In practice the administration would face the danger of failing to satisfy either its natural supporters or traditional opponents.

Cooptation

The administration could embrace neoliberal policies wholeheartedly on the assumption that it is the only practical option available to them. The forces opposed to the PT both within and outside Brazil are huge and connect across the military, mainstream cultural institutions, landowners and dominant economic classes. Faced with such serious opposition it might make sense to accept these constraints and argue that it is better that it is Lula overseeing such policies than representatives of Brazil's traditional political classes who have shown they to be thoroughly corrupt and indifferent to the position of the impoverished majority. Such a strategy would mean sacrificing the alternate networks of social and political communication that have served to build the PT in return for mainstream media acceptance as simply another party of business and governance. The problem with this is that it runs the serious danger of thoroughly discrediting not only the PT but the legitimacy of any claims to be able to challenge neoliberalism put forward by other social and political movements in the South. The stakes are necessarily high for the Lula administration and they transcend the formal boundaries of Brazilian political culture (Udry 2002).

Resistance

The final option open to the Lula administration is one of resistance to neo-liberalism and its supporters. Such a strategy would rely upon the network of support that is already in place for the PT but would have to extend beyond the boundaries of Brazilian political culture to work with like-minded groups across the region. To have a chance of success such a strategy would rely on the ability of the Lula administration to communicate its goals to its natural supporters in a way that is able to overcome the propaganda of the mainstream capitalist media, embodied most clearly in Brazil in the Globo Corporation. The PT has adopted a Gramscian strategy according to many of its supporters that will see it moving carefully to extend its counter-hegemonic network in a manner that will enable it to challenge ruling class interests (Branford and Kucinski 2003).

These possible futures should not be seen as clear distinction but more of a continuum of positions along which Lula's administration might situate themselves. The choices that the administration makes will dictate which battle it thinks is winnable in Brazilian political culture. Compromise means an attempt to use the mechanisms of the state to transcend class conflict by appealing to something bigger than the individual or the class: the nation. The practical import of such a strategy is that it means limiting what is offered to the administration's supporters in return for modest and utterly contingent support from its opponents. Cooptation would mean that the administration had chosen in office to side with its political enemies against its supporters that in practice the Lula administration will have changed sides in a class war. There are precedents for this in recent Brazilian political culture. Former President Fernando Cardoso, for example, was one of the original founders of the Dependency school in South America that was anti-capitalist and argued that the North systematically exploited the South in trade relations. Cardoso chose ultimately to switch sides in the class war and become candidate and ultimately President on behalf of the business-led Social Democratic Party. Finally, resistance means an attempt at mobilising a widespread popular cultural rebellion against neoliberalism that builds an alliance both within and outside Brazil's state boundaries. Whether the will or the desire is there for such a battle on the part of the administration seems questionable to say the least. Thus far the Lula administration has trod an uneasy path of compromise, trying to maintain its image in the capitalist press as modest and competent managers of capital, whilst trying to deliver some goods for its long-standing supporters.

Notes

1 For detailed analysis of post-dictatorship Brazilian presidential elections see the US Library of Congress website at www.lcweb2.loc.gov/frd/cs/brtoc.html.

2 The American tradition of media studies has been dominated by positivist model building. A good recent example can be found in this paper by Loo and Reibel, 'Television News and the 1990s Crime Problem', www.nssa.us/nssajrnl /NSSJ2003%2020_2/html/12Loo_Dennis.htm.

Global solidarity and the communications revolution – resisting state and capital

Introduction: the rise of the movements for global social justice

> It meets my tests of reactionary utopianism . . . (Christopher Hitchens, interview with *The Stranger*, 17–23 January 2002)

The end of the millennium has seen the emergence of a unique social movement in world history. At times called the anti-globalisation or anti-capitalist movement, this movement became most clearly defined at the WTO conference in Seattle in 1999. It has come to represent a global social movement that has sought to articulate and promote the interests of a cross-section of the world's population, drawn usually but not exclusively from the poorest and least empowered sectors. For this reason and for the purposes of this chapter we describe this movement made up of disparate groups as the emergence of the Movements for Global Social Justice (MGSJ).[1] The controversy that the movement has generated comes not just from established interests in state and capital but also from erstwhile radical movements and writers such as Hitchens who have long argued for a global solidarity movement promoted through some variant of socialism, usually but not always associated with the Marxist-Leninist tradition. To such critics the MGSJ represents the worst kind of rainbow coalition believing it to have no coherent principles and a lack of seriousness to its activities encapsulated in the carnival-style opposition that has been developed at mobilisations such as those in Seattle, Prague, and Genoa (Friedman 2000). This chapter will situate the MGSJ in the context of the communications revolution embodied in new forms of Information and Communication Technology (ICT). The argument being made is that for the MGSJ to manifest itself in the historically unique form we see it in, would not have been possible without such a technological infrastructure. There is a deeper political irony here in that, as the post 9/11 political landscape has shown, the use of ICT has been a weapon for states to control populations with greater forms of surveillance such as the emergence of biometrics (Reid 2003), email interception (Reilly 2003), mobile phone monitoring and website activity tracking (Hentoff 2003).[2]

This, of course, is reliant upon significant cooperation between state and capital, the latter of which profit from the massive state investment in the new technologies of social control and discipline. An incongruous situation arises when the ICT revolution also empowers those who would resist this tendency. The more quickly state and capital produce new ways in which to monitor, survey, categorise and register populations through a variety of information-driven mechanisms, the more they enable the comparatively powerless opposition groups to respond by using many of the same tools to organise acts of resistance. As Manfred B.Steger points out:

> Ironically, the 'Battle of Seattle' showed that many of the new technologies hailed by globalists as the true hallmark of globalisation could be employed in the service of antiglobalist forces and their political agenda. For example the Internet has enabled the organizers of events such as Seattle to arrange for new forms of protest such as a series of demonstrations held in concert in various cities around the globe. Individuals and groups all over the world can utilize the internet to readily and rapidly recruit new members, establish dates, share experiences, arrange logistics, identify and publicize targets – activities that only fifteen years ago would have demanded much more time and money. (Steger 2001: 122)

The end of the Cold War has ushered in a period of neoliberal ideology that has largely dominated formal party politics globally but has also created the opportunity for those groups committed to social justice to organise in new forms. The Cold War period saw the establishment of a rigid political, economic and military structure that split the world largely, though not completely, into two camps, each dominated by their respective hegemon, the USA and the USSR. Whenever indigenous movements emerged arguing for independence from this framework they were generally either crushed directly or indirectly by these hegemons. Examples abound and are well known from Poland, Hungary, Czechoslovakia to South America, Congo, Central America (Chomsky and Herman 1979; Halliday 1989). To be a social movement in either bloc arguing for independence or social justice often brought about the most brutal forms of repression. In the Western bloc under US tutelage this was justified on the basis that such groups were communist sympathisers who would undermine the freedoms enjoyed in the West. Similarly in the Eastern bloc repression of opposition was based upon the need to defend socialism from the subversion of the capitalist world. However, the end of the Cold War has created the opportunity for new forms of social and political organisation to occur and organise in ways that would not have been possible during it. The emergence in Brazil of the Workers' Party and the Lula (Luiz Ignacio Lula da Silva) Presidency would most certainly not have happened during either the time of the dictatorships or even in the immediate aftermath of the return to democratic governance, post-1985. One of Brazil's largest corporate media outlets, Globo TV, organised a vicious campaign against Lula's presidential candidacy in successive elections and did everything in its power to oppose the Workers' Party (see Wilkin and Beswick, chapter 7 in this volume). So it is reasonable to observe that political openings are in place that have allowed the MGSJ to emerge.

The aim of this chapter is to illustrate the significance of this movement, to examine the ways in which ICT is essential to its mode of organisation, and in particular to focus upon the way in which the Seattle protests helped to galvanise and define their identity, leading to the emergence of the World Social Forum. Thus it will set out an analysis of the movement before looking at the way in which it was formed in the moment of the World Trade Organisation ministerial meeting in Seattle. This chapter will then consider the significance of Indymedia (alternatively know as Independent Media Centre or IMC) and its contribution to the movement, while also examining its ability to challenge state and capital. It will conclude by considering the grounds for longevity of the movement, particularly in the aftermath of 9/11 when states have sought to reassert their authority over political dissent by massive assaults on civil liberties.

Part one: understanding the MGSJ

The MGSJ emerged at the end of the millennium from a diverse number of groups connected by shared concerns including:

- The power of capital to reorganise social and economic life by the deepening of commodification into more areas than ever before. This is typified by the rise of Trade Related Intellectual Property Rights (TRIPS) through the GATT system and subsequently the WTO. In practice TRIPS have enabled corporations in the core capitalist states to deepen their control over the world's resources (Correa 1999).
- The integration of state power through new arrangements, both formal and informal, of policing and surveillance of civil populations.
- The undermining of people's right to determine and defend their own culture, values and beliefs when they conflict with the values of neoliberalism, capitalism and liberal democracy.

Thus the tendencies that fed the breakthrough of the MGSJ or that coalesced around Seattle have their roots in diverse social movements that can be traced back into contrasting locations. For example, the 1990s saw a worldwide opposition by farmers in the South to the GATT round and the liberalisation of agriculture that effectively posed a threat to the livelihood not only of the farmers themselves but to peasant communities that make up a significant sector of the world's population. As *Third World Resurgence* (based in Malaysia) and *Corporate Watch* (based in the UK) have noted, this movement, connecting a huge proportion of the world's non-white population, went largely ignored and unreported in the Western dominated global media network (Khor 1999). Elsewhere movements based around environmental concerns in Europe and North America, trade unions, women's rights, the rights of indigenous peoples, landless peoples and human rights along with myriad other concerns were struggling to deal with issues that ultimately required a global and systemic analysis and response if they were to be challenged with any success. In their different and often contradictory ways these groups were trying to give expression to new forms of solidarity that would enable them to direct their critique and action against the major structural framework underpinning the neoliberal version of the New World Order, as it came to be known. Specifically, the focus of attention for those concerned with global social justice[3] had to be directed against the international state system and capitalism itself (two factors that have served to provide the backdrop against which modernity has been formed). They also pose strict limits on the possibility of global social change and social justice, if by the latter we mean the prioritising of the satisfaction of human needs over private profit, and the promotion of universal human rights over those of distinct national interests. To push for global social justice is to raise fundamental questions about the legitimacy of state and capital that cannot be brushed away or ignored. As structural factors that both constrain and enable social action in the new world order, state and capital rest on principles that are ultimately opposed to global social justice. The national interest and the pursuit of private profit and power cannot be reconciled with the demand for the satisfaction of universal human need and human rights.

Thus in the 1990s we saw these different groups beginning to make contact with each other to organise their opposition to state and capital. A common criticism of the MGSJ is that it is largely a Northern-based body built by relatively privileged actors in the core capitalist states rather than those in the impoverished parts of the global South. Even if this were true it is a rather curious criticism in that it presupposes that there must be something *a priori* wrong with a critique of the state and capital that emerges in the core capitalist states. Any movement should only be judged on the basis of its analysis, principles and actions. To dismiss it on the grounds that it is not a product of movements in the South is to be guilty of an irrational and ideological discrimination. Nevertheless, this argument is inaccurate, the major initiatives behind the emergence of the MGSJ can be seen as being two-fold: the impact of the Zapatistas in Chiapas, Mexico from New Year's Day 1994 with their imaginative attempt to use the means of communication to promote a vision of resisting oppression and promoting solidarity that transcended their concern simply for the rights of the indigenous population of the region to a connection to subjugated peoples globally (Midnight Notes Collective 2003); and the global protest movements, rooted largely in the South, against the final GATT Round (The Uruguay Round) and its attempts to liberalise agriculture and entrench TRIPS (Trade Related Intellectual Property Rights), to the detriment of those farmers in the South who had, over centuries, cultivated and disseminated the seeds and practices that had gone into food and pharmaceutical production (Khor 1996; Shiva 1997). What this build-up to Seattle shows is that the MGSJ is not simply a movement based around a particular local, national or regional framework, but that its ambitions are genuinely global. This new coalition was formed in Chiapas in 1996 at the first Intercontinental Encuentro for Humanity and Against Neoliberalism. At this international meeting organised by the Zapatistas, thousands of representatives from social, political and environmental groups discussed global issues and were able to articulate their opposition to becoming another disposable commodity within the global economy (The Zapatistas 2002). This was followed up in 1998 by a meeting in Geneva of activists from seventy-one countries, all of whom were involved in practises at the grassroots level. Out of this emerged the loose decentralised network known as People's Global Action Against Free Trade and the WTO (abbreviated to People's Global Action or PGA). The intention was to organise transnational opposition to both transnational capital (one of the slogans of the movement is 'resistance will be as transnational as capital' (Notes from Nowhere 2003: 29)) and the reconstruction of state power and authority at a level beyond the limited democratic participation allotted to individuals within the nation-state. The manifesto that emerges from PGA is forthright and clearly a critique of both the logic of capital and state:

> 1. A very clear rejection of capitalism, imperialism and feudalism; all trade agreements, institutions and governments that promote destructive globalisation.
> 2. We reject all forms and systems of domination and discrimination including, but not limited to, patriarchy, racism and religious fundamentalism of all creeds. We embrace the full dignity of all human beings;
> 3. A confrontational attitude, since we do not think that lobbying can have a major impact in such biased and undemocratic organisations, in which transnational capital is the only real policy-maker;
> 4. A call to direct action and civil disobedience, support for social movements' struggles, advocating forms of resistance which maximise respect for life and oppressed peoples' rights, as well as the construction of local alternatives to global capitalism;
> 5. An organisational philosophy based on decentralisation and autonomy.[4]

How, though, does this movement differ from earlier social movements? And by earlier social movements we are referring to two distinct types, firstly, traditional or old social movements, which tended to be grounded in a class identity while at the same time being more institutionalised and vertically organised, with a specific headquarters, location, leadership and membership, trade unions being the most global example here. Second, we refer to new social movements as described by Alberto Melucci and Clause Offe (Melucci 1995; Offe 1985). New social movements, are most commonly associated with the groups that emerged in the West in the 1960s and 1970s with their concern over such issues as human rights, nuclear weapons, sexuality, gender and the environment. Often seen as the preserve of sections of the middle classes in Europe and North America they had, by the 1990s, become to a certain degree familiar, legitimate and an important component of formal political structures (Ray 1993; Della Porta et al. 1999). Greenpeace is a good example of an organisation that has strived to marry its commitment to radical activism with a need to develop a more insider-based approach that might influence the political and economic institutions that they criticise. At the most extreme, groups that were part of the earlier waves of social movements were criticised in the 1990s for becoming severely compromised by their relations with the state and political parties. This crisis of identity is one that has come to concern these groups as they strive to maintain a distinct and oppositional identity apart from existing structures of governance. Ian Clark makes the point that there is a view within the global South that sees some segments of civil society in the North (such as international non-governmental organisations) as tainted by their nearness to conventional political powers, so much so that they 'should be regarded not as part of the resistance movement . . . but instead as the shock troops of Empire, and hence an integral part of the fabric of governance' (Clark 2003: 78; see also Hardt and Negri 2000).

While we recognise common features, attributes and points of overlap between earlier and contemporary forms of social movements, there are, in fact, clear distinctions that hinge on two factors: (1) the failure of traditional forms of anti-capitalist political ideology and (2) the emergence of the ICT revolution that has transformed the mode of organisation for contemporary social movements. For the contemporary social movements embodied in the MGSJ, the nature of their organisation is quite different. There is no centralised hierarchy directing movement activities. What mobilisations in places such as Seattle and Genoa illustrate is that such a movement is capable of organising relatively spontaneously around local groups who would act on behalf of the wider movement without the necessity of any formalised hierarchical leadership structures. Thus in Seattle the local Direct Action Network and in Genoa the Genoa Social Forum were both crucial in establishing the infrastructure that enabled the protests to take place. Membership is not determined by fees or commitment to a single issue or goal. By necessity the MGSJ has to embrace and reconcile diverse goals and aims if it is to realise the broad vision of attaining the satisfaction of universal human needs and human rights. In addition, it is clear that MGSJ is not bound by commitment to past political ideologies. The failure of Marxist and social democratic forms of socialism has freed many of the younger activists within the movement who are not ideologically constrained by any form of historical or emotional commitment to a particular doctrine. It is often noted that the current movement seems to have borrowed more from anarchism than Marxism in terms of its decentralised organisation, its recognition of multiple forms of oppression and its commitment to activism over the need to build a party or intellectual base for its key thinkers (Graber 2002; Chesters 2003).

The limitations of this movement are equally clear and much focused upon by their opponents. The weaknesses tend to take two distinct forms:

Ideology

> To put several hundred such people in a big hotel with instructions to 'determine the facts behind the assertions of anti-globalisation protesters' and 'recommend policies to address the most contentious issues' would be great fun for outsiders. It would be like watching scorpions in a bottle. It is wrong to imagine that the protesters agree even among themselves'. (Martin Wolf, 'Responding to the Anti-globalisation Protestors', *Financial Times*, 4 September 2001)

There is no single coherent ideological framework that can unite the MGSJ. As was seen at Seattle, the movement embraces orthodox trade union groups led by traditional, hierarchies of authority demanding protection for US workers from foreign competition, alongside those groups committed to global forms of social justice. Where traditional political parties based in particular nation-states have been built around coherent constitutional and institutional frameworks, the MGSJ is very different. In part this reflects its ambitions which are to build a movement that can express the concerns of people from very different cultures and with strikingly different needs. Of course it can be argued that both Liberalism and Socialism in both their Marxist and Social Democratic forms, have historically been global movements. In practice, however, neither Liberalism nor Socialism have been able to overcome either the boundary of the nation-state and the national interest and their universal principles have run aground against the imperialist interests of the nation-states in which they have been based. Historically both China and the Soviet Union sacrificed internationalism for national interest in the manner of any great power. Likewise the US and the UK were only really committed to principles of liberal economic theory when they were the most powerful trading nations in the world and in a position to reap the rewards of free trade (Wilkin 2001). As soon as this window of control began to narrow both the US and the UK sought to replace this with a state-managed capitalist trading system that protected the interests of the core capitalist states against the global South. So to criticise the MGSJ for a lack of ideological coherence is also a criticism that could be laid against the established political ideologies that shaped state politics in the twentieth century and continue to do so in the twenty-first century.

Organisation and representation

A second strand of criticism has been that, without formal organisation, the MGSJ is not in a position to bargain and negotiate with existing political and economic interests. Who, in effect, are their leaders and whom do they represent? This is an understandable but misguided criticism. The MGSJ does not, thus far, espouse the need for leaders in the classic political sense. In this respect it owes more to anarchism than it does to liberal, socialist or conservative political traditions. The question of representation is more pertinent. For example *The Economist* questioned whether the MGSJ represents 'a dangerous shift of power to unelected and unaccountable special interest groups?' (*The Economist*, Editorial: 'The Non- governmental Order', 1 December 1999).[5]

Although rhetorically groups such as the Zapatistas have claimed to speak for diverse oppressed groups, the wretched of the earth perhaps, in Frantz Fanon's terms (Fanon 1965), it is far from clear that the movement has legitimacy in any traditional political sense. This is not altogether surprising, it is not seeking a mandate for governance so much as creating a vehicle for dissent in an era where politics has become so constrained that it is impossible to find a government or major international organisation that does not espouse commitment to some variant of neoliberal orthodoxy (Hamilton 2003). Where this does happen, with governments in Argentina, Haiti, Brazil and Venezuela, for example, traditional forms of imperialist pressure are brought to bear in order to discipline the government and population, in the form of capital flight, military coup, the fomentation of protest and unrest through the sponsorship of or support for pro-Western clients in the country. To become part of the mainstream political landscape would be a severe problem for the MGSJ as it would immediately open itself up to the kind of control by state and capital that it seeks to resist. The question of representation remains, however, and the extent to which the movement remains open, free, and committed to democratic principles, will help to answer the question posed by *The Economist* editorial.

This section sets out the background to the MGSJ. What we now intend to do is examine it in practice through the example of the Seattle protests in order to illustrate the ways in which the movement has used ICT to organise its activities and to promote democratic practice. Contrary to the assumptions implicit in *The Economist* editorial, the MGSJ is interested in deepening and extending democracy, not undermining it, if by democracy we mean the control by people over all aspects of their lives. For a liberal propaganda outlet such as *The Economist* it is not possible to go beyond the formalities of liberal democracy to consider democracy in the workplace, for example. However, the MGSJ, there can be no *a priori* constraints on the meaning of democracy. So what does Seattle mean for the movement and the part that ICT plays in its organisation?

Part two: breaking through – the importance of Seattle

> It is hard to know which was worse – watching the militants dress parade their ignorance through the streets of Seattle, or listening to their lame-brained governments respond to the 'arguments'. (*The Economist*, Editorial: 'Clueless in Seattle', 4 December 1999)

> What we saw in Seattle across the tumultuous day stretching from November 28 through December 3, 1999, and then in Davos, Switzerland, Washington, D.C., Philadelphia, Los Angeles and Prague was the flowering of a new radical movement in America and across the world, rambunctious, anarchic, internationalist, well informed and in many ways more imaginative and supple than kindred popular eruptions in recent decades'. (Alexander Cockburn and Jeffrey St. Claire, Five Days that Shook the World, p. 1)

The protests at Seattle organised around the WTO meetings proved to be a defining moment in the emergence of the MGSJ. As the above quotations illustrated, it both provoked the ire and scorn of establishment interests and also provided a galvanising moment for others who saw in it a glimmer of the possibilities of a new form of global solidarity that would enable a plurality of voices to listen, learn and understand the nature of their respective goals and work accordingly for mutual aid and benefit. Historically movements for social change that are driven from below rather than above have been vulnerable to all kinds of divisions around ideology, tactics, strategies, gender and nationality. The promise of the MGSJ was that it had brought together disparate groups with a view to promoting communication and organisation amongst them. In this section we will draw out the symbolic significance of Seattle for the movement, how it sought to organise and the integral part that ICT plays in this and in the rise of the Indymedia network that Seattle brought into being.

Building Seattle

There is no doubt that the Seattle protests took the world's media, political and economic elites by surprise.[6] However, it would be a mistake to see this as being simply a spontaneous outpouring of dissent at the policies of the WTO. On the contrary, the protests were the result of skilful planning, organisation and communication, largely organised through the local Seattle Direct Action Network. This is a good example of the decentralised nature of the MGSJ. Setting itself up as an alternative to the formal meetings of the WTO, World Bank, the International Monetary Fund (IMF), NATO, the World Economic Forum or the G8, it aims to challenge the agenda of those meetings wherever they occur, and it is the local (to the areas where these gatherings, meetings and summits take place) activist networks that seek to organise the response. We will also point out here how a form of ICT such as the internet has been a key organising tool for such mobilisations. Realizing that the internet was originally developed by the US Department of Defence[7] as a means of communication, command and control during a potential nuclear war is another example of the way in which ICT has become a mechanism to aid opposition groups in organising and challenging the authority of states. The obvious advantage that the internet brings to those organising such protests is that it allows for instant, diverse, multiple and global communication. Thus the organisers of Seattle were able to set their sights high. Although it was dominated by representatives from North America and Europe, it was important that at least a cross-section of groups from the South were able to be present and to be seen. Critics understandably have pointed out that the meetings were dominated by white people and this is an important challenge for the MGSJ (Martinez 1999). If it is to succeed in its aims it must find ways of bringing together a representation of all those interests collected under its mantle. That said, as we have demonstrated above, it would be churlish to say that the movement is simply limited by the representation at Seattle. Seattle is an early attempt to organise such a movement, an essential event in its beginning. It is one of the movements starting points[8] and as such brings out all manner of weaknesses and contradictions. These, however, are issues to be addressed and not necessarily barriers that cannot be transcended.

The aims and ambitions of the organisers and participants at the Seattle protests were great. This was not simply to be a traditional march-and-rally-type protest. On the contrary, the movement has tried to develop a very different form of opposition that communicates a more libertarian spirit. Not only were the protestors there for the duration of the trade negotiations, they also wanted to turn the occasion into a meaningful democratic forum. Although the overall goal of forcing the abandonment of the negotiations was achieved the ambitions of the MGSJ were much broader. Thus throughout the week a variety of meetings and events were held to bring together the protestors, the local Seattle community and the elites gathered at the meetings. WTO organisers had even arranged public forums to defend themselves from the criticism of the protestors, although as the Seattle press suggested, by and large the official spokespeople lost their case (Paulson 1999; Henwood 1999; George 2000).[9] Whether this was because of the arguments, the audience or the weight of opposition is not noted. Equally, the protests enabled a range of diverse groups to discuss, organise and find grounds for solidarity that they might once have thought unlikely, if not impossible. The significance of Seattle, then, is that having happened once, it laid the foundations for the emergence of an active international civil society that could challenge state and capital anywhere and everywhere. Traditional spatial and temporal constraints, whilst not completely removed, were certainly proving to be far less effective in undermining opposition to state and capital.[10]

The idea being expressed here was that not only was there a moral and emotional opposition to the impact of WTO polices but that there is also an intellectual analysis being developed that could put forward a coherent critique of these institutions. *The Economist*'s line was not entirely representative of the mainstream Western media coverage of the Seattle protests but it raises an interesting point about the importance of power and representation in global politics. It far easier to dismiss the protestors at Seattle as 'a rabble' when compared to the collectively suited and manicured representatives of the world's governments and corporations. Indeed, the power of representation is a key battleground for the movement in that legitimacy is not simply an outcome of electoral mandates but is also reflected in the very details of the appearance of the elites gathered at Seattle: a cursory glance of the group pictures that go with any such global gatherings, meetings or summits reveals a uniformity of appearance that represents power, authority and legitimacy – conservative grey or black suits, neat hair, overwhelmingly men (an added irony when it is considered that one of the criticisms of the movement is that it is male dominated). The ideological importance of appearance in bestowing legitimacy upon the elites and their spokespeople has been noted in some depth by Cynthia Enloe in her work on gender, identity and international relations (Enloe 2004). By contrast the MGSJ was composed of such diverse bodies as the United Steelworkers of America (USWA), The Topless Santa Cruz Lesbian Avengers (who commented, 'When we got here, the steelworkers weren't very queer-friendly. As the week wore on, they got more comfortable with us. My nipples stand in solidarity with the steelworkers and the Teamsters and all the labouring peoples' (Henwood 1999)), Asian Indigenous Woman's Network, People for Fair Trade, and the Chilean Ecological Network. It is estimated that no fewer than 700 groups were represented at the protests (Thomas 2000: 66–67). The issue here is not that the media wilfully communicate the idea that the protestors at Seattle are necessarily a rabble or 'ignorant', in *The Economist's* words.[11] Rather, so ingrained in global political culture are the symbols of what constitutes a credible, legitimate, authoritative figures (the men in suits we discussed earlier) that it is almost impossible to break through that barrier. This is precisely what power and authority convey in the current phase of global politics, a series of symbols and norms that are conforming to an ideal-type of authoritative figure. As Beder notes elsewhere in this volume (chapter 6), the rise and integration of public relations into the political and economic world serves to reinforce this narrowing of representation and legitimacy. Simply put, in part it doesn't matter what the protestors say, they just don't look right. They are already starting from a disadvantaged position in terms of how they are represented by the media. The TV camera is not neutral in how it highlights *what the protestors are*, it also highlights *what they are not*. They do not look like the world's political and economic elites. They may not even look like the norm of reasonable people. This is a major communicative task for the movement and it has sought to use imaginative tactics to challenge and shatter the consensus surrounding neoliberalism and representations of what is normal and acceptable. Whether it is in the form of pie-throwing anarchists targeting representatives of the world's political and economic elites for ritual humiliation by flan-flinging (Biotic Baking Brigade 2004), or through the organising public meetings to bring together diverse groups so that a dialogue can emerge and perhaps a consensus can be reached on key issues, the MGSJ has had in part to fight a guerrilla war against the power of PR and the management of image, authority and legitimacy. So how can the MGSJ hope to challenge the elite driven norms and values of the global corporate media?

Part three: Indymedia – resisting the corporate mainstream

Indymedia is a form of alternative media that was created in direct opposition to the mainstream corporate media. As we will demonstrate, it asserts its independence from both state and capital, and holds values and uses organisational strategies that are a challenge to those of mainstream media outlets. As we saw in Part two, Indymedia was originally set up to give a different version of the events in Seattle to that of the mainstream media. Since that time, it has been challenging the mainstream media's coverage in areas as diverse as the war on Iraq, the implementation of the Kyoto Treaty, and socio-political changes in Argentina. Also, and arguably more significantly, it covers issues and events that the major media will vaguely note or refuse to touch such as the suffering caused by privatisation in South Africa, the curtailing of civil liberties since 9/11, and forms of resistance to state and capital that are occurring all the time. It produces newspapers,[12] radio programmes, and documentaries covering protest activities[13] but it is mainly know for its website which has received literally millions of visits since it was set up in 1999. It offers forms of representation that subvert conventional images of authority and legitimacy.

Those within the Indymedia network reject the major media for a number of reasons. The first is that media outlets are corporate enterprises and therefore primarily driven by profit. To protect and increase these profits they are cautious about or altogether avoid material that raises questions about the established socio-political order, as by avoiding broadcasting or printing contentious material they make themselves more appealing to advertisers (Schudson 1993; Herman and Chomsky 1995; Soley 1997). This is essential because for those corporations in both broadcast and print media, advertising is their main source of profits. Secondly, major media organisations are hierarchically structured. Their output is carefully controlled by editors, managers and executives who tend to share certain values, political perspectives, and understandings of the world (Gans 1979; Herman 1986; McQuail 1987). While voices of dissent may occasionally make their way into the mainstream media their appearance makes up no more that a negligible portion of overall media output. It must be stated here that mainstream media output is not completely homogenous and unable to consider anything beyond what is ideologically acceptable to elite interests, there are certain outlets that are more open to social justice issues and those who advocate them, however, they will not provide the kind of dissenting views and perspectives that are provided by Indymedia.[14] Third, the mainstream media are heavily reliant on the politicians, bureaucrats, think tanks (such as the Cato Institute, Adam Smith Institute, RAND Corporation, and Brookings Institution), PR firms, and academics as sources of information (Lee and Solomon 1991; Stauber and Rampton 1995; Ewen 1996; Solomon 1999; Dolny 2001; McCullagh 2002; Cottle 2003). These sources give official (in the case of representatives of the state) or establishment approved (in the case of non-state sources) versions of events and perspectives on significant issues. Generally, this results in media output being homogenised, sanitised and supportive of the status quo (see Beder, chapter 6 in this volume).

In contrast, Indymedia is not driven by the profit motive. Instead, it is totally dependent on the voluntary efforts of journalists, photographers, sound recordists, web designers, computer technicians and documentary makers, who give their time and resources in order to free Indymedia from the burden of market imperatives. It is, therefore, able to criticise transnational corporations, the state and international financial institutions to an extent that the mainstream media are not able to do because of their economic constraints. Furthermore, Indymedia is built on a decentralised network, in other words, it is not based on an organisational model where local offices answer to a central headquarters. Starkly contrasting the structure of the corporate media, the decentralised network that makes up Indymedia operates in a non-hierarchical way so that control by editors, managers and executives does not become an issue. What appear in place of hierarchical structures are two organisational layers that help preserve its independence. First, there is a vast and growing network of local Indymedia sites all maintaining their autonomy within the wider network. Next, each of these local sites is run collaboratively by media activists within the particular geographical area covered by the site. This two-fold layering helps to ensure the avoidance of the kind of centralisation and careful regulation (in terms of the values, beliefs and meanings) that constrict the output of the mainstream media and assure that it will fall within the established editorial parameters. What this decentralisation within Indymedia does is encourage 'immense freedom, creativity and innovation on the part of each local centre and each individual contributor, while each still remains connected to a network for the sharing of ideas, visions, analysis research stories and even hardware' (Nogueira 2002: 294).

For reasons we have just outlined, Indymedia is able to give space to forms of resistance to state and capital that the mainstream maintains a blind spot to. Indymedia aims to offer an alternative to what it sees as the ideologically narrow vision of the mainstream media. In seeking out critical views, marginalised voices and perspectives from the grassroots, Indymedia creates media output that represents, reflects and encourages heterogeneity within what may be understood as global civil society.

Of course there are problems with Indymedia that are inherent to its mode of organisation. For example, by encouraging diversity it also suffers the problems of fragmentation. Having so many local sites and such an extensive variety of media activists connected within a decentralised network, while in some ways being a virtue, may also potentially lead to problems with decision making and editorial policy. Another problem is that contributions may seem unprofessional in their presentation because Indymedia's production values may appear inferior to those of the mainstream. Drawing out further points on the power of representation (see Part two above), Indymedia's lack of concern for glossy corporate production values may mean that it is prevented from being seen as having the kind of authority and legitimacy that the mainstream enjoys. However, what is seemingly a weakness for Indymedia may also be a strength. This is because its production values and ethos counters the kind of uniform and formulaic output of the mainstream. In avoiding the conventions that that the mainstream adheres to, it provides information and reporting with a degree of sincerity, immediacy and authenticity the mainstream cannot attain.

A lack of resources is also a perennial problem for genuinely grassroots non-profit- making endeavours such as Indymedia. Indymedia web-based reports are accessed free of charge. And unlike prominent non-governmental organisations such as Oxfam, Amnesty International and Greenpeace, Indymedia does not carry out any fundraising campaigns to support its efforts. Therefore, because it receives very limited financial backing, Indymedia is reliant on donations of labour, equipment and physical space for the maintenance and expansion of its network. Finally, Indymedia also suffers from constraints on its distribution capabilities. As already indicated, the network is rapidly expanding but the majority of its output is still web based, therefore, its distribution is somewhat limited to those with access to the internet. However, it does make efforts to span this digital divide as Indymedia journalist Jeff Perlstein explains:

> We were especially concerned with the way the Internet has grown and how access by a certain segment of the population has grown, and so there's an issue of what's called a 'digital divide' [wherein the vast majority of the world does not have internet or even telephone access]. So we set about to do this innovative thing, linking high and low technologies, or old and new technologies . . . For example, we posted audio, video, text, and photos, all these different mediums, to the site, and would easily download. Then community

radio stations, cable access stations, even community based organizations internationally could download and distribute them. (as quoted in Notes from Nowhere 2003: 232)

The following section will examine the relationship between Indymedia and the MGSJ by considering: (1) How it reflects the movement in its structure and values; (2) The way it contributes to the self-awareness, ideas and practical action of the movement.

In structural terms, Indymedia mirrors the anti-hierarchical organisational form of the mass movement. Espousing egalitarian and direct democratic principles, both the movement and the media network reject the idea of having established positions within a hierarchical framework. Because they adhere to the principle of promoting autonomy, they dismiss the idea that permanent leaders are needed to organise and direct a movement of resistance. What Indymedia promotes and practises instead is a belief in the idea of people working collaboratively and relating to one another on an equal basis. Also in terms of structure, like the MGSJ, Indymedia is decentralised and global. The direct action and do-it-yourself (or DIY) ethos[15] of the movement spills over into Indymedia; as one of its rallying cries suggests, 'Don't hate the media, be the media'. Media activists within the organisation do not accept the picture of the world that the mainstream project. So combining it critique of the major media with their DIY ethos, they grab hold of their cameras, keyboards and pens and make their objections through creative, autonomous and direct interventions. ITC has helped to enable those within the movement to make their own media. New and affordable computer, video, satellite and digital technologies have allowed activist to create media to a standard of quality and level of distribution that until recently would only have been obtainable by well funded corporate outlets.

Indymedia contributes to the self-awareness, ideas and practical action of the movement in a number of ways. By reporting on the movement's activities and facilitating communication between its various parts, Indymedia helps to give the MGSJ a sense of itself. It raises the movement's awareness of its global dimensions, accomplishments and capabilities. On any visit to the website you can get a sense of the diversity and scale of the movement by receiving information about campaigns, actions and demonstrations that are occurring in places as far removed from each other as Manila, Ambazonia and Vancouver. For example, an activist in Istanbul can go onto her/his local Indymedia site and gain a sense of solidarity with other activists in Moldova, Guadalajara and Tel Aviv. By reporting on and documenting the movement's activities in all its shapes and sizes (not just the large scale, high-profile mobilisations such as those that took place in Seattle, Genoa or Quebec) it gives visitors to the site a knowledge of the considerable quantity and forms of resistance that are happening globally. Moreover, it has the potential to widen the movement, by informing the uninitiated of recent achievements and future activities they may in turn be inspired to become active within it. Through the information, discussions and debates the Indymedia site offers it can arm activists with empirical ammunition that will strengthen their own arsenal of arguments and ideas. And finally, it is an invaluable tool for organising local, regional and international campaigns, actions and demonstrations. Indymedia sites function as very practical tools for those who wish to become involved the activities of the movement. Provided one has internet access, she or he is only a few clicks away from practical information such as contact numbers and internet links to groups within the movement, event schedules, maps and legal information that will help them to take part in protest activities.

The provision of infrastructure by the ITC revolution enables the MGSJ, aided by the Indymedia network, to organise a loose, decentralised framework for analysis and activism as a means to challenge the interests of state and capital. With respect to Audre Lorde, the master's tools are, to some extent, being used to dismantle the master's house.[16]

Indymedia goes far beyond being simply an alternative media outlet. It is a highly political intervention in that it contests conventionally accepted versions of events and the political trajectories they lead to. In response to these accepted versions and trajectories, Indymedia challenges those who receive its dissenting reports, images and assessments to become politically engaged themselves. And this may contribute to the greater normative aim of attempting to change these political trajectories and point them in directions that will lead to deepening degrees of social justice. In its own words: 'The Independent Media Center is a network of collectively run media outlets for the creation of radical, accurate, and passionate tellings of the truth. We work out of a love and inspiration for people who continue to work for a better world, despite corporate media's distortions and unwillingness to cover the efforts to free humanity' (www.indymedia.org/en/static/about.shtml).

Conclusions: a radical departure?

> The world's political structures are completely obsolete . . . the critical issue of our time is the conceptual conflict between the global optimisation of resources and the independence of nation-states. (Jacques Maison Rouge, former Chief Officer for European Operations of IBM and of the European Bank for Reconstruction and Development)[17]

Maison Rouge's observation is made from the perspective of the elite interests that he represents and is meant to be a critique of the way in which states need to dismantle the barriers that stand in the way of a properly functioning capitalist market economy. However, the truth that he raises cuts in different directions. The world's political structures are considered to be obsolete for those in the MGSJ just as much as for the capitalist investors Maison Rouge promotes. State structures no longer offer a significant mechanism to protect the world's working and non-working populations from the demands of capitalism or the coercive and disciplining mechanism of the state. Global social justice runs against the grain of the two major structures that have shaped the modern world system: the national interest of imperialist states and the private interest and pursuit of profit of capital. For the movement to attain its goals something fundamental has to happen to transform the way in which politics, economy and culture are produced and reproduced. Unintentionally Maison Rouge sets out the fault line for the global socio-political struggle taking place. However, is it realistic to talk of the movement as being an example of global resistance? Perhaps it makes more sense to describe it as a project for global resistance that is in the making. Thus far the movement has been using and refining a communication infrastructure that allows it to promote dialogue between different groups within the MGSJ, organise its activities and agitate against the state and capital. Communication is both essential to its activities and the means by which a new political agenda can be formed that is genuinely beyond the spatial and temporal constraints of state, nation and capital. It is, if you like, a work in progress.

Indymedia has unarguably had great success already, far surpassing the expectations of its founding contributors. There has never been an independent media network of anything like the scope that Indymedia has attained already. By its bringing together of activists, facilitating of mass mobilisations (in given areas as well as synchronous worldwide protests) and documenting a resistance movement on a global scale, Indymedia has made great gains compared with the achievements of earlier forms of independent media. As for the MGSJ, mobilisations of so many people and of such diversity would be difficult to understand as anything but successful in social movement terms. And while the post-9/11 socio-political climate may have compounded risks and difficulties for those protesting, especially in the US where the curtailment of civil liberties has been especially aggressive (Chang 2002), mobilisations such as those witnessed in Miami contesting the Free Trade Area of the Americas (FTAA) in November 2003 and New York against the Republican Party National Convention in August 2004 would indicate that the determination to resist the neoliberal agenda has not diminished. The same is true of Indymedia which despite having suffered violent attacks by the state during mobilizations in Italy and France/ Switzerland as well as harassment and free speech assaults by the FBI, still shows a complete determination to present perspectives contesting the status quo and record the history of the MGSJ. The significance of international events such as Seattle, Genoa, Quebec and Prague as well as a host of the nationally based protests is to symbolise that, in a time where political debate is largely denuded of substance in the mainstream political parties, alternative spaces for dialogue and action are being developed globally, outside those institutions.

Notes

1 Clearly there is no agreement amongst these groups over a suitable generic title and the one we use here is merely for analytic convenience and is not intended to suggest a homogeneity that does not exist in theory or practice.

2 Legislation which has extended the surveillance powers of the state such as the USA PATRIOT Act in the US and the Anti-Terrorism, Crime and Security Act of 2001 in the UK were passed in the post-9/11 anti-terrorist hysteria. The implications for basic civil liberties has been extremely worrying.

3 We are aware of the contested nature of the term 'social justice', recognizing that it is used by those within the movement who believe the capitalist system can be reformed as well as those within the movement who believe social justice is not possible within a global economic system structure by capitalist social (in the broadest sense) relations.

4 For information on the PGA consult its website at www.nadir.org/nadir/initiativ /agp/index.htm.

5 See also Applebaum 2001.

6 We use 'elite' as a general term to denote those in positions of power that benefit from the prevailing socio-political relations and therefore seek to preserve those relations as they exist. Elites hold positions within the realm of the state and capital as well as civil society. They act as representative spokespeople for dominant class alliances.

7 At the time the internet was known as Advanced Research Projects Agency Network or ARPANET. See Hauben 2004.

8 As noted earlier the movement has its roots in the South, but even in the North there were significant mobilisations pre-dating Seattle such as the 1998 protests against the WTO in Geneva or the concerted multi–geographic mass actions against the G8 summit in Cologne on 18 June 1999.

9 For reports of the events at the WTO ministerial meetings see any of the following: *WTO Watch; Seattle Daily Journal of Commerce; Seattle Times*.

10 The hostility of the business press can in part be reasonably interpreted as recognition of this fact.

11 Though there is much evidence to suggest that the US press coverage in the mainstream media is overwhelmingly a propaganda outlet for elite interests and interpretations of Seattle. Interestingly, there has been the occasional glimmer of recognition with in the mainstream media and certain academic institutions in the US that the rest of the world does not share the self-perception of its role in world order as set out by its political elites. See *Newsweek* on anti-Americanism (31-1-2000). As *Newsweek*'s coverage and subsequent letters page response reveal, critiques of US State and corporate power are often taken to be anti-Americanism. The failure to recognise this distinction is the knee-jerk response of well meaning (and less well-meaning) liberals around the world.

12 It mainly produces newspapers for large protests events but some Independent Media Centres such as Indymedia in New York City have been producing newspapers regularly. Their bi-weekly, called the *Indypendent*, is now reaching tens of thousands.

13 For example see Indymedia's coverage of the Seattle protests: *Showdown in Seattle: Five Days that Shook the WTO*, 1999, Indymedia's look at resistance in

Argentina: *The Land, the Street and the Square*, 2001, or its reporting on the Zapatistas' arrival in Mexico City *A Storm from the Mountain: The Zapatistas take Mexico City*, 2001.

14 For example the coverage of the events in Seattle by more progressive outlets such as the *Guardian* and the *Independent* in the UK accepts many of the rest of the mainstreams assumptions and prejudices about the movement. See their coverage from 30 November 1999 to 4 December 1999.

15 This DIY ethos, which is very much a part of the MGSJ, can be traced back to protest movements of the late 1980s/early 1990s (if not further). See Mckay1996. and Mckay 1999.

16 Lorde also warns that, 'They may allow us to temporarily beat him at his own game, but they will never enable us to bring about genuine change'. Lorde 1984.

17 As quoted in Mulgan 1991 at p. 220.

The global public sphere: fourth estate or new world information disorder?

Recent years have witnessed major change in the technological and political environments within which news and information media operate. The introduction of transnational satellite broadcasting in the 1980s with Cable News Network (Flournoy 1992), and the emergence of the internet as a global mass medium in the 1990s have produced an unprecedented expansion, acceleration and pluralisation of information flow across the world. Western-based companies such as CNN and BBC World are accessed by hundreds of millions of viewers, while Al Jazeera and other non-Western providers have also expanded their reach and influence, especially since September 11 and the onset of the 'war on terror'. Online, by the end of 2002 there were nearly 600 million regular users of the internet worldwide, and rapid expansion continues. In China alone there will be an estimated 300 million net users by 2008. Online journalism sites have proliferated since the pioneering days of the early 1990s (McNair 1998), and now most print and broadcast media outlets have an online presence. In addition to the digitisation of established media organisations there are, amongst the millions, soon to be billions, of net users worldwide, tens of thousands of online diarists, columnists and web loggers (bloggers), all filling the internet with news, commentary and analysis of variable quality.

Within media and communication studies assessments of the implications of this emerging global news network have varied from deep pessimism to utopian optimism. The former has been concerned with the negative political consequences of imbalances in information flow, viewing globalised news as, for example, 'one of the most important instruments of domination, a currency of power' (Boyd-Barrett and Kishan Thussu 1992). The flow of transnational information has been perceived to be one sided, top-down, West-East, North-South, contributing to the maintenance of what is characterised as Anglo-American cultural imperialism. UNESCO's New World Information and Communication Order (NWCIO) agenda was informed by this perspective, viewing globalisation as a negative cultural trend because it is dominated by America and a handful of other countries, which have used control of information to pursue their national strategic interests against the competing pressures of anti-capitalist development and local democracy.

This analysis resonated in the post-Second World War era of East-West superpower conflict, when the world was divided into two ideologically hostile camps, and information was a key instrument of propaganda. Since the end of the Cold War, however, the concept of the NWICO, and with it that of cultural imperialism has fallen out of favour, replaced by greater recognition of the progressive potential of free flows of news and information on the countries of the post-Soviet and developing world, especially those with authoritarian political systems which had long sought protection from 'cultural imperialism' in order to preserve the interests of local elites.[1] Some observers have shifted their critical ground to emphasise the negative effects of 'the implantation of the commercial model of communication' (Herman and McChesney 1997) associated with cultural globalisation. Rather than reflecting concern about the consequences, real or imagined, of Anglo-American domination on those societies which are currently experiencing cultural globalisation, anxiety is here premised on the assumption that commercialisation is in itself an inappropriate model for global media development, if compared for example with public service broadcasting of the British type. Commercialisation is assumed to work against the establishment of the free and independent media required to support properly functioning democracies. As the internet has expanded, however, some sociologists and media scholars have expressed more optimistic positions. Writing in 1996 E. R. Girardet observed that

> today, authoritarian regimes such as those in Saudi Arabia, China, or Iran are finding that they cannot enjoy the benefits of modern communications without allowing minority (or majority) ethnic, tribal, religious, political or generational groups to dip into the Internet or tune into outside BBC, CNN, or MTV satellite broadcasts for news and entertainment. For the first time, hundreds of millions, if not billions, of people around the world are enjoying the freedom of access to outside information sources over which their governments have no control. (1996: 53)

From this perspective the evolution of satellite and internet technology creates possibilities for the establishment at the global level of the kind of rational communicative space described by Jürgen Habermas (1989) in his classic formulation of the public sphere. Just as newspapers formed what eighteenth-century English philosopher Edmund Burke termed a 'fourth estate', facilitating the bourgeois revolutions and the development of democracy within the nation states of early modern Europe (Eisenstein 1983), contemporary sociologists of communication are speculating on the possibility that rolling news and online media may advance the prospects of democracy and human dignity across the world. Underpinning their optimism is the fact that from China to Iran, and Cuba to Afghanistan, the emergence of new information and communication technologies (NICTs) has made political

environments more volatile, less predictable, and less amenable to traditional forms of state control of the media. Some adherents to this optimistic
view are motivated by post-Cold War ideological triumphalism of the kind
which regards the global march of democracy and market capitalism as
unstoppable. Others argue that, notwithstanding its continuing dominance
by big transnational capital, the current generation of digitised, interactive
NICTs, linking the speed and capacity of computers with the global reach of
satellites, usher in a qualitatively new era of human communication, with
major implications for social and cultural evolution in the coming decades.
Whatever their ideological motivation, the optimists are linked by their
belief that digitisation and democratisation are linked processes, and that
globalised journalism can act as a force for social and political progress.

A third perspective, lying somewhere between the pessimistic and the
optimistic positions, asserts that the capacity of NICTs to act as a global
fourth estate for the twenty-first century depends on the circumstances prevailing in individual countries. William Atkins and others have cautioned
that the presence of new media technologies in a particular country or region
cannot by itself generate democracy. As he puts it, 'media information can
only contribute to change if other social, political and economic conditions
are at a particular stage and are receptive to the information and able to act
upon it' (2002: 68). Kalathil and Boas agree that 'information technology is
challenging and helping to transform authoritarianism. Yet information
technology alone is unlikely to bring about its demise' (2003: x). Ingrid
Volkmer argues that 'the media act as reflectors of a global reality which is
otherwise inaccessible and yet which increasingly shapes the context for the
identity of political communities within a new global public sphere' (2002:
237). Such assessments assume that the progressive impact of these new
media cannot be taken for granted, and cannot be predicted in isolation from
consideration of the local political, economic and cultural factors which constrain or encourage their adoption, and which shape their use.

This chapter shares that caution. It focuses on the potential of NICTs and
their use by journalists, not just for global democratisation but for new
forms of despotism – not least the modern McCarthyism of some of the democratic world's more populist media as they find their capacity to interro-
gate, expose and vilify presidents and prime ministers, princes and priests,
hugely enhanced by the communicative power of NICTs. It argues that real-
time news and online media have the potential to unleash disorder and
chaos, as much as the rational critical scrutiny expected of the ideal fourth
estate. NICTs, I will suggest, may destabilise power as much as democratise
it, with consequences which may be negative or positive, depending on
circumstances. Moreover, these impacts may be felt in advanced capitalist
democracies as much as authoritarian societies. Before the rise of the internet to its present level of saturation McKenzie Wark discussed cultural globalisation in terms of 'the unpredictable movement of information', noting

that 'the immediacy of information can create crises' (1994). In 1995 Paul Virilio wrote of 'the sudden bewildering Babel clamour of the world-city, the untimely mix of the global and the local' (1997). Media researchers have been working for at least a decade on 'the CNN effect' (Gowing 1994; Natsios 1996; Robinson 2002), referring to the impact of relatively unedited real-time news coverage on policy-makers in democratic countries. In previous work I have argued for a notion of cultural chaos as potentially helpful in understanding the unpredictability and uncertainty of the emerging global information environment (McNair 1998, 2003), echoing Hamelink's view that the time has come for media sociology to 'accept that contradiction and chaos are indeed the very characteristics of reality' (1998: 65). In assessing the potential of NICTs and the emerging global media system to act as a fourth estate, or as something rather less noble, this chapter aims to embody that spirit.

Mapping the global media

In the five hundred years or so since the invention of the first newspapers (Raymond, 1996) the evolution of journalistic media has been governed by one inexorable trend – what Anthony Giddens has called the erosion of *time-space distantiation* (1990). In simple terms, the gap in time between an event's taking place and its cultural manifestation as news or some other form of journalism (feature articles, commentary, documentary, etc.) has shrunk, from the weeks and months experienced by the typical sixteenth century correspondent to the instantaneous transmission (give or take a fraction of a light second) of an event such as the September 11 attacks on the World Trade Centre. News is no longer just something that happened in the past. It can be happening right now, even as we watch coverage of it live on TV or by video stream on the internet.

Time-space distantiation also refers to the *geographical* separation between events and their reportage. Thanks to the enhanced realism of contemporary media, and assuming that the required newsgathering resources are in place, people sitting at home in London or Glasgow can now experience events happening anywhere in the world with an unsettling immediacy. During the Iraqi war of 2003, for example, BBC News 24 broadcast live footage of Saddam's soldiers in Baghdad pursuing suspected American airmen shot down over the city. Thousands of miles away British viewers watched these pictures and heard these sounds, experiencing a virtual proximity to the action which, though illusory in the sense that one could not be hurt by a stray bullet, or smell the burning oil, felt real to a degree which no previous generation of media audience has experienced. A BBC news crew led by foreign editor John Simpson was caught up in a 'friendly fire' incident in northern Iraq which killed one of its own members. The incident was broadcast live as it happened, blood-smeared camera lens and all. In another dramatic example, a Sky News reporter accompanied British troops at night as they entered an Iraqi house in pursuit of the enemy, emerging again with one of the troops on fire. Viewers watched as his colleagues wrestled success-fully to put the flames out before serious injury was caused to the soldier.

Never before in the history of war reportage had audiences on the home front been brought by their media so close in time or space to the action. Such unnerving proximity was possible because portable newsgathering technologies have allowed greater intimacy and 'up closeness' by journalists, while the spread of satellite broadcasting, cable and computing technology have facilitated the enhanced speed of news processing and dissemination. Coalition authorities had agreed to allow reporters to be 'embedded' with units fighting on the ground, and the stage was set for an unprecedentedly 'real' media war, with as yet unresearched consequences for audiences who witnessed the spectacle from the comfort of their living rooms thousands of miles away.[2]

If NICTs have driven the increased speed and intimacy of global news, the altered geo-political environment of the post-Cold War era has facilitated changes in its content which are at least as significant. Global radio news outlets such as the BBC World Service, Voice of America, Radio Free Europe and Radio Moscow had been broadcasting to the world for decades with a mixture of disinterested journalism, cultural diplomacy and highly motivated propaganda in which services were operated, covertly or otherwise, as instru-ments of state foreign policy. In this era, as Mikhail Gorbachev famously con-ceded after the failure of the coup of August 1991 which signalled the final dissolution of the Soviet Union, only the BBC World Service enjoyed the rep-utation for universal objectivity which allowed it to be relied on as an inde-pendent and reliable source of information just about anywhere in the world. With the end of the Cold War, however, and in the wake of the global ideo-logical realignment which followed, the crude anti- or pro-capitalist propa-ganda which had been the hallmark of many global broadcasters became redundant and anachronistic. At the same time as new technology created the infrastructural foundation for the emergence of a global public sphere, post-Cold War politics necessitated greater ideological flexibility on the part of news organisations. The emergence of a global news market further encour-aged the abandonment of propaganda by any organisation seeking to sell journalism as a commodity to global publics.

This new era began with the launch of Ted Turner's Cable Network News (CNN) in 1980. Though slow to gain credibility and audiences, Turner's CNN demonstrated its usefulness with live, often exclusive coverage of such events as the 1986 *Challenger* space shuttle disaster and the first Gulf War of 1991. Its growing success led in the 1990s to the launch of competitor ser-vices by such as BBC World, Rupert Murdoch's Star TV and many others, including Al Jazeera, the Qatar-based Arabic language channel launched in

1996 and which rose to global prominence after 9/11. Today in Britain the viewer of cable or digital TV has access to three UK-produced 'rolling' news services (BBC News 24, Sky News, ITV News Channel), and others produced overseas, including CNN, Al Jazeera, Fox News and CNBC.

UK and US-based news organisations dominate this information marketplace, as they always have, but in the political environment of the twenty-first century satellite TV and radio broadcasting accommodates an unprecedentedly diverse range of editorial perspective, simply because organisations, whether based in Atlanta, Qatar or Dubai, must operate in a marketplace of many providers and demanding audiences. Organisations such as CNN and Star TV have refined their services to better compete in local markets such as India and China (in the case of Star TV, producing criticism of Murdoch's News Corporation that it kowtows to the Chinese Communists). The Voice of America radio service, currently broadcasting in fifty-three languages, has sought to lose its image as an old-style Cold War propagandist and build a reputation for balance and objectivity of the type long enjoyed by the BBC. In 2002 the US government launched a new Arabic language radio service, Middle East Radio Network, 'designed to appeal to the younger Arab audience and to counter-balance the growing wave of anti-Americanism in the Arab world' (El-Nawawy and Iskandar 2002: 193). Such moves reflect not just the changed ideological conditions of the twenty first century, but have been a response to the growing influence of Al Jazeera and other Arab-language broadcasters. To the frustration of some, and the satisfaction of others, these organisations have often articulated editorial positions on the issues raised by September 11 and the war on terror which are very different from those of, say, CNN or Fox. Whatever the latter organisations may deliver to their domestic audiences in the USA (and the unqualified patriotism of some US broadcasters post-9/11 has been a subject of much critical commentary [Zelizer and Allan 2002]), pro-American journalistic cheerleading does not suffice in a competitive global marketplace which includes credible competition broadcasters such as Al Jazeera.

In the 1990s satellite TV and radio were joined by a new medium for the distribution of news and information, the World Wide Web. Developed with scientific and military applications in mind (Naughton 1999), the World Wide Web went mainstream in the late 1990s, forming an information superhighway with global reach and mass accessibility. From a slow start, by the beginning of the twenty-first century an online presence was practically mandatory for established print and broadcast media, turning them all, in effect, into global as well as national media. A newspaper published in Scotland or San Francisco could be read online in Australia or Japan. If BBC TV and radio programmes were available only in the UK and Ireland, BBC Online could deploy streaming technology to make them available to anyone in the world with access to an internet-capable computer.

In addition to providing a new platform for the dissemination of journalistic material which originated in newspapers and broadcast media, the internet added new elements of interactivity and accessibility to the environment, allowing users to engage with their media of choice in new ways. BBC Online, for example, functions as a gateway to a host of programme-related services and resources, as well as providing users with opportunities to feedback to producers, or to communicate with each other through chatrooms and e-mail.

Of at least as much importance, the internet has also allowed resource poor organisations and enthusiastic individuals – hitherto excluded from all but the letters pages of mainstream news media – to have a presence not just as consumers and critics but as serious producers of journalism. If satellite broadcasting continues to be capital intensive and thus restricted to a relatively small number of providers (albeit many more than have ever been present in the global public sphere before), the emergence of the internet has been accompanied by an explosion of independent news and information sites, from commercially developed online gossip and commentary columns such as those operated by Matt Drudge[3] and Andrew Sullivan,[4] to the tens of thousands of web logs run by non-journalists. The most famous of these has been Salam Pax, the 'Baghdad blogger', whose dispatches from inside Iraq became part of the mainstream media coverage of the war.

NICTs and the fourth estate

Does this emerging global network amount to a transnational public sphere; a globalised fourth estate capable of strengthening democracy at a global level? What do we mean by these terms, and are the ideas they express, so central to the classic models of liberal democracy which developed after the bourgeois revolutions of early modern Europe, relevant or appropriate to the twenty-first century?

Let's first recall their origins in the coffee house cultures of seventeenth-century European cities, where the 'public sphere' was born as a media space within which individuals could for the first time come together in common contemplation, through their use of print media, of the great issues and debates of the day. The bourgeois revolutions which overthrew Europe's absolute monarchies in France, Germany, Britain and elsewhere introduced, on the one hand, the principle of intellectual freedom – in particular, freedom of the press, at that time the main communicative channel where competing intellectual positions could be aired and tested. Integral to this freedom, an index of its existence, were the ability and willingness of the media to critically scrutinise political power. Where the absolute monarchies had prohibited meaningful press criticism of their activities, the struggles which led to the emerging democracies of early modern Europe developed a role for journalists as watchdogs over the potential abuses of power.

If power corrupted, and the new democrats of the European enlightenment believed that it did, journalism could act as a 'fourth estate' to identify
and expose corruption, and to protect newly enfranchised citizens from its
negative consequences, such as a return to the despotism of feudal regimes.
This 'defeudalisation' of political power, meaning the facilitation of its transparent display before the people rather than its imposition upon them, was
the essential feature of Habermas's public sphere, and has remained the normative role of the journalistic media in a democracy ever since. Without the
presence of a properly functioning fourth estate, well-resourced and adver-
sarial, pluralistic and independent of the state, democracy is inconceivable
at worst, disabled at best. Not only does such a media system check and
balance political and other forms of power which might seek to subvert
democracy; it provides the citizen with information and knowledge on the
basis of which his or her democratic rights will be exercised. Who to vote
for? Which party to support? Which issues to prioritise when making these
judgments? In a democracy it is the responsibility of the journalistic media
to address all of these questions with honesty, accuracy and fairness – with
objectivity, as journalists have defined their key professional ideal since the
nineteenth century.

If the ideal is to be fully realised in practice, the fourth estate – the proprietors, editors and journalists who staff its constituent elements – must be
not just legally free to confront political power, but willing to do so in a
manner which inspires the trust and confidence of the public whom it exists
to serve. The example most often cited is the Watergate scandal of the early
1970s, in which reporters Carl Bernstein and Bob Woodward of the
Washington Post pursued President Richard Nixon to the point of impeach-
ment, and forced his resignation amidst allegations of criminal conspiracy.
Here was the classic case of a democratically elected political leader prone
to corruption and abuse of power, but subjected to effective critical scrutiny
by journalists. Many other examples of the watchdog function of the press
being successfully enacted could be mentioned, and there can be little serious
objection to the conclusion that, on balance and overall, the most conscien-
tious of the journalistic media have contributed substantially to the creation
and maintenance of democratic institutions wherever they exist in the world,
from Britain and the USA to South Africa and post-Soviet Russia.

The Watergate example is not typical, however, and there been many criticisms of the failures and limitations of the media in their role as fourth
estate, not least from media and communication scholars. These have
focused on the constraining influence of capital, or its absence, in prevent-
ing journalists from scrutinising power as they might wish to. Marxist theo-
rists from the nineteenth century onwards have of course questioned the
entire premise of the fourth estate as an independent sphere of elite scrutiny,
preferring to think of objectivity as a bourgeois myth, and the media as ideological instruments in the hands of the ruling class. Chomsky and Herman's

propaganda model for analysing coverage of the US media exemplifies this perspective, arguing that Watergate and other cases have been tokenistic and illusionary, serving as ideological diversions designed to mask the deeper reality of a media system which is bound in key ways to the American military-industrial complex and does its bidding, as in coverage of the Vietnam war, or the more recent conflict in Iraq. The media function not as watchdogs in this model, but as the propaganda division of a 'national security state' (1979), hostile to domestic dissent and overseas opposition to the progress of American capitalism. The Chomsky-Herman approach, in common with most left and Marxian-influenced critiques of the workings of the fourth estate, presumes that there is an alternative to both capitalism and the 'bourgeois' ideology underpinning it; an alternative which is more democratic, but which is being masked by the workings of the liberal media, at home and overseas, as they carry out the ideological functions of the capitalist state.

Like the cultural imperialism thesis, the propaganda model was born of the particular ideological polarities of the Cold War, and formed against the specific background of the USA, where media have been highly commercialised and pro-business for centuries. In countries with strong public service broadcasters, such as the UK, critics instead stressed the hegemonic role of the media in securing ideological reproduction. Media freedom was perceived from this perspective as a legitimising device to secure the consent of the population into believing what news media told them about industrial disputes, the nature of the Soviet threat and other key issues (Glasgow University Media Group 1976, 1980). Broadcast impartiality of the type practised in its purest form by the BBC was viewed as a refined version of the older notion of objectivity, and the work of many media scholars, including this writer, sought to deconstruct and critique it (McNair 1988), and to reveal news as a form of ideology (in the Marxian sense), servicing the British state during the Cold War.

In the 1980s and early 1990s the left critique of the fourth estate in Britain was fuelled by the presence of obvious right-wing bias. Stridently pro-Thatcher proprietors such as Rupert Murdoch and Conrad Black seemed to confirm the obvious limitations of the fourth estate idea, and to negate British democracy with their apparent contempt for the views of the 30–40 per cent of the public who, even at the nadir of Labour's electoral fortunes in the early 1980s, still supported the party.

Explanations for the propaganda model in the US, or UK press bias, focused on the power of big capital to control media, and to prevent alternative views from emerging. Commercialisation was seen as the enemy of editorial diversity, and the workings of the market as inherently pro-conservative. Advertisers were alleged to suppress potentially critical news content. Powerful political actors were able to use the patronage of the state to counteract the watchdogs of the media. Moreover, the increased importance of public opinion in the twentieth century had resulted in the growth of a 'fifth estate', a public relations industry whose members worked to shape, influence and if possible control the range of possible interpretations to be drawn by audiences from their consumption of journalism. PR had evolved from the combination of mass media and mass democracy, and the resultant need to restrict the range of meanings which might be drawn by citizens from their consumption of journalism. For Habermas, and the scholarly tradition influenced by him, the growth of public relations was synonymous with the 're-feudalisation' (1989) of the public sphere, and the weakening of the fourth estate's capacity to fulfil its democratic functions. Journalists became lazy and dependent on sources as they were fed with press releases, pseudo-events, photo-opportunities and spin, themselves corrupted by the new profession of news and media management.

If these criticisms resonated through the four decades of the Cold War, they required revision as the political and technological trends of the late twentieth century made themselves felt. As a result of the introduction of NICTs discussed above, entry costs to news media fell, and the producer–consumer relationship changed. Cheaper media production and new forms of dissemination meant more media outlets, which enhanced the power of the consumer by increasing choice. Proprietors could not presume to bombard audiences with their preferred readings of events and, in the absence of alternative viewpoints, get away with it. More media meant enhanced media literacy, and increasing levels of awareness of the limitations of journalism as a cultural form. Survey evidence suggests that media consumers in the twenty-first century still want to believe in the reliability and trustworthiness of their journalism, but are less likely to take it for granted, or to be fooled into doing so by the co-conspirators of a 'national security state'.

At the level of ideology, as noted above, the end of the Cold War began the erosion of the alignments of left–right, east–west, capitalist–communist which had structured the global politics of the twentieth century. Francis Fukuyama called it the end of history, but it was really the beginning of a new phase of history, in which the focus of ideological struggle moved away from class-based movements to struggles between organisations and belief systems based on ethnicity, sexuality, nationalism and religious belief. The failure of 'actually existing socialism' everywhere on the planet, combined with capitalism's apparently endless capacity for reinvention and growth, threw left critiques into disarray. In such conditions such ideas as 'ruling class' and 'dominant ideology' seemed insufficiently flexible to describe the complexity of national and global politics. Rupert Murdoch's previously pro-Tory newspapers jumped ship for the Labour Party in time for the 1997 election, because this was in tune with his readers' opinions (McNair 2000). Chomsky and Herman's propaganda model explained will the pattern of US coverage of central American death squads in the Reagan era, but was less helpful in understanding the coverage of a conflict such as that in the former

Yugoslavia, or the first Gulf War in which the USA, the USSR and China were all part of the international coalition (if some more enthusiastic than others) which threw Saddam Hussein out of Kuwait. September 11 and the war on terror saw unusual alliances being formed on all sides, with labels of 'left' and 'right' no longer a reliable predictor of where people stood. In these conditions the notion of a 'national security state' unproblematically flooding the US people and those of the world in general with pro-American propaganda, aided and abetted by a compliant media, made little sense outside the pages of a Michael Moore polemic. Indeed, Michael Moore's fiercely anti-Bush books were bestsellers in America, where there huge mainstream success presented an excellent example in itself of the increasingly complex and contradictory realities of journalistic culture in advanced capitalism.

NICTs, democratic societies and the fourth estate

For all the limitations of the fourth estate as it has classically been conceived, however, there are grounds for recognising not only that the concept retains its relevance in the multi-channel, multi-platform media environment of the twenty-first century, but that the classic functions of the liberal media are being strengthened as NICTs evolve. If the democratic role of journalism is to act as a watchdog over power, then in a media environment of accelerated, expanded, pluralised information flow, where censorship by national authorities becomes steadily more difficult to achieve and there is ever greater competition for audiences, that role is strengthened by default. Recent British political history provides many examples of the media exercising effective critical scrutiny over political elites, setting the agenda of public debate with stories about official corruption, the excesses of spin, racism in the police force, and the legitimacy of the UK government's decision to go to war in Iraq. Alongside the established print and broadcast media, these stories have been 'given legs' by the relentless reportage of 24-hour real-time news channels, and a host of new online media, flooding the public sphere with information in such quantities, and at such speed, that no elite group can take its dominance of the news agenda or public debate for granted. Governments, big business, public bodies, all are constantly in reactive, response mode, usually assisted by public relations professionals. Control of the communication environment is still the goal of political actors, but that goal is increasingly difficult to achieve in the evermore volatile and turbulent environment of real-time news and the internet. There is a lot of time and space to fill in these proliferating channels, and thus journalists are under huge pressure to dig for newsworthy stories, unearth scandals and probe minor rhetorical inconsistencies in search of a major deception. Competition for audiences and influence provides incentive to get the scoop, and if not to get it, at least to share in it.

And as if the real-time capabilities of the mainstream media were not unsettling enough for political actors, the public sphere is now also crowded with alternative, independent voices of all kinds. Dutch scholar Kees Brants observed in 1998 that the rise of the internet provided 'examples of non-hierarchical, bottom-up and voluntary networks, where everybody is welcome to raise issues, participate in debate with complete strangers and put information on the network' (see Brants 1998: 177). Notwithstanding the commercialisation of the network which has accompanied its explosion into mass consciousness, the internet continues to present a media platform of historically unprecedented capacity and accessibility. Moreover, its roots in military thinking make it resistant to state censorship and other constraints used in the past to banish unwanted messages from the media. Censorship and repression of the internet remains an option for governments across the world, and has been a tactic adopted by democratic societies in the policing of child pornography and other unwelcome inhabitants of cyberspace, as well as a weapon against political dissenters who use the net in dictatorships such as Saddam-era Iraq, Cuba and China. No government, however, no matter how authoritarian its measures, can entirely prevent unruly online phenomena such as Salaam Pax and the Drudge Report, which first disseminated the news of Bill Clinton's difficulties with Monica Lewinsky. Alongside trends in TV and radio, there has been what Andrew Sullivan describes (referring to the USA in particular, but applicable elsewhere) as 'a fracturing of the media in which cable, the internet and talk radio have given every constituency its own echo chamber'.[5]

The media in advanced capitalist societies, then, are more numerous, more accessible and more diverse than they have ever been, because the combined impact of technology, economics and geo-political trends has made it that way. Added to this is the fact that since the Second World War, and especially towards the end of the twentieth century, the traditional deference towards elites which characterised capitalism for most of its history has been eroded. Politicians, celebrities of sport and screen, senior figures in all walks of life, are all subject to critical scrutiny of their activities as never before. To this extent the continuation of the media's fourth estate role into the twenty-first century is inevitable. Politicians have become less secure in power, not more.

It can also be argued that they have become too free, as exemplified by the stories which circulated about Prince Charles's sexuality in the British and global media in November 2003. As former prime minister John Major put it in a newspaper column, 'how is it possible to ignite worldwide interest in something so obviously untrue? Are we now in a world in which peephole journalism will print anything – true or false, that is said by anyone – sick or otherwise, on the grounds that the subject is a public figure and therefore the public has a "right to know"?'[6] Mr Major, himself a frequent target of the fourth estate when in government, was highlighting the fact that the forces outlined above have produced a situation in which scrutiny of elites power may become invasive and predatory, leading to negative consequences for the practice of good government, as well as a society's moral health. The speed and ubiquity of the modern media means that sources are often unchecked, analysis of facts is thin, and rumours can spread faster than their veracity can be checked, with extremely damaging consequences for some individuals. Addressing these concerns, while protecting the rights of journalists to effectively scrutinise power, will be one of the key challenges for politicians, legislators and human rights activists in the years to come.

NICTs, authoritarian societies and global democratisation

Whether or not the rise of NICTs and their impact on the fourth estate may turn out to be a mixed blessing for the advanced democracies, they have even greater potential for change in the remaining authoritarian societies of the world. The spread of 24-hour news channels and the emergence of online media has eroded the cultural and ideological isolation of authoritarian political systems, from the Soviet Union in the late 1980s (McNair 1989) to the Islamic states of the Middle East today. The global spread of NICTs has the potential to facilitate economic, social and political modernisation (although, as we have seen, the pessimistic perspective asserts that these processes represent a further stage in American cultural imperialism and the construction of 'MacWorld'). It is perhaps best to avoid both dystopian and utopian extremes of thinking and hypothesise that the impact of NICTs will be neither straightforwardly progressive nor conservative, and that they will have outcomes which are inherently unpredictable, because contingent on local environmental factors which shape their development and use.

In Iran and some of the Arab states, for example, growing pressure for democratisation is certainly fuelled by the presence of the internet and satellite broadcasting, which has steadily eroded if not yet eliminated censorship of debate and dissent. In China, on the other hand, which has embraced the internet as a tool for economic growth, the Communist government has successfully maintained control over dissent. As Kalathil and Boas see it, 'although Premier Zhu Rongji exhorted the media in 2001 to act as the watchdog of government, encouraging the exposure of corruption and government misdeeds, state regulations and actions have presented a conflicting image. Progressive publishing houses have been reined in, while journalists continue to be harassed and imprisoned for exposing official wrongdoing' (2003: 19). In the aftermath of the SARS epidemic of 2003, and in the face of a public health crisis caused by the spread of HIV and AIDS in China, the authorities were reported to be harassing journalists who sought to report the story.[7] In China, despite the enthusiastic adoption of NICTs as part of a modernisation strategy, the emergence of an effective fourth estate is still far from certain. In Singapore, a wealthy capitalist society with a semi-authoritarian regime, the people appear to consent to restrictions on their use of NICTs which prevent the media from acting as a fourth estate. In Burma, where there is a substantial domestic and expatriate opposition to the ruling regime, NICTs have provided a campaigning resource. They have also helped to create a 'more transparent environment in which the [regime] is likely to find its actions highly scrutinised by the international community' (Ibid., 98).

Conclusion

To what extent can authoritarian regimes continue to constrain the spread of externally produced news media within their territories? If a global public sphere has come into existence (and transnational coverage of the recent war in Iraq suggests that it has), has it, and will it in the future, facilitate democratisation in countries hitherto excluded from or resistant to it? Or will it act as a vehicle, as some critics argue, for further imperialistic expansion by the big players of the Anglo-American cultural economy? What will be the long-term impact on democratic societies of a global public sphere characterised by communication chaos and anarchy rather than order and elite control?

The hard research work required in order to provide convincing answers to these questions is just beginning. In the meantime, I have drawn a picture of a global media system characterised by accelerated, expanded and relatively unconstrained information flow. This new world information disorder, if we may think of it in that way, is crowded and chaotic, unruly and subversive of authority, despite efforts to tame it through commercialisation and incorporation in the cultural mainstream. At times it functions as a fourth estate in the traditional sense – critical, considered, responsible in its attempts to scrutinise and improve the democratic process, and to facilitate processes of democratisation in countries where authoritarianism still prevails. At times it behaves like the anti-globalisation protestor who throws a molotov cocktail at a city-centre burger joint in the belief that he is fighting a war against capitalism. In some countries NICTs are clearly contributing to a pro-democracy environment. In others the eventual outcome of their introduction is less certain. If the nature of satellite and digital technology justifies a degree of optimism about the prospects of progressive political evolution across the globe in the twenty-first century, it does not guarantee it. Recent years have shown that if despotisms and authoritarian regimes are everywhere in decline, there is life in them yet. As for the democracies of the advanced capitalist world, the line between the welcome critical scrutiny of a fourth estate boosted by the communicative power of NICTS, and the less welcome chaos of communication witnessed in a story such as the Clinton-Lewinsky scandal or the scandal which engulfed Prince Charles in late 2003 is easily crossed. Whether this will be good or bad for the evolution of democratic politics remains to be seen, and depends not least on what journalists, editors and proprietors elect to do with the new powers of critical scrutiny the onward march of communication technology has provided them.

Notes

1 The cultural imperialism thesis is not dead, though, especially amongst those observers who see globalisation as merely its latest manifestation. In 1998 one scholar argued that 'the cultural product of the international television news agencies serves to perpetuate a western hegemony hostile to developing nations . . . The globalisation of television news is producing an international public sphere, but one dominated by mainstream Anglo-American ideologies conveyed in the texts of internationally distributed television news' (Paterson 1998: 95).
2 For a discussion of the cultural impact of this development, written during the 2003 Iraqi war, see B. McNair, 'This terrifying spectacle may provide a vital TV service', *Scotland On Sunday*, 30 March 2003. (online version, www.scotlandon sunday.com/weekinreview.cfm?id=376172003).
3 See www.drudgereport.com/. Drudge's site contains links to hundreds of other online columnists.
4 See www.andrewsullivan.com/. For a portal giving access to some of the online columns popular in early 2004 see www.instapundit.com/.
5 A. Sullivan, 'Battle lines deepen in the US', *Sunday Times*, 9 November 2003.
6 J. Major, 'We're hurting ourselves as well as Charles', *Sunday Times*, 16 November 2003.
7 X. Dong, 'China Crisis', *Guardian*, 1 December 2003.

Bibliography

ABC News (2003) 'Fear and Relief: Jessica Lynch Was about to be Rescued; She Thought She Was about to be Killed', ABCNews.com, 11 November, www.abcnews .go.com/sections/Primetime/US/Jessica_Lynch_031111–1.html.

Ad Council (1976a) 'Chambers of Commerce Get Involved', *Economic Communicator*, September/October, 7.

Ad Council (1976b) 'Corporate Effort: Economic Education', *Economic Communicator*, May, 1, 4–5.

Ad Council (1976c) 'Corporate Materials to Build Economic Understanding', *Economic Communicator*, July, 3.

Ad Council (1976d) 'On the Issues', *Economic Communicator*, September/October, 3.

Ad Council (1976e) 'Program to Last Three to Five Years', *Economic Communicator*, May, 1, 6.

Adams, R. (2003) 'American Presidents All Mixed Up', *Guardian*, 29 January.

Adelman, K. (2002) 'Why Now? A Better Question Is Why Wait?', Foxnews.com, www.foxnews.com/story/0,2933,65146,00.html.

Adorno, T. and Horkheimer, M. (1997) *Dialectic of Enlightenment*, London, Verso.

Agence French Press (2004) 'Bush to Encounter Latin America's New Left at Monterrey Summit', 12 January, www.commondreams.org/headlines04/0112–03.htm.

Agencia Brazil (2003) 'Brazil's Lula to Bush: Stop Subsidies', September, www.brazzil.com/2003/html/articles/sep03/p111sep03.htm.

Agger, B. (1989) *Fast Capitalism*, Urbana, University of Illinois Press.

Alexander, J. and Jacobs, R. (1998) 'Mass Communication, Ritual and Civil Society', in T. Liebes and J. Curran (eds), *Media, Ritual and Identity*, London and New York, Routledge, pp. 23–41.

Allan, S. (2002) 'Reweaving the Internet: Online News of September 11', in B. Zelizer and S. Allan (eds), *Journalism After September 11*, London and New York, Routledge, pp. 119–140.

Allan, S. (2004) 'The Culture of Distance: Online Reporting of the Iraq War', in S. Allan and B. Zelizer (eds), *Reporting War: Journalism in Wartime*, London and New York, Routledge, pp. 347–374.

Allan, S. and Matheson, D. (2004) 'Online Journalism in the Information Age', *Knowledge, Work and Society*, 1(3).

Allan, S. and Zeliver, B. (eds) (2002) *Journalism After September 11*, London, Routledge.

Allemang, J. (2003) 'Where Everybody is a War Reporter', *The Globe and Mail*, 29 March, www.globeandmail.com.

Alterman, E. (1994) 'Fighting Smart', *Mother Jones* 19(4), 59–61.

Anderson, B. (1991) *Imagined Communities*, rev. edn, London, Verso.

Andrews, P. (2003) 'Is Blogging Journalism?', *Nieman Reports*, Fall, 63–64.

Applebaum. (2001) 'Who Elected the Anti-capitalist Convergence?' *Slate Magazine*, 23 April, 2001, slate.msn.com/default.aspx?id=104829.

Aragão, P. C. (2004) 'Brazil: Mergers and Acquisitions', *International Financial Law Review*, July 2004.

Arcenenaux, C. L. (2001) *Bounded Missions: Military Regimes and Democratisation in the Southern Cone*, Pennsylvania, The Pennsylvania State University Press.

Armstrong, D. (2002) 'Dick Cheney's Song of America: Drafting a Plan for Global Dominance', *Harper's*, October, 305 (1829), 76–83.

Ashford, N. (1997) 'Politically Impossible? How Ideas Not Interests and Circumstances, Determine Public Policies', *Policy*, Autumn, 21–5.

Atkins, W. (2002) *The Politics of Southeast Asia's New Media*, London, RoutledgeCurzon.

Avery, N. (1993) 'Stealing from the State', *Multinational Monitor*, September, www.essential.org/monitor/hyper/issues/1993/09/mm0993_10.html.

Babich, P. (2000) 'Spinning Free Trade: The Battle for Public Opinion', *Making Contact, National Radio Project*. 5 July. www.radioproject.org/archive/2000/0027.html.

Baiocchi, G. (ed.) (2003) *Radicals in Power: The Workers' Party and experiments in urban democracy*, London, Zed Books.

Balanyá, B., et al. (2000) *Europe Inc. Regional and Global Restructuring and the Rise of Corporate Power*. London, Pluto Press.

Barber, B. (1995) *Jihad vs. McWorld*. New York, Times Books.

Barnhart, A. (2003) 'On TV, Bombing Induces Awe', *Kansas City Star*, 22 March, www.kansascity.com/mld/kansascity/.

Bart, P. (2003) 'Iraq Passes Its Screen Test', Variety.com, 13 April, www.variety.com/index.asp?layout=print_story&articleid=VR1117884504&categoryid=1019.

Barthes, R. (1993) *Mythologies*, London, Vintage.

Bauder, D. (2001) 'Geraldo Rivera Goes from CNBC to Fox', *Associated Press*, 1 November, www.news.excite.com/news/ap/011101/19/ent-fox-rivera.

Bauder, D. (203) 'Embedded War Reporters: Experiment Passes Muster', *The Globe and Mail*, 23 April, B12.

Baudrillard, J. (1992) *The Illusion of the End*, Cambridge, Polity Press.

Baudrillard, J. (1995) *The Gulf War Did Not Take Place*, Indiana, Indiana University Press.

Bauman, Z. (1992) *Postmodern Ethics*, Oxford, Blackwell.

BBC News Online (2002) 'Brazil's New Political Map', http://news.bbc.co.uk/1/hi/world/americas/2304849.stm.

BBC News Online (2003a) 'Sony in 'Shock and Awe' Blunder', *BBC News Online*, 16 April, http://news.bbc.co.uk/1/hi/business/2951859.stm.

BBC News Online (2003b) 'CBS Backs Down on Lynch Movie', *BBC News Online*, 21 July, http://news.bbc.co.uk/2/hi/entertainment/3083235.stm.

BBC News Online (2004a) '40 Years of The Sun', http://news.bbc.co.uk/nolpda/ukfs_news/hi/newsid_3654000/3654446.stm.

BBC News Online (2004b) 'Brazil Battles Sharp Market Slide', http://news.bbc.co.uk/1/hi/business/3701619.stm.

Beard, A. (2003) 'US TV Counts the Cost of War', *Financial Times*, 7 April, 18.

Beaverstock, J., Smith, R., and Taylor, P. (1999) 'A Roster of World Cities', *Cities*, 16 (6), 445–458.

Beder, S. (1996) *The Nature of Sustainable Development*, 2nd edn, Melbourne, Scribe Publications.

Beder, S. (2000) *Selling the Work Ethic: From Puritan Pulpit to Corporate PR*, London, Zed Books.

Beder, S. (2002) *Global Spin: The Corporate Assault on Environmentalism*, 2nd edn, Devon, Green Books.

Beder, S. (2003) *Power Play: The Fight to Control the World's Electricity*, Melbourne and New York, Scribe Publications and the New Press.

Beder, S. and Gosden, R. (2001) 'Wpp: World Propaganda Power', *PR Watch* 8(2), 9–10.

Bednarski, P. J., and Higgins, J. M. (2003) 'Heyward: Objectivity a Function of Fairness', Broadcastingandcable.com, 24 March, www.broadcastingcable.com/CA286552.htm.

Bedway, B. (2003) 'Why AP Counted Civilian Deaths in Iraq', *Editor and Publisher*, 24 July, www.editorandpublisher.com/editorandpublisher/headlines/articles_display.jsp?vnu_content_id=1920081.

Bekaert, G., Harvey, C. and Lundblad, T. (2003) 'Equity Market Liberalization in Emerging Markets', *Review*, July/August, 53–84, http://research.stlouisfed.org/publications/review/03/07/Bekaert.pdf, accessed 2 September 2003.

Bell, D. (1988) *The Third Technological Revolution and its Possible Socio-Economic Consequences*, lecture given to the University of Salford, 3 March.

Bell, S. and Warhurst, J. (1992) 'Political Activism among Large Firms', in S. Bell and J. Wanna (eds), *Business-Government Relations in Australia*, Sydney, Harcourt Brace Jovanovich, pp. 57–65.

Bellos, A. (2003) 'Roberto Marino', *Guardian*, 8 August, www.guardian.co.uk/brazil/story/0,12462,1014553,00.html.

Bellos, A. (2004) 'Lula Throws Brazilians More Promises as Problems Mount', *Guardian*, 28 April, www.guardian.co.uk/international/story/0,3604,1204816,00.html.

Benjamin, W. (2004) *Illuminations*, London, Pimlico.

Bennett, W. L. (1990) 'Toward a Theory of Press State Relations in the United States', *Journal of Communication*, 40 (2), pp. 103–25.

Bergsten, C. F. (2000) 'The Backlash against Globalization', The Trilateral Commission www.trilateral.org/annmtgs/trialog/trlgtxts/t54/ber.htm.

Bhagwati, J. (1998) 'The Capital Myth: The Difference between Trade in Widgets and Dollars', *Foreign Affairs*, 77 (3), 7–12.

Bhaskar, R. (1998) *The Possibility of Naturalism*, London, Routledge.

Biotic Baking Brigade (2004) *Pie Any Means Necessary*, Edinburgh, AK Press.

Bodi, F. (2003) 'Al-Jazeera Tells the Truth About War', *Guardian*, 28 March.

Borges, J. L. (1999) *The Total Library: Non Fiction 1922–1986*, London, Penguin.

Boseley, S. (2004) '100,000 Iraqi Civilians Dead, Says Study', *Guardian*, 29 October.

Bourdieu, P. (1977) *Outline of a Theory of Practice*, Cambridge, Cambridge University Press.

Bourdieu, P. (1990) *In Other Words: Essays Toward a Reflexive Sociology*, Stanford, Stanford University Press.

Bourdieu, P. (1991) *Language and Symbolic Power*, in John B. Thompson (ed.), trans. by G. Raymond and M. Adamson, Cambridge, MA, Polity Press.

Bourdieu, P. (1993) *The Field of Cultural Production: Essays on Art and Literature*, New York, Columbia University Press.

Bourdieu, P. (1998a) *Acts of Resistance: Against the Tyranny of the Market*, New York, The New Press.

Bourdieu, P. (1998b) *Practical Reason: On the Theory of Action*, Stanford, Stanford University Press.

Bowman, S. and Willis, C. (2003) *We Media*. Reston, Va: The Media Center at The American Press Institute. www.hypergent.net/wemedia/.

Boyd-Barrett, O. and Thussu, D. K. (1992) *Contra-flow in Global News: International and Regional News Exchange Mechanisms*, London, John Libbey.

Boyd-Barrett, Rantanen, T. (1998) (eds), *The Globalization of News*, London, Sage.

Branford, S. (2003) 'Brazil: The Debt Crisis', *New Internationalist Magazine*.

Branford, S. and Kucinski, B. (2003) *Politics Transformed: Lula and the Workers Party in Brazil*, London, Latin American Bureau.

Branford, S. and Rocha, B. (2002) *Cutting the Wire: The Story of the Landless Movement in Brazil*, London, Latin American Bureau.

Brants, K. (1998) 'With the Benefit of Hindsight: Old Nightmares and New Dreams', in K. Brants, J. Hermes. and L. van Zoonen (eds), *The Media In Question*, London, Sage, pp.169–180.

Broadway, F. (1978) 'Defending Free Enterprise: An Approach to the Schools', in M. Ivens (ed.), *International Papers on the Revival of Freedom and Enterprise* , London, AIMS, pp. 63–4.

Brown, R. (2003) 'Spinning the War: Political Communications, Information Operations and Public Diplomacy in the War on Terrorism', in D. K. Thussu and D. Freedman (eds), *War and the Media: Reporting Conflict 24/7*, London, Sage, pp. 87–100.

Bruce, I. (2003) 'Al Qaeda Chiefs Told US They Had No Links with Saddam: Bin Laden Ruled out Iraq Sanctuary Offer' (*Glasgow) Herald*, 10 June, 2.

Buckley, C and Liebovitz, A. (2002) 'War and Destiny: The White House in Wartime', *Vanity Fair*, February.

Burbach, R. (2002a) 'Brazil on the Verge of a Peaceful Revolution', *Spotlight*, www.redress.btinternet.co.uk/rburbach11.htm.

Burbach, R. (2002b) 'Brazil's Lula Checks Bush', *CounterPunch*, 13 December, www.counterpunch.org/burbach1213.html.

Burbach, R. (2004) 'Rebuffing the IMF: Brazil Begins to Throw Off Austerity Plans', *Counterpunch*, 25 March, www.counterpunch.org/burbach03252004.html.

Burke, K. (1954) *Permanence and Change: An Anatomy of Purpose*, Indianapolis, Bobbs-Merrill.

Burkeman, O. (2004) Terrorism Actually (accessed 9 September 2004).

Burkeman, O., Black, I., Wells, M., Smith, S. and Whitaker, B. (2003) 'Television Agendas Shape Images of War', *Guardian*, 27 March, Home Pages, 7.

Burston, J. (2003) 'War and the Entertainment Industries: New Research Priorities in an Era of Cyber-Patriotism', in D. K. Thussu and D. Freedman (eds), *War and the Media: Reporting Conflict 24/7*, London, Sage, pp. 163–175.

Calvino, I. (2003) *Hermit in Paris: Autobiographical Writings*, London, Jonathan Cape.

Cardoso, F. (2004) 'Fernando Henrique Cardoso Reflections and Lessons from a Decade of Social and Economic Reforms', *World Bank Online*, http://info .worldbank.org/etools/bspan/PresentationView.asp?PID=980&EID=328.

Carey, A. (1995) *Taking the Risk out of Democracy*, ed. Andrew Lohrey, Sydney, UNSW Press.

Carroll, J. (1992) 'Economic Rationalism and Its Consequences', in John Carroll and Robert Manne (eds), *Shutdown: The Failure of Economic Rationalism and How to Rescue Australia*, Melbourne, The Text Publishing Company, pp. 7–26.

Carter, G. (2002) 'The War Room', *Vanity Fair*, February.

Cassy, J, and Milmo, D. (2003) 'Ad Slots Empty as Brands Avoid War', *Guardian*, 21 March, City Pages, 23.

Castells, M. (1996) *The Rise of the Network Society*. Oxford, Blackwell.

Castells, M. (1997) *The Power of Identity*. Oxford, Blackwell.

Castells, M. (2000a) *End of Millennium*. Oxford, Blackwell.

Castells, M. (2000b) *The Rise of the Network Society*, 2nd edn, Oxford and Malden, MA, Blackwell.

Castells, M. (2001) *The Internet Galaxy*, Oxford, Oxford University Press.

Castilho, C. (2004) 'Globo: Death of a Brazilian Media Empire?', Mediachannel.org, progressivetrail.org/articles/040405Castilho.shtml.

CBS News (2003) 'Iraq Faces Massive Missile U.S. Barrage', CBSNews.com, 24 January, www.cbsnews.com/stories/2003/01/24/eveningnews/main537928.shtml.

Chang, L. and Hutzler, C. (2003) 'CCTV Aims To Be China's CNN', *The Globe and Mail*, 27 March, B12.

Chang, N. (2002) *Silencing Political Dissent: How Post-September 11 Anti-Terrorism Measures Threaten Our Civil Liberties*, New York, Seven Stories Press.

Chesters, G. (2003) 'Shape Shifting: Civil Society, Complexity and Social Movements', *Anarchist Studies*, 11 (1).

Chinni, D. (2003) 'Jessica Lynch: Media Myth-Making in the Iraq War', journalism.org, www.journalism.org/resources/research/reports/war/postwar/lynch.asp, accessed 26 July.

Chomsky, N., Herman, E. (1979) *The Political Economy of Human Rights*, Boston, Massachusetts, South End Press.

Chossudovsky, M. (1992) 'The Global Creation of Third World Poverty', *Third World Resurgence*, January, 13–20.

Chossudovsky, M. (2003) 'Brazil: Neoliberalism with a 'Human' Face?', *Global Research*, www.globalresearch.ca/articles/CHO303C.html.

Chunovic, L. (2003) 'War: Sponsors Take Wait-and-See Stance', *Electronic Media*, 30 September, 10.

Church, R. (2003) 'Interview with Salman Pax', CNN International, Transcript Number: 100302cb.k18, 3 October.

Clark, I. (2003) 'Legitimacy in Global Order', *Review of International Studies*, December, 29 (1).

Cockett, R. (1994) *Thinking the Unthinkable: Think-Tanks and the Economic Counter-Revolution 1931–1983*, Harper Collins.

Cohen, N. (2000) *Cruel Brittania*, London, Verso.

Connolly, W. E. (1992) *Identity/Difference: Democratic Negotiations of Political Paradox*, Ithaca, NY, Cornell University Press.

Correa, C. M. (1999) *Intellectual Property Rights, the WTO and Developing Countries: The TRIPS Agreement and Policy Options*. New York, Zed Books.

Correa, C. M. (2000) *Intellectual Property Rights, the WTO and Developing Countries: The TRIPS Agreement and Policy Options for Developing Countries*, London, Zed Books.

Cottle, S. (2003) *News, Public Relations and Power*, London, Sage.

Cowen, R. (2003) 'Die-ins Target War and News Media', *The Record*, www.commondreams.org/headlines03/0328-10.htm.

Cozens, C. (2003) 'Hoon Claims PR Victory', media.guardian.co.uk, 28 March, http://media.guardian.co.uk/marketingandpr/story/0,7494,924642,00.html.

Curran, J. and Seaton, J. (2003) *Power Without Responsibility*, London, Routledge.

Dao, J. (2003) 'Private Lynch Comes Back Home to a Celebration Fit for a Hero', *New York Times*, 23 July, A1.

Dassin, J. (1998) *Torture in Brazil*, Austin, University of Texas Press.

David, M. (2005), *Science in Society*, London, Palgrave.

David, M. and Kirkhope, J. (2004) 'New Digital Technologies: Privacy/Property, Globalization and Law', *Perspectives on Global Development and Technology*, 3 (4), 437–449.

de Jonquieres, G. (1998) 'Network Guerillas', *Financial Times*, 30 April, MAI discussion list.

de Rato, Rodrigo (2004) 'IMF Managing Director Rodrigo de Rato's Statement at the Conclusion of His Visit To Brazil', *IMF Press Release* No. 04/186, www.imf.org/external/np/sec/pr/2004/pr04186.htm.

de Staal, G. D. (2003) 'Brazil: No Economy Without Democracy', *Le Monde Diplomatique*, December, http://mondediplo.com/2003/12/11brazil.

Debord, G. (1995) *The Society of the Spectacle*, trans. by Donald Nicholson-Smith, New York, Zone Books, 1995.

Deibert, R. (1997) *Parchment, Printing, and Hypermedia: Communication in World Order Transformation*. New York, Columbia University Press.

Deibert, M. (2004) 'Lula Continues to Play a Beautiful Game for Brazil', *Guardian*, 13 September.

Deleuze, G. *Desert Islands and Other Texts (1953–1974)*, New York, Semiotexte.

Deleuze, G. and Guattari, F. (1984) *Anti-Oedipus: Capitalism and Schizophrenia*, London, Athlone Press.

Della Porta, D., Kriesi, H. and D. Rucht, D. (1999) (eds), *Social Movements in a Globalising World*, London, Macmillan.

Der Derian, J. (2001) *Virtuous War: Mapping the Military-Industrial-Media-Entertainment Network*, Boulder, Colorado, Westview Press.

Desai, R. (1994) 'Second-Hand Dealers in Ideas: Think-Tanks and Thatcherite Hegemony' *New Left Review* (Jan.-Feb.) 203, 27–64.

DeYoung, K. (2001) 'U.S., Britain Step Up War for Public Opinion', *Washington Post*, 1 November, A1.

Dodge, T. (2003) 'An Iraqi in Cyberspace', *The Time Literary Supplement*, 24 October.

Doherty, A. and Hoedeman, O. (1994) 'Knights of the Road'. *New Statesman & Society*, 7 (327). 27–29.

Donly, M. (2001) 'Think Tanks Y2K: Progressive Gain but Right Still Cited Twice as Often', *Extra*, July/August.

Downey, J., and Murdock, G. (2003) 'The Counter-Revolution in Military Affairs: The Globalization of Guerilla Warfare', in D. K. Thussu and D. Freedman (eds), *War and the Media: Reporting Conflict 24/7*, London, Sage, pp. 70–86.

Dudley, S. (2002) 'Lula Needs a Miracle', *The Progressive*, October, http://static.highbeam.com/t/theprogressive/october012002/lulaneedsamiracle/.

Easton, B. (1988) 'From Reaganomics to Rogernomics', in Alan Bollard (ed.), *The Influence of United States Economics on New Zealand*, Wellington, NZ-US Educational Foundation and the New Zealand Institute of Economic Research, pp. 69–95.

ECLAC (2004) *A Decade of Social Development in Latin America*, www.eclac.cl/cgibin/getProd.asp?xml=/publicaciones/xml/1/14801/P14801.xml&xsl=/dds/tpl-i/p9f.xsl.

The Economist (1989), 'Of Policy and Pedigree', 6 May, 52–54.

The Economist (1996) 'The Mall of Dreams', 4 May, 23.

The Economist (1999a) 'Clueless in Seattle', 4 December.

The Economist (1999b) 'The Non-Governmental Order', 1 December.

The Economist (2003) 'Lula: Twixt Inflation and Recession', 19 June.

Edelman, M. (1988) *Constructing the Political Spectacle*, Chicago, University of Chicago Press.

Eisenstein, E. (1983) *The Printing Revolution in Early Modern Europe*, Cambridge, Cambridge University Press.

El-Nawawy, M. and Iskandar, A. (2002) *Al-Jazeera*, Boulder, Westview Press.

Elliott, M. (2002) 'Brazil's Election: Something to Celebrate?', *Time Magazine*, 14 October.

Ellis, R. (2003) 'The Surrender of MSNBC', AllYourTV.com, February 25, www.allyourtv.com/0203season/news/02252003donahue.html.

Enloe, C. (2004) 'Masculinity, War, Oil and Torture', *Left Business Observer*, No. 108.

Epstein, G. and Power, D. (2003) 'Rentier Incomes and Financial Crises: An Empirical Examination of Trends and Cycles in Some OECD Countries', www.networkideas.org/feathm/apr2003/Gerald_Power.pdf, accessed on 2 September 2003.

Ericson, R. V., Baranek, P. M. and Chan, B. L. (1989) *Negotiating Control: A Study of News Sources*, Toronto, University of Toronto Press.

ERT (2003a) 'Acheivements', European Round Table of Industrialists, 23 June, www.ert.be/pg/eng_frame.htm.

ERT (2003b) 'ERT Highlights 1983–2003'. Brussels: European Round Table of Industrialists, June www.ert.be/pdf/ERT%20Highlights.pdf.

ERT (2003c) 'The European Round Table of Industrialists', European Round Table of Industrialists, 23 June. www.ert.be/.

Ewen, S. (1996) *PR! A Social History of Spin*, New York, Basic Books.

Fanon, F. (1965) *The Wretched of the Earth*, London, MacGibbon & Kee.

Farhi, P. (2003) 'For Broadcast Media, Patriotism Pays', *Washington Post*, 28 March, C1.

Feldmann, L. (2003) 'The Impact of Bush Linking 9/11 and Iraq', csmonitor.com, 14 March, www.csmonitor.com/2003/0314/p02s01–woiq.html.

Feulner, E. J. (1985) 'Ideas, Think-Tanks and Governments: Away from the Power Elite, Back to the People', *Quadrant*, November, 22–26.

Financial Times (2003) 'The United States of Television', 21 July.

Fishman, M. (1980) *Manufacturing the News*, Austin, University of Texas Press.

Flournoy, D. (1992) *CNN World Report: Ted Turner's International News Coup*, London, John Libbey.

Foerde, J. (2002) 'The Monterrey Consensus: A Failure to Challenge the Status Quo', in Women's Environment & Development Organization (ed.), *Women in Globalization*, www.wedo.org.ffd/ffdreport.doc, accessed 12 December 2003.

Foucault, M. (1977) *Language, Counter-memory, Practice: Selected Essays and Interviews*, ed. with an introduction by Donald F. Bouchard and trans. by Donald F. Bouchard and Sherry Simon, Ithaca, NY, Cornell University Press.

Foucault, M. (1980) *The History of Sexuality, Vol. I: An Introduction*, New York, Vintage.

Foucault, M. (1991a) *The Foucault Effect: Studies in Governmentality*, ed. by Graham Burchell, Colin Gordon and Peter Miller , Chicago, University of Chicago Press.

Foucault, M. (1991b) *Remarks on Marx*, New York, Semiotexte.

Foucault, M. (2004) *Society Must Be Defended*, London, Penguin.

Friedmann, T. (1999) *The Lexus and The Olive Tree*, New York, Farrar, Straus and Giroux.

Friedmann, T. (2000) *The Lexus and the Olive Tree*, London, Harper/Collins.

Gallagher, D. F. (2002) 'A Rift Among Bloggers', *The New York Times*, 10 June.

Gans, H. (1979) *Deciding What's News: A Study Of CBS Evening News, Newsweek, and Time*, New York: Pantheon.

Gellner, W. (1995) 'The Politics of Policy 'Political Think Tanks' and Their Markets in the U.S.-Institutional Environment'. *Presidential Studies Quarterly*, 25 (3), 497–510.

Gentile, C. (2004) 'Brazil's Landless Movement Heats Up', *Washington Times*, 8 April, www.washtimes.com/upi-breaking/20040407–061506–2886r.htm.

George, S. (2000) 'Fixing or Nixing the WTO', *Le Monde Diplomatique*, January, www.corpwatch.org/trac/feature/wto/6–george.html

Gereffi, G. and Korzeniewicz, M. (1994) *Commodity Chains and Global Capitalism*, Westport, Conn. Praeger.

Giddens, A. (1990) *Consequences of Modernity*, Oxford, Blackwell.

Gillmor, D. (2004) *We the Media*, Cambridge, O'Reilly Media.

Gini, A. R. and Sullivan, T. J. (1989) 'A Critical Overview', in A. R. Gini and T. J. Sullivan (eds), *It Comes with the Territory: An Inquiry Concerning Work and the Person*, New York, Random House, pp. 1–35.

Girardet, E. R. (1996) 'Reporting Humanitarianism: Are the New Electronic Media Making a Difference?', in Robert I. Rotberg and Thomas G. Weiss (eds) *From Massacres to Genocide: Media, Public Policy and Humanitarian Crises*, Washington, D.C., Brookings Institution, pp. 45–67.

Glasgow University Media Group (1976) *Bad News*, London, Routledge & Kegan Paul.

Glasgow University Media Group (1980) *More Bad News* London, Routledge & Kegan Paul.

Glasner, J. (2003) Big Win for File-Swap Services, www.wired.com/news/business/0,1367,58636,00.html, accessed 8 June 2004.

'The Good Think-Tank Guide' (1992). *The Economist,* 321 (7738), 49–53.

Gowan, P. (1999) *The Global Gamble: Washington's Faustian Bid for World Dominance,* London, Verso.

Gowing, N. (1994) *Real-time Television Coverage of Armed Conflicts and Diplomatic Crises,* Harvard University Press.

Grabel, I. (2002) 'Neoliberal Finance and Crisis in the Developing World', *Monthly Review,* 53 (1), 34–45.

Graber, D. (2002) 'The New Anarchists', *New Left Review* (Jan.–Feb.) vol. 13.

Gramsci, A. (1971) *Selections from the Prison Notebooks,* London, Lawrence & Wishart.

Granneman, S. (2003) 'Al-Jazeera, the First Amendment, and Security Professionals', *SecurityFocus*.com, 22 April.

Gray, P. (2003) 'Al-Jazeera Suffers DoS Attack', News.ZDNet.co.uk, 27 March.

Gray, J. (2004) *Heresies: Against Progress and Other Illusions,* London, Granta.

Grefe, E. A. and Linsky, M. (1995) *The New Corporate Activism: Harnessing the Power of Grassroots Tactics for Your Organization,* New York, McGraw-Hill.

Greider, W. (1997) *One World, Ready or Not: The Manic Logic of Global Capitalism,* New York, Simon & Schuster.

Greimas, A. J. (1987) *On Meaning: Selected Writings in Semiotic Theory,* Minneapolis, University of Minnesota Press.

Group of Ten (2001) Report on the Consolidation of Financial Sector, www.imf. org/external/np/g10/2001/01/Eng/.

Habermas, J.(1989) *The Structural Transformation of the Public Sphere,* Cambridge, Polity Press.

Hackett, R., and Zhao, Y. (1998) *Sustaining Democracy: Journalism and the Politics of Objectivity,* Toronto, Garamond Press.

Halliday, F. (1989) *Cold War, Third World,* London, Radius.

Halton, E. (1995) *Bereft of Reason: On the Decline of Social Thought and Prospects for its Renewal,* Chicago, University of Chicago Press.

Hamelink, C. J. (1998) 'World Communication: Conflicting Aspirations for the Twenty-first Century', in Brants et al. (eds), *The Media In Question,* London, Sage pp. 64–76.

Hamilton, C. (2003) *Growth Fetish,* London, Pluto Press.

Hardt, M and Negri, A. (2000) *Empire.* Cambridge, MA, Harvard University Press.

Harper's (2003) 'Shock and Awe', *Harper's,* June, 306 (1837), 18.

Harvey, D. (1989) *The Condition of Postmodernity: An Enquiry into the Origins of Cultural Change,* Oxford, Blackwell.

Harvey, D. (1989) *Conditions of Postmodernity,* Cambridge, MA, Blackwell.

Harvey, D. (2003) *The New Imperialism,* Oxford, Oxford University Press.

Hassan, R. (2004) *Media, Politics and the Network Society,* Maidenhead and New York, Open University Press.

Hauben, M. (2004) *History of the ARPANET,* www.dei.isep.ipp.pt/docs/arpa.html.

Hay, C. (2002) *Political Analysis,* London, Palgrave.

Heard, L.S. (2004) 'Innocents are Paying the Price in Iraq', Gulf News Online Edition, 14 September.

Henry, J. S. (2003) *The Blood Bankers,* New York, Four Walls, Eight Windows.

Henwood, D. (1999) *Left Business Observer,* December, www.panix.com/~dhenwood/ seattlefriday.html.

Hentoff, N. (2003) 'War on the Bill of Rights', *In These Times*, 5 September.

Herman and Chomsky (1979) *The Washington Connection and Third World Fascism*, Boston, South End Press.

Herman, E. S. (1986) 'Gatekeeper vs. Propaganda Models: A Critical American Perspective', in P. Golding, G. Murdock and P. Schlesinger (eds), *Communicating Politics: Mass Communications and the Political Process*, New York, Holmes & Meyer.

Herman, E. S., and Chomsky, N. (1988) *Manufacturing Consent*, New York, Pantheon.

Herman, E. S., and Chomsky, N. (1995) *Manufacturing Consent: The Political Economy of the Mass Media*, New York, Vintage.

Herman, E. and McChesney, R. (1997) *The Global Media: The New Missionaries of Global Capitalism*, London, Cassell.

Hernandez, A. (2004) 'Brazil's New Deal Foreign Policy', *Peacework*, February, http://www.afsc.org/pwork/0402/040211.htm.

Himmelstein, J. L. (1990) *To the Right: The Transformation of American Conservatism*. Berkeley, CA, University of California Press.

Hinchberger, B. (2004) 'Brazil's Media Monopoly', *Multinational Monitor*, multinationalmonitor.org/hyper/issues/1991/01/mm0191_12.html.

Hitchens, C. (2002) interview with *The Stranger*, 17–23 January.

Hoedeman, O. and Doherty, A. (2002) 'Joining Forces: Big Business Rallies after Seattle', in E. Lubbers (ed.), *Battling Big Business: Countering Greenwash, Infiltration and Other Forms of Bullying*, Devon, UK, Green Books, pp. 64–77.

Holson, L. M. (2003) 'Saving the Drama For the Audience', *New York Times*, 6 July, C1.

Houston, W. (2003a) 'War Coverage More Objective Here than in U.S.', *The Globe and Mail*, 22 March, A10.

Houston, W. (2003b) 'Independent Reporters Jailed, Mistreated', *The Globe and Mail*, 5 April, A8.

Hudson, M. (2003) 'America's Monetary Imperialism', *Global Dialogue*, 5 (1/2), 73–81.

Industry Trust for IP Awareness Limited (2004) Revealing the True Face of DVD Piracy, London, Industry Trust for IP Awareness Limited.

Infoplease (2004) 'Gap Between Rich and Poor', www.infoplease.com/ipa/A0908770.html.

Inter-American Commission on Human Rights (2004) 'Report on the Situation of Human Rights in Brazil', www.cidh.org/countryrep/brazil-eng/chaper%202%20.htm.

Iskandar, A. and El-Nawawy, M. (2004) 'Al-Jazeera and War Coverage in Iraq: The Quest for Contextual Objectivity', in S. Allan and B. Zelizer (eds), *Reporting War: Journalism in Wartime*, London and New York, Routledge, pp. 315–332.

Ivens, M. (ed.) (1978) *International Papers on the Revival of Freedom and Enterprise,* London, AIMS.

James, C. (2001) 'Power Brokers', *The Advertiser*, 28 April, 63.

Jameson, F. (1991) *Postmodernism, or the Cultural Logic of Late Capitalism*, Durham, Duke University Press.

Jessop, B. and Sum, N-L. (2001) 'Pre-Disciplinary and Post-Disciplinary Perspectives', *New Political Economy*, 6 (1), 89–102.

Johnson, B. (2004) *Just Who are the Bad Guys?*, *Guardian* Online Supplement, 23 September.

Jones, T. (2003) 'Media Giant's Rally Sponsorship Raises Questions', *Chicago Tribune*, 19 March 19, 6.

Kafala, T. (2003) 'Al-Jazeera: News Channel in the News', *BBC News Online*, 29 March.

Kahney, L. (2003) 'Media Watchdogs Caught Napping', *Wired News*, 17 March.

Kahney, L. (2001) 'Amateur Newsies Top the Pros', *Wired News*, 15 September.

Kakutani, M. (2003) 'Shock, Awe and Razzmatazz in the Sequel', *New York Times*, 25 March, E1.

Kalathil, S. and Boas, T. C. (2003) *Open Networks, Closed Regimes: The Impact of the Internet on Authoritarian Rule*, Washington, D.C., Carnegie Endowment for International Peace.

Kampfner, J. (2003) 'The Truth about Jessica', *Guardian*, 15 May, Features Pages, 2.

Kaplan, R. (1996) The Ends of the Earth, New York, Random House.

Keane, J. (1991) *The Media and Democracy*. Cambridge, Polity Press.

Keck, E. M. (1991)*The Workers' Party and Democratisation in Brazil*, New Haven and London, Yale University Press.

Kelley, M. (2003) 'Pentagon Likely to Keep Embedding Plan', *Editor and Publisher*, 17 June, www.editorandpublisher.com/editorandpublisher/headlines/article_display.jsp?vnu_content_id=1915837.

Kellner, D. (1992) *The Persian Gulf TV War*, Boulder, Colorado, Westview Press.

Kellner, D. (2001) *The Postmodern Adventure: Science, Technology and Cultural Studies at the Third Millennium*, London, Routledge.

Kellner, D. (2003a) 'September 11, Spectacles of Terror, and Media Manipulation: A Critique of Jihadist and Bush Media Politics', *Logos*, Winter, www.logosonline.home.igc.org/kellner_media.htm.

Kellner, D. (2003b) *From 9/11 to Terror War: The Dangers of the Bush Legacy*, New York, Rowman and Littlefield.

Kelsey, J. (1999) *Reclaiming the Future: New Zealand and the Global Economy*, Wellington, Bridget Williams Books.

Kemeny, L. and Rush, D. (2003) 'Music Gets The Blues', *Sunday Times*, Business Focus, 1 June, 5.

Kenna, K. (2003) 'Americans Pay Price for Speaking Out', *Toronto Star*, 9 August, A22.

Kennedy, P. (1993) *Preparing for the Twenty-First Century*, New York, Random House.

Kepp, M. and Zellner, M. (2000) 'The Empires Strikes Again – Brazil's Globo', *Latin Trade*, April.

Kepp, M. (2002) 'Massive M and A Madness?', *Latin Trade*, October.

Ketupanet (2004) *Media Profiles*, 'Globo', www.ketupa.net/globo.htm.

Khor, M. (1999) 'The Revolt of Developing Nations', *Corporate Watch*, www.corpwatch.org/feature/wto/b-khor.html.

Khor, M. (1996) *The Uruguay Round and Third World Sovereignty*, Penang, Third World Network.

Kim, Y.-H. (2002) 'Globalization and Financial Crises in Seoul, South Korea', in R. Grant and J. Short (eds), *Globalization and the Margins*, London, Palgrave, pp. 170–190.

King, J. (2003) 'Bush Limits Pay Increases for Many Federal Workers', *CNN*, 27 August, www.edition.cnn.com/2003/ALLPOLITICS/08/27/bush.federal.pay.

Kingstone, P. R. (1999) *Crafting Coalitions for Reform: Business Preferences, Political Institutions and Neoliberal Reform in Brazil*, University Park, PA, The Pennsylvania State University Press.

Kull, S. (2003) 'Misperceptions, the Media and the Iraq War', Program on International Policy Attitudes (PIPA), October, www.pipa.org/OnlineReports /Iraq/Media_10_02_03_Report.pdf.

Kull, S., Ramsay, C. and Lewis, E. (2003) 'Misperceptions, the Media, and the Iraq War', *Political Science Quarterly*, 118 (4), pp. 569–598.

Kundera, M. (1991) *Immortality*, London, Faber and Faber.

Kurtz, H. (2003a) 'Embedded, And Taking Flak', *Washington Post*, 31 March, C1.

Kurtz, H. (2003b) 'Embedded Reporter's Role In Army Unit's Actions Questioned by Military', *Washington Post*, 25 June, C1.

Kurtz, H. (2003c) 'The Press Gets Pumped', washingtonpost.com, 3 April, www. washingtonpost.com/wp-dyn/articles/A19046–2003Apr3.html.

Langfield, A. (2002) 'Democratizing Journalism', *Online Journalism Review*, www. orj.org, 3 April.

Lee, M. A. and Solomon, N. (1992) *Unreliable Sources: A Guide to Detecting Bias in the News Media*, New York, Carol Publishing Group.

Levine, R. M. and Crocitti, J. L. (eds) (1999) *The Brazil Reader*, London, Latin American Bureau.

Liderdigital (2002) 'Brazilian TV O Globo HQ Declare Chapter 11 to Get Rid of Debts', http://digest.liderdigital.com/noticias/detalle_noticia.php?id_noticia=15.

Livingston, S. and Lance Bennett, W. (2003) 'Gatekeeping, Indexing, and Live-Event News: Is Technology Altering the Construction of News?', *Political Communication*, 20, 363–380.

Loo, D. D. and Reibel, M. (2003) 'Television News and the 1990s Crime Issue', www.nssa.us/nssajrnl/NSSJ2003%2020_2/html/12Loo_Dennis.htm.

Lorde, A. (1984) *Sister Outsider*, Freedom, California, Crossing Press.

Luke, T. W. (1997) 'At the End of Nature: Cyborgs, "Humachines", and Environments in Postmodernity', *Environment and Planning. A*, 29.

Luke, T. W. (1996) 'Governmentality and Contra-Governmentality: Rethinking Sovereignty and Territoriality After the Cold War', *Political Geography*, 15 (6/7), 491–507.

Luke, T. W. (1993) 'Discourses of Disintegration, Texts of Transformation: Re-Reading Realism in the New World Order', *Alternatives*, 18, 229–258.

Luke, T. W. and Geároid Ó. Tuathail, G. Ó. (1997) 'On Videocameralistics: The Geopolitics of Failed States, the CNN International, and (UN) Governmentality', *Review of International Political Economy*, 4, 709–733.

Lule, J. (2004) 'War and Its Metaphors: News Language and the Prelude to War in Iraq, 2003', *Journalism Studies*, 5 (2), 179–190.

McCool, G. (2003) 'NY Police Admit Keeping Anti-War Protest Database', *Reuters*, 10 April, www.commondreams.org/headlines03/0410–07.htm.

McCullagh, C. (2002) *Media Power: A Sociological Introduction*, Basingstoke, Palgrave.

MacDonald, G. (2003) 'CNN Medical Reporter Becomes Unlikely Hero', *The Globe and Mail*, 5 April, A8.

McGuigan, J. (1999) *Modernity and Postmodern Culture*, Buckingham, Open University Press.

Mckay, G. (1996) *Senseless Acts of Beauty: Cultures of Resistance since the Sixties*, London, Verso.

Mckay, G. (1999) *DIY Culture: Party and Protest in Nineties Britain*, London, Verso.

McKinnon, R. (1973) *Money and Capital in Economic Development*, Washington, D.C., Brookings Institution.

McMahon, P. (2002) *Global Control: Information Technology and Globalization Since 1845*, Cheltenham, Edward Elgar.

McNair, B. (1988) *Images of the Enemy*, London, Routledge.

McNair, B. (1989) 'Glasnost and Restructuring in the Soviet Media', *Media, Culture & Society*, 11 (3), 327–351.

McNair, B. (1998) *The Sociology of Journalism*, London, Arnold.

McNair, B. (2000) *Journalism and Democracy*, London, Routledge.

McNair, B. (2003) 'From Control to Chaos: Towards a New Sociology of Journalism', *Media, Culture & Society*, 25 (4), 547–555.

McQuail, D. (1987) *Mass Communications Theory: An Introduction*, 2nd edn, London, Sage.

Madeley, J. (2000) *Hungry for Trade: How the Poor Pay for Free Trade*, Global Issues Series, London and New York, Zed Books.

Mann, C. C. (2003) The Year the Music Dies, www.wired.com/wired/archive /11.02/dirge.html (accessed 14 October 2004).

Marshall, A. (2002) 'The Marshall Plan', *Wired*, 11 February, www.wired.com /wired/archive/11.02/marshall_pr.html

Martin, H.-P., and Schumann, H. (1998) *The Global Trap: Globalization & the Assault on Democracy & Prosperity*, London, Zed Press.

Martinez (1999) 'Where was the Color in Seattle?', *Color Lines Magazine*, www. Zmag.org/CrisesCurEvts/globalism/Seattlecolor.htm

Marx, K. (1995) *Capital,* Oxford, Oxford University Press.

Matheson, D. (2004) 'Weblogs and the Epistemology of the News: Some Trends in Online Journalism', *New Media and Society*, 6 (4), 493–518.

Mead, W. (2000) 'The Case for Capitalism', *World Link* September/October.

Melucci, A. (1995) 'The New Social Movements Revisited: Reflections on a Sociological Misunderstanding', in Louis Maheu (ed.), *Social Movements and Social Classes: The Future of Collective Action*, London, Sage.

Mermin, J. (1999) *Debating War and Peace: Media Coverage of U.S. Intervention in the Post-Vietnam Era*, Princeton, Princeton University Press.

Midnight Notes Collective (2003) *Auroras of the Zapatistas*, London, Pluto Press.

Milbank, D. (2004) 'Bush Defends Assertions of Iraq-Al Qaeda Relationship', *Washington Post*, 18 June, A9.

Milbank, D. and Deane, C. (2003) 'Hussein Link to 9/11 Lingers in Many Minds', *Washington Post*, 6 September, A1.

MIT (2004) Globo as the World's Fourth Largest Media Network, web.mit.edu/12.000/www/m2006/teams/r1/possible_media_outlets.htm.

Moeller, S. D. (2004) 'Media Coverage of Weapons of Mass Destruction', paper produced for the Center for International and Security Studies at Maryland (CISSM), 9 March, University of Maryland, www.cissm.umd.edu/documents/WMDstudy_ short.pdf.

Moore, B. and Carpenter, G. (1987) 'Main Players', in Ken Coghill (ed.), *The New Right's Australian Fantasy*, Fitzroy, Victoria: McPhee Gribble and Penguin Books.

Moses, L. (2003) 'Gen. Franks a Fan of Embedding', *Editor and Publisher*, 29 April, www.editorandpublisher.com/editorandpublisher/headlines/article_display.jsp?vnu_content_id=1876177.

Mowlana, H., Gerbner, G. and Schiller, H. I. (eds) (1992) *Triumph of the Image: The Media's War in the Persian Gulf-A Global Perspective*, Boulder, CO, Westview Press.

Mulgan, G. (1991) *Communication and Control*, Cambridge, Polity Press.

Murphy, C. N. (1999) 'Inequality, Turmoil and Democracy: Global Political-Economic Visions at the End of the Century', *New Political Economy*, 4 (2), 289–304.

Nacos, B. L. (2002) *Mass-Mediated Terrorism: The Central Role of the Media in Terrorism and Counterterrorism*, New York: Rowman and Littlefield.

Nagourney, A. and Elder, J. (2003) 'Threats and Responses: The Poll', *New York Times*, 11 March, A1.

Natsios, A. (1996) 'Illusions of influence: The CNN effect in complex emergencies', in Robert I. Rotberg and Thomas G. Weiss (eds), *From Massacres to Genocide: The Media, Public Policy and Humanitarian Crises*, Washington, D.C., Brookings Institution, pp. 149–168.

Naughton, J. (1999) *A Brief History of the Future: The Origins of the Internet*, London, Weidenfeld & Nicolson.

New Musical Express (2004) BPI Court Victory, www.nme.com/news/110194.htm (accessed 14 October 2004).

News Corporation (2004) 'Press Release', www.newscorp.com/news/news_221.html.

Nineham, C. (1995) 'Is the Media All Powerful?', *International Socialism*, Issue 67.

Notes from Nowhere (2003) (eds) *We are Everywhere: The Irresistible Rise of Global Anticapitalism*, London, Verso.

Noguereira, A. (2002) 'The Birth and Promise of the Indymedia Revolution', in B. Shepard and R. Hayduck (eds), *From Act Up to the WTO: Urban Protest and Community Building in the Era of Globalisation*, London, Verso.

Offe, C. (1985) 'New Social Movements: Challenging the Boundaries of Institutional Politics', *Social Research* (Winter) 52 (4).

Ohmae, K. (1990) *The Borderless World: Power and Strategy in the Interlinked Economy*, New York: Harper and Row.

Ortellado, P. (2002) 'Brazil: Between Hope and Fear', Znet, www.zmag.org/content/showarticle.cfm?SectionID=48&ItemID=2665.

O'Shaughnessy, H. (2002) 'The Boy for Brazil?', *Observer Newspaper*, 6 October.

Ostrum, M.A. (2003) 'Net Plays Big Role in War News, Commentary', *The Mercury News*, 28 February.

Outing, S. (2001) How Online Journalists can Recover Lost Ground, *Poynter.Org.*, 11 September.

Outing, S. (2003) 'Stop the Presses!', *Editor & Publisher*, 26 March.

Painter, J. (2004) 'No Turmoil as South America Goes Left', BBC News Online, 2 November, news.bbc.co.uk/2/hi/americas/3975663.stm.

Parenti, M. (1986) *Inventing Reality: The Politics of the Mass Media*, New York, St Martin's Press.

Paterson, C. (1998) 'Global Battlefields', in Boyd-Barratt and Rantanen (eds), *The Globalization of News*, pp. 79–103.

Patomäki, H. (2001) *Democratizing Globalization: The Leverage of the Tobin Tax*, London, Zed Books.

Paulson, M. (1999) 'Business Leaders Fight Back Against Anti-WTO Forces', *Seattle Post*, 24 September.

Peet, R. (2003) *The Unholy Trinity*, New York, Zed Books.

Peirce, C. (1955) *Philosophical Writings of Peirce*, ed. by Justus Buchler , New York, Dover.

Perez, C. (2002) *Technological Revolutions and Financial Capital*, Cheltenham, Edward Elgar.

Petras, J. (2002) 'U.S. Offensive in Latin America: Coups, Retreats, and Radicalization', *Monthly Review*, May 2002.

Petridis, A. (2004) *Lord of the Rings*, www.guardian.co.uk/arts/fridayreview/story/0,1220860,00.html (accessed 9 September 2004).

Pew Internet & American Life Project (2003) 'The Internet and the Iraq War', Project Report, 1 April.

Pew Internet & American Life Project (2004) 'The Internet as a Unique News Source', 8 July, www.pewinternet.org/.

Pickerill, J. (2004) *Representing Resistance: The Practices and Constructions of Indymedia*. Imaging Social Movements Conference, Ormskirk, Edge Hill College.

Power, T. J. (2000) *The Political Right in Postauthoritarian Brazil*, University Park, PA, The Pennsylvania State University Press.

Priest, D, and Milbank, D. (2003) 'President Defends Allegations On Iraq', *Washington Post*, 15 July, A1.

Priest, D., Booth, W. and Schmidt, S. (2003) 'A Broken Body, a Broken Story, Pieced Together', *Washington Post*, 17 June, A1.

Project for Excellence in Journalism (2003) 'Embedded Reporters: What are Americans Getting?', www.journalism.org/resources/research/reports/war/embed/default.asp.

Pynchon, T. (1973) *Gravity's Rainbow*, New York, Viking Compass.

Rampton, S., and Stauber, J. (2003) 'Trading Fear', *Guardian*, 12 July, Weekend Pages, 32.

Rangwala, G., and Whitaker, R. (2003) '20 Lies About the War', *The Hamilton Spectator*, 14 July, C1.

Ray, L. (1993) *Rethinking Critical Theory: Emancipation in the age of Global Social Movements*, London, Sage.

Raymond, J. (1996) *The Invention of the Newspaper*, Oxford, Clarendon Press.

Reich, R. (1991) *The Work of Nations: Preparing Ourselves for Twenty-first Century Capitalism*, New York, Knopf.

Reid, P. (2003) *Biometrics and Network Security*, New York, Prentice Hall.

Reilly, K. (2003) 'Warning You Are Being Watched', *In These Times*,19 September .

Ricci, D. (1993) *The Transformation of American Politics: The New Washington and the Rise of Think Tanks*, New Haven, Yale University Press.

Rich, F. (2003) 'The Spoils of War Coverage', *New York Times*, 13 April, B1.

Rippa, S. A. (1984) *Education in a Free Society: An American History*, New York, Longman.

Roberts, P. (2003) 'Al-Jazeera Hobbled by DDOS Attack', *Infoworld.com*, 26 March.

Robins, K. and Webster, F. (1999) *Times of the Technolculture: From the Information Society to the Virtual Life*, London and New York, Routledge.

Robins, W. (2001) News Web Sites Could Not Compete with TV, *Editor and Publisher*, 11 September.

Robinson, P. (2002) *The CNN Effect: The Myth of News, Foreign Policy and Intervention*, Routledge.

Rorty, R. (1998) *Truth and Progress; Philosophical Papers Volume 3*, Cambridge, Cambridge University Press.

Rosenau, J. (1980) *The Scientific Study of Foreign Policy*, New York, Nichols Publishing Company.

Rosenau, J. M. (1990) *Turbulence in World Politics: A Theory of Change and Continuity*, Princeton Princeton University Press.

Rosenbaum, D. E. (2001) 'Since Sept. 11, Lobbyists Put Old Pleas in New Packages, *New York Times*, B1.

Rosenthal, P. (2003) 'Awe Arrives, But Not With Human Angle', *Chicago Sun-Times*, 22 March, www.suntimes.com/output/rosenthal/cst-nws-tv22.html.

Rubin, J. (2002) 'Brazil's democracy takes a chance', *New York Times*, 23 October.

Rutenberg, J. (2001) 'Hollywood Seeks Role in the War', *New York Times*, 20 October, B9.

Rutenberg, J. (2003a) 'Battle Rages Between Fox News and MSNBC', *New York Times*, 3 April, C6.

Rutenberg, J. (2003b) 'Cable's War Coverage Suggests a New 'Fox Effect' on Television', *New York Times*, 16 April, B9.

Rutenberg, J. (2003c) 'To Interview Former P.O.W., CBS Dangles Stardom', *New York Times*, 16 June, A1.

Rutherford, P. (2004) *Weapons of Mass Persuasion: Marketing the War against Iraq*, Toronto, University of Toronto Press.

Sader, E. and Silverstein, K. (1991) *Without fear of being Happy: Lula, The Workers' Party and Brazil*, London, Verso.

St John, W. (2003a) 'Akamai Cancels a Contract for Arabic Network's Site', *The New York Times*, 4 April.

Sale, K. (1993) *The Green Revolution: The American Environmental Movement, 1962–1992*, New York, Hill and Wang.

Salladay, R. (2003) 'Peace Activism: A Matter of Language', *San Francisco Chronicle*, 7 April, A19.

Saloma, J. S. (1984) *Ominous Politics: The New Conservative Labyrinth*, New York, Hill and Wang.

Sampson, A. (1996) *Company Man: The Rise and Fall of Corporate Life*, paperback edn, London, HarperCollinsBusiness.

Sayer, A. (1992) *Method in Social Science*, London, Routledge.

Schmidt, S., and Loeb, V. (2003) 'She Was Fighting to the Death', *Washington Post*, 3 April, A1.

Schudson, M. (1993) *Advertising, the Uneasy Persuasion: Its Dubious Impact on American Society*, London, Routledge.

Seelye, K. Q. (2002) 'Pentagon Plays Role in Fictional Terror Drama', *New York Times*, 31 March, A1.

Seib, P. (2004) *Beyond the Front Lines: How the News Media Cover a World Shaped by War*. New York, Palgrave Macmillan.

Seidman, G. W. (1990) *Manufacturing Militance: Workers' Movements in Brazil and South Africa, 1970–1985*, London, University of California Press.

Sennett, R. (1996) *Flesh and Stone: The Body and the City in Western Civilization*, London, Faber and Faber.

Sethi, S. P. (1977) *Advocacy Advertising and Large Corporations*. Lexington, MA, Lexington Books.

Sharkey, J. E. (2003) 'The Television War', *American Journalism Review*, May, 18.

Sharma, S. (2003) *The Asian Financial Crisis*, Manchester, Manchester University Press.

Shaw, E. (1973) *Financial Deepening in the Economic Development*, Oxford, Oxford University Pres.

Shenon, P. (2003) 'Report on USA Patriot Act Alleges Civil Rights Violations', *New York Times*, 21 July, A1.

Shenon, P., and Marquis, C. (2004) 'Panel Finds No Qaeda-Iraq Tie; Describes a Wider Plot for 9/11', *New York Times*, 17 June, A1.

Shepard, B., and Hayduck, R. (eds.) (2002) F*rom Act Up to the WTO: Urban Protest and Community Building in the Era of Globalisation*, London, Verso.

Shiva, V. (1997) *Biopiracy: The Plunder of Nature and Knowledge*, Boston, Massachusetts, South End Press.

Sidaway, J., and Bryson, J. (2002) 'Constructing Knowledges of "Emerging Markets": UK-Based Investment Managers and their Overseas Connections', Environment and Planning A, 34 (3), 401–416.

Sinclair, T. (1994) 'Passing Judgement: Credit Rating Proceses as Regulatory Mechanisms of Governance in the Emerging World Order', *Review of International Political Economy*, 1 (1), 133–159.

Singh, K. (2000) *Taming Global Financial Flows*, London, Zed Books.

Skidmore, T. E. (1967) *Politics in Brazil, 1930–1964*, New York, Oxford University Press.

Skidmore, T. E. (1988) *The Politics of Military Rule in Brazil, 1964–1985*, New York and Oxford, Oxford University Press.

Skidmore. T. (1997) *The Politics of Military Rule in Brazil 1964–1985*, Oxford, Oxford University Press.

Smith, J. A. (1991) *The Idea Brokers: Think Tanks and the Rise of the New Policy Elite*, New York, Free Press.

Socialist World (2003) 'Recession and Corruption', www.socialistworld.net/index2. html?/eng/2004/04/01brazil.html.

Soederberg, S. (2002) 'The New International Financial Architecture: Procrustean Bed for Emerging Markets?', *Third World Quarterly*, 23 (4), 607–620.

Soley, L. (1997) 'The Power of the Press has a Price',. July/August. *Extra*.

Solomon, N. (1999) *The Habits of Highly Deceptive Media: Decoding Spin and Lies in the Mainstream News*, Monroe, Maine, Common Courage Press.

Sontag, S. (2004) 'What Have We Done?', *Guardian*, 24 May, www.commondreams. org/views04/0524–09.htm.

Stanley, A. (2001) 'Battling the Skepticism of a Global TV Audience', *New York Times*, 1 November, B4.

Stauber, J. S. and Rampton, S. (1995) *Toxic Sludge is Good for You: Lies, Damn Lies and the Public Relations Industry*, Monroe, Maine, Common Courage Press.

Steger, M. B. (2001) *Globalism: The New Market Ideology*, Lenham, MA, Rowman & Littlefield.

Stein, R. (2004) '100,000 Civilian Deaths Estimated in Iraq', *Washington Post*, 29 October.

Stepan, A. (1989) *Democratising Brazil*, Oxford, Oxford University Press.

Strupp, J. (2003) 'Was Press Asleep on Pre-War WMD Issue?', *editorandpublisher. com*, 12 June, www.editorandpublisher.com/editorandpublisher/headlines/article _display.jsp?vnu_content_id=1910998.

Sum, N.-L. (2001) 'An Integral Approach to the Asian "Crisis": The (Dis-) Articulation of the Production and Financial (Dis-)Order', *Capital and Class*, 74, 141–166.

Sum, N.-L. and Jessop, B. (2004) *Towards Cultural Political Economy*, Cheltenham, Edward Elgar.

Sum, N.-L. (2002) 'The Material, Strategic and Discursive Dimensions of the "Asian Crisis" and Subsequent Developments', in P. Masina (ed.) *Rethinking Development in East Asia*, London, Curzon, pp. 53–78.

Strange, S. (1986) *Casino Capitalism*, Oxford, Blackwell.

Thomas, J. (2000) *The Battle in Seattle: The Story Behind and Beyond the WTO Demonstrations*, Golden, Colorado, Fulcrum Publishing.

Thussu, D. K. (2002) 'Managing the Media in an Era of Round-the-Clock News: Notes from India's First Tele-War', *Journalism Studies*, 3 (2), 203–212.

Tugend, A. (2003) 'Pundits for Hire', ajr.org, May, www.ajr.org/Article.asp?id=2995.

Tumber, H. and Palmer, J. (2004) *Media at War: The Iraq Crisis*, London, Sage.

Udry, C.-A. (2002) 'The Workers' Party in Power', *Workers' Liberty*, December, www.workersliberty.org/comment/reply/669.

Ullman, H. K., and Wade, J. P. (1996) *Shock and Awe: Achieving Rapid Dominance*, Washington: NDU Press Book, www.dodccrp.org/shockIndex.html.

Urry, J. (2003) *Global Complexity*, Cambridge, Polity.

USCIB (1998) 'Summary of U.S. Council Recommendations for the May WTO Ministerial'. US Council for International Business, May, www.uscib.org/ wtost.asp.

Virilio, P. (1984) *War and Cinema: The Logistics of Perception*, London, Verso.

Virilio, P. (1990) *Popular Defense and Ecological Struggles*, New York, Semiotexte.

Virilio, P. (1994) Bunker Archaeology, Princeton Architectural Press, New York.

Virilio, P. (1997) *Open Sky*, London, Verso.

Virilio, P. (2003) *The Unknown Quantity*, London, Thames and Hudson.

Vogel, D. (1989) *Fluctuating Fortunes: The Political Power of Business in America*, New York, Basic Books.

Volkmer, I. (2002) 'Journalism and Political Crises in the Global Network Society', in B. Zelizer and S. Allan (eds), *Journalism After September 11*, London and New York, Routledge, pp. 235–242.

Volkmer, I. (2002) Journalism and Political Crises in the Global Network Society', in B. Zelizer and S. Allan (eds), *Journalism After September 11*, London and New York, Routledge.

Wade, R. and Veneroso, F. (1998) 'The Asian Financial Crisis: The High Debt Model Versus the Wall Street-Treasury-IMF Complex', *New Left Review*, 228, 3–23.

Walker, R. B. J. (1993) *Inside/Outside: International Relations as Political Theory*. Cambridge, Cambridge University Press.

Wallerstein, I. (2003) 'Brazil and the World System: The Era of Lula', fbc.binghamton.edu/120en.htm.

Wanna, J. (1992) 'Furthering Business Interests: Business Associations and Political Representation', in S. Bell and J. Wanna (eds), *Business-Government Relations in Australia*, Sydney, Harcourt Brace Jovanovich, pp. 66–79.

Ward, S. (2003) 'In Bed With the Military', *Media*, Spring, 10 (1), pp. 6–7.

Wark, M. (1994) *Virtual Geography*, Indiana, Indiana University Press.

Weaver, R. K. (1989) 'The Changing World of Think Tanks', *PS: Political Science and Politics*, 22 (Sept.). 563–78.

Weber, S. (2002) 'War, Terrorism, and Spectacle', *South Atlantic Quarterly*, 101 (3), 449–458.

Webster, F. (2003) 'Information Warfare in an Age of Globalization', in D. K. Thussu and D. Freedman (eds), *War and the Media: Reporting Conflict 24/7*, London, Sage, pp. 57–69.

Whitaker, B. (2003) 'Al-Jazeera Cause Outcry with Broadcast of Battle Causalities', *Guardian*, 24 March.

Whoriskey, P. (2003) 'In Lynch Country, a Puzzled Kind of Pride', *Washington Post*, 22 July, A1.

Wilkin, P. (2001) *The Political Economy of Global Communication*, London, Pluto Press.

Williamson, J. (1994) 'In Search of a Manual for Technopols', in J. Williamson (ed.) *The Political Economy of Policy Reform*, Washington, DC, Institute for International Economics, pp. 9–28.

Willis, J. (2003) 'The War, Brought to You by the White House', *Guardian*, 20 June, Leader Pages, 21.

Wolf, M. (2001) *Financial Times*, 'Responding to the Anti-globalisation Protestors', 4 September.

Wolff, M. (2003) 'Live From Doha', NewYorkmetro.com, 7 April, www.newyork metro.com/nymetro/news/media/columns/medialife/n_8545/index.html.

Woolgar, S. (1988) *Science: The Very Idea*, London, Tavistock.

Woolgar, S. (2002) *Virtual Society? Technology, Cyberbole, Reality*, Oxford, Oxford University Press.

Woolley, B. (1999) 'Let the Good Times Roll', *60 Minutes*, 5 September.

World Economic Forum. 2000, 'World Economic Forum', WEF. www.weforum.org/. *World Bank Report* 2004. web.worldbank.org/WBSITE/EXTERNAL/COUNTRIES/LACEXT/BRAZILEXTN/0,menuPK:322351~pagePK:141132~piPK:141107~theSitePK:322341,00.html

York, G. (2003) 'Independent Journalists' Work Severely Hampered', *Globe and Mail*, 3 April, A7.

Yuen, E., Katsiaficas, G. and Burton Rose, D. (2001) (eds) *The Battle of Seattle: The New Challenge to Capitalist Globalization*, New York, Soft Skull Press.

The Zapatistas (2002) *Zapatista Encuentro: Documents from the 1996 Encounter for Humanity and Against Neoliberalism*, New York, Seven Stories Press.

Zelizer, B. and Allan, S. (eds) (2002) *Journalism After September 11*, Routledge.

Zerbisias, A. (2003) 'Spinmeisters in Need of Fodder', *Toronto Star*, 27 July, D10.

Index